THE TRAGEDY OF
KIRK O' FIELD

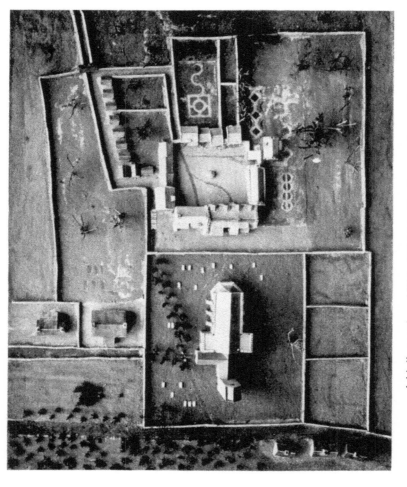

A bird's-eye view of Kirk o' Field, looking from south to north.

THE TRAGEDY OF KIRK O' FIELD

BY

MAJOR-GENERAL R. H. MAHON
C.B., C.S.I.

CAMBRIDGE

AT THE UNIVERSITY PRESS

1930

CAMBRIDGE
UNIVERSITY PRESS

University Printing House, Cambridge CB2 8BS, United Kingdom

Cambridge University Press is part of the University of Cambridge.

It furthers the University's mission by disseminating knowledge in the pursuit of education, learning and research at the highest international levels of excellence.

www.cambridge.org
Information on this title: www.cambridge.org/9781316613177

First published 1930
First paperback edition 2016

A catalogue record for this publication is available from the British Library

ISBN 978-1-316-61317-7 Paperback

CONTENTS

PAGE

Prefatory note   ix

Introductory   xi

Works referred to in the text   .   .   .   xv

PART I

CHAP.

  I. A Reconstruction of the Scene of the Tragedy   .   1

 II. The Physical Impossibilities of the Accepted
     Narratives   45

III. The Rationale of the Plot   .   .   .   79

PART II

IV. Cause   201

Index   279

ILLUSTRATIONS

PLATES

The model. A bird's-eye view of "Kirk o' Field" .   *frontispiece*

  I   The model. Kirk o' Field in 1513 .   . *facing page* 4

  II   The model. Kirk o' Field after 1558 .   .   ,,   76

  III   The model. Kirk o' Field after the explosion .   ,,   156

IN THE TEXT

Elevation and plan of Kirk o' Field   .   .   . *page* 5

Kirk o' Field precincts   .   .   .   ,,   11

S.E. corner of the old college quadrangle   .   . ,,   14

Superimposed plans of Kirk o' Field and its precincts, the old and present University buildings .   .   . ,,   16

Plan and Section of the "Old Provost's House" and the "Salle" .   .   .   .   .   . ,,   28

A portion of "The Picture" of 1567 showing personal effects of Darnley, chair, etc., found by his body   .   . ,,   110

PREFATORY NOTE

WHEN Major-General Reginald Mahon retired from the Army after the War he devoted himself to a study of the tragedy of Kirk o' Field and what led up to it. An Irishman and a Protestant, he had no bias in favour of the Queen, nor was he affected by the opinions of historians for or against her. Long years ago, when we were both on the Army Head-Quarters staff in India, he used to tell me that, while his instinct was to disbelieve her traducers, his reason satisfied him that only by prolonged research and study of original sources could light be thrown on a problem rarely approached without controversial heat.

So he set to work exploring, without any idea where his researches would lead him.

In 1923 the Cambridge University Press published the result of his first work—*The Indictment of Mary Queen of Scots as derived from a manuscript in the University Library at Cambridge*, a free rendering in Scots of Buchanan's *De Maria*. In this volume General Mahon traced the connection between Buchanan's work and its later developments and the three papers by the Earl of Lennox, and compared them with each other.

In 1924 appeared the second volume of the Trilogy, *Mary Queen of Scots, a study of the Lennox narrative in the University Library at Cambridge*. This document, which is given *in extenso*, is of course important as one of those on which the indictment of the Queen was based. General Mahon compares this source with the 'Detection,' and shows how they agree and how they differ. He also devotes one section to the Queen's life in France, and another to the Glasgow letters and their significance. Replying to hostile criticisms later, he stated that his object was "to give reasons why it is wrong to present the Queen as a potential Messalina in the years preceding the tragedy of February 1567 and...to show that the case requires fresh examination."

Having grave doubts as to the truth of much which was written by Lennox and Buchanan, General Mahon then turned to a study of the locale of Kirk o' Field and of the manner in which the explosion was carried out, and with the greatest care analysed the sources of information in France, Germany, and Italy, of which little use had previously been made.

So careful was he of detail that he built a scale model of the precincts of "St Mary in the Fields," taken from the picture, now in the Museum of the Public Record Office, which was drawn soon after the event for the information of Cecil. This model was then photographed from various aspects, and the results serve to illustrate this, the last volume of his Trilogy— *Kirk o' Field*.

The last chapter of the work, which he entitled "The Cause," shows that the plot was a part of the Counter-Reformation movement, aimed against Mary and the Protestant nobles. Darnley and Lennox and Balfour were aware of it, and the latter at least was the active agent. Bothwell became aware of it the evening before the explosion and, with the knowledge of her Captain of the Guard, prevented her being present.

Darnley, who had already decided to leave Kirk o' Field, was caught in the act of doing so and strangled; who was responsible for this is not certain—there were enough Scottish peers who had reason to dread his assumption of the Crown to guarantee a sudden end for him sooner or later.

And so Kirk o' Field resolved itself into a plot within a plot; and the only person who was innocent of either was the Queen.

General Mahon died simultaneously with the completion of his manuscript. No one knew better than he that the present work would meet with adverse, as well as favourable, criticism; but since he, unlike many "Marian" writers, gave authorities for his statements, he was prepared to meet attacks. In any attempt to defend him, his friends, alas, will not be equipped with his knowledge.

BRUCE SETON

May 1930

INTRODUCTORY

"THE whole scheme of the *Discourse* is to surround fiction by undoubted truths with such apparent simplicity and carelessness, but in fact, with such consummate skill and depth of design, that the reader is beguiled into an unsuspecting belief of the whole narration. The fidelity of the story is, in both cases, vouched by the introduction of depositions and documents which give an air of candour and authority, but which might be garbled at the discretion of the writer without fear of detection as the originals were in his power."

The *Discourse* otherwise known as *The King's Book* is the work attributed to James I of England, descriptive of the Gunpowder Plot of 5th November, 1605. The words quoted are those of David Jardine in his Narrative of that plot. They embody so completely the nature of the records which pass as evidence in the gunpowder plot of February 1567 that I venture to use them as a fitting introduction to this part of my work. To my mind, though I have yet to show my reasons, the circumstances, even the object, of both plots, were closely similar—to remove an obstacle to the Counter-Reformation. In 1605 it was James, Mary's only child, who was aimed at; in 1567 it was Mary *and not Darnley* whose life was sought. A bold statement; as I have said, it is what I have to justify[1].

The *dramatis personæ* in the two cases were curiously alike in the class of life from which they came. Catesby, Wright, Winter, Percy, may be compared with Balfour, Hepburn, Hay, Ormistoun; and in Guy Fawkes, soldier of fortune and versed in the art of mining, we will find a counterpart in Captain Cullen, equally soldier of fortune, and similarly instructed. Father Garnet's place is taken in our story, unless I am much mistaken, by Father Edmund Hay. There is another name which should be mentioned here, Anthony Standen, the elder. In *our* time,

---

[1] The *Discourse*, together with King James' speech to Parliament, are to be read in vol. IV. of the *Harleian Miscellany*, at pp. 245 ff.

gentleman of Darnley's household, though absent in Rome, or at least on the Continent, at the time of the plot; in 1605 recently returned from Rome, bearer of presents to the leading Catholic gentry; whilom correspondent of Walsingham under an assumed name[1]; doubtful character, of whom one would wish to know a great deal more. Anthony, the younger, his brother, was with his master at the time of the execution of the plot, but had been *fortunate* enough not to be at Kirk o' Field at the critical moment.

To present a reasonably brief and yet sufficiently complete account of the plot of 1567 is a matter of great difficulty. The records bristle with such an array of improbable situations, so many impossibilities, such contradiction of assertion, such a mixture of truth and falsehood, that those who have written on either side of the question have scarcely found room in spacious volumes to express their views. Frankly, were it not that the "evidence" contains, as in a palimpsest, the faint trace of a different and truer story overlaid by the coarse invention that we have to deal with, it would not be worth while to refer to it at all. Even as it is, I think we can arrive at a conclusion by following only a few of the threads, and choosing those which have been neglected, wholly or partly, by others.

With this aim I propose to divide the subject in Part I of this work into three chapters; the first, a reconstruction of the site of the tragedy; the second, an exposition of the physical impossibilities of the official narrative; the third, to draw together the facts, principles and reasons which emerge from a consideration of the plot itself; this latter I have called the rationale of the plot. As to the first, it is the usual course in an important criminal trial in modern times to present to the jury as complete a schedule of detail involving time, space, and surroundings as can be made; this has been neglected hitherto in dealing with Kirk o' Field. As to the second, I do not intend to weary the reader by any repetition of the well-worn arguments; for the most part, what is now advanced by me is a new field of enquiry. The last, the most difficult of the three, is intended to carry the

---

[1] Add. MS. Brit. Mus. 3581, ff. 129, 136–144, 146.

reader with me through the actual course of what must have happened, and the genesis, reasons and facts underlying it.

In Part II I propose to review the whole matter and to consider the Cause. At the outset I want to tell the reader where I am going. I believe that it will be easier to appreciate the facts as they appear if they be related to a known scheme, rather than to accumulate numerous details and then announce the purpose.

My story is this: Kirk o' Field was deliberately chosen as the place to which Darnley should return, by conspirators led by Sir James Balfour, instigated as to the object, but not necessarily as to details, by Father Edmund Hay. The Earl of Lennox and his son, Darnley, were both aware of, and conniving in, the attempt, which was only one of several which had, so far, failed. The object was to destroy the Queen, who had refused to adopt the measures put before her to effect the Counter-Reformation; the Regency, possibly the Kingship, would then be assumed by Darnley.

The *modus operandi* was to mine the large reception room which we will call, for short, the Salle; in it the Queen and many of the nobles were expected to assemble on her return from Holyrood after the wedding party. The match was to be fired, and Darnley to escape, on the approach of the returning party. The plot, however, had leaked out. The Queen was warned not to return; but a large party did approach the place, and the conspirators carried out the programme in the belief that the moment had arrived. Darnley was met in the south garden, escaping, and was there strangled, a consent to his capture having been wrung from the Queen when the plot was opened to her.

The dwelling-house, which will be called the Old House, was not mined; to do so would have been almost impossible, for the space was confined, not easily accessible for the purpose, and extremely dangerous from the presence of fires. But, and this is one of the difficulties, the plot included a dumb show, reasonably public, of carrying explosives to the Old House immediately before the real business commenced. The obvious intention was that Darnley, escaped, could fabricate a story against, probably, the Earl of Moray and the Protestant party generally. I have referred to this secondary phase in the plot as "dumb show." I think it likely that no explosive was actually put in the Queen's chamber, but that all the necessary motions of carrying a barrel of powder, etc., were gone through, so that the fact could be vouched for by a hundred witnesses when required. Possibly powder was actually carried; it does not greatly matter.

The Queen, dazed by the shock, reduced to a mental state not far, at times not at all, removed from insanity, became the shuttlecock of the factions. Each party, after the manner of the Scots of the period, sought to make capital from a catastrophe which came as an unexpected gift. To Moray it meant a Regency; to the nobles, a minority; to Cecil and Lethington, renewed hopes of a Union with England; and to Bothwell— honest, I think, for a brief space—an early formed hope of Kingship. Excepting as to the last of these, it was necessary that Mary, though shattered, should first be obliterated. That, too, was accomplished.

Neither Bothwell, nor Moray, nor the Douglases were responsible for the explosion, but all were represented at the execution of the real culprit, the first, perhaps in person, though I doubt if he reached the scene until the deed was done. If he had, it would have made no difference, for not one of them would raise a finger to save Darnley.

Beyond, and in the shadow, stood the Catholic party, realizing that the Counter-Reformation must come now or never; but this phase, though touched on in this part, properly belongs to Part II of this book.

WORKS REFERRED TO IN THE TEXT

OFFICIAL PUBLICATIONS

Accounts of the High Treasurer. 1564.
Calendar of State Papers relating to Scotland.
Calendar of State Papers relating to Foreign Affairs.
Calendar of State Papers relating to English Affairs, in the Archives of Venice.
Calendar of State Papers relating to English Affairs, in the Archives of Simancas.
Calendar of Border Papers.
Calendar of Documents relating to Scotland.
Register of Privy Seal.
Register of Privy Council Scotland.
Miscellaneous State Papers 1501–1726, ed. by Earl of Hardwicke 1778.

CAMBRIDGE PAPERS (University Library)

Press Mark Dd.3.66. Buchanan's Indictment.
    ,,   Oo.7.47/8. The Lennox Narrative.
    ,,   Oo.7.47/11. The Lennox Narrative.
    ,,   Oo.7.47/5.

OTHER WORKS, WITH DATE OF COPY USED

AUTHOR OR EDITOR	TITLE OF WORK	ABBREVIATION USED
Anderson, James	*Collections relating to Mary Queen of Scots*	*Collections*
Arnot	*Criminal Trials*	Arnot
Bain, Joseph	*State Papers relating to Scotland and Mary Queen of Scots 1547–1603*	Bain
	Biometrika	*Biometrika*
Bishop of Ross, Leslie	*Paralipomena ad Historiam*	*Paralipomena*
Boog-Watson	*Closes and Wynds of Old Edinburgh* (Old Edinburgh Club, XII)	Boog-Watson
	The Book of Articles	In full
Buchanan, George	*History of Scotland*	In full
,,	*The Detection*	*Detection*
	Cabala sive Scrinia Sacra. 1691	*Cabala*
Camden, William	*History of the Reign of Elizabeth*	Camden

AUTHOR OR EDITOR	TITLE OF WORK	ABBREVIATION USED
Chalmers, George	*Life of Queen Mary*	Chalmers
Conn, G.	*Life of Mary*	Conn
Crawford, Thomas	*History of the University of Edinburgh.* 1640	Crawford
Dalzel, Andrew	*History of the University of Edinburgh*	Dalzel
de Pimodan	*La mère des Guises*	In full
	Diurnal of Occurrents (Bannatyne Club)	In full
	Early views and maps of Edinburgh 1544–1852 (R. Scots Geographical Society)	In full
	Edinburgh Burgh Records	In full
Ferrière, H. de la	*Lettres de Catherine de Médici.* 1885	Lettres C. de M.
Forbes-Leith, W.	*Narratives of the Scottish Catholics.* 1885	Forbes-Leith
Fouqueray, H.	*Histoire de la Compagnie de Jésus.* 1910	Fouqueray
Froude	*History*	Froude
Gachard	*Correspondance de Philippe II sur les affaires des Pays-Bas*	Gachard
Goodall, Walter	*Examination of letters said to have been written by Mary Queen of Scots.* 1744	Goodall
Gordon, Sir Robert	*The Earldom of Sutherland.* 1813	Gordon
Grant, Sir A.	*History of the University of Edinburgh*	In full
Grant, J.	*Old and New Edinburgh*	In full
	Granvelle papers	In full
	Harleian MSS. British Museum	In full
Hay Fleming, D.	*Mary Queen of Scots*	In full
Henderson, T. F.	"Mary Stuart," *Dict. of Natl. Biography*	In full
,,	*Casket Letters and Mary Queen of Scots*, 2nd ed. 1890	Henderson
	History of King James the Sext	In full
Hosack, John	*Mary Queen of Scots and her accusers.* 1870	Hosack
,,	*The Book of Articles* (Hopetown MSS.). 1870	In full

AUTHOR OR EDITOR	TITLE OF WORK	ABBREVIATION USED
Hume, Martin	*Spanish Calendar of Letters and Papers relating to England—Simancas*	*Simancas*
Jebb	*Vita Mariae*	Jebb
Jerrano, D. L.	*Correspondencia Diplomática entre España y la Santa Sede.*	Corr. Dip.
Keith, Robert	*History of the affairs of Church and State in Scotland.* 1844	Keith
Klarwill, von	*Queen Elizabeth and some foreigners.* 1928	In full
Knox, John	*History of the Reformation in Scotland*	Knox
Labanoff, A.	*Lettres de Marie Stuart.* 1844	Labanoff
Laing, David	*Collegiate Churches of Midlothian* (Bannatyne Club, 1861)	In full
,,	*Charters of St Giles* (Bannatyne Club, 1859)	In full
,,	*Registrum domus de Soltre* (Bannatyne Club, 1861)	In full
Laing, Malcolm	*History of Scotland*	Laing
Lang, Andrew	*History of Scotland*	Láng
Leslie, John	*Defence of Queen Mary's honour*	In full
	Les affaires du Conte de Boduel 1568 (Bannatyne Club)	In full
Mahon, R. H.	*The Indictment of Mary Queen of Scots.* 1923	*Indictment*
,,	*Mary Queen of Scots and the Lennox MS.* 1924	*Lennox*
Melville, Sir James	*Memoirs*	Melville
Merriman	*Rise of the Spanish Empire*	Merriman
Mignet, F. A.	*History of Mary Queen of Scots*	Mignet
	Miscellany of the Bannatyne Club	In full
Moir-Bryce, W.	*The Black Friars of Edinburgh*	In full
,,	*Book of the Old Edinburgh Club II*	In full
Motley, J.	*Rise of the Dutch Republic.* 1878	Motley
Nau, Claude	*Memoirs of Mary Queen of Scots*, ed. Rev. J. Stevenson, 1883	Nau

AUTHOR OR EDITOR	TITLE OF WORK	ABBREVIATION USED
Pastor, L. von	*Geschichte der Päpste* (Also translation)	Pastor, *Gesch.* Pastor, tr.
Paul, Sir J. Balfour	*Scots Peerage*	In full
Pitcairn, Robert	*Criminal Trials in Scotland* (Maitland Club 1833)	In full
Pollen, Joseph	*Papal negotiations with Mary Queen of Scots.* 1901 (Scottish Hist. Society)	Pollen
Prescott	*Ferdinand and Isabella*	In full
Ranke, von	*Geschichte*	von Ranke
Raumer, Fred von	*Elizabeth and Mary*	von Raumer
Robertson, Joseph	*Inventaires de la Royne d'Escosse* (Bannatyne Club, 1863)	*Inventaires*
Robertson, William	*History of Scotland*	Robertson
Rodocanachi, E.	*Renée de France*	In full
Rouer, R. de	*Lettres de Fourquevaux*	In full
	Lettres de Charles IX à M. de Fourquevaux	In full
Seeley, Sir John	*The growth of British Policy*	Seeley
	Sloane MSS. Brit. Museum	In full
Stevenson, Joseph	*Selections from unpublished MSS.* (Maitland Club, 1837)	*Selections*
Strickland, Agnes	*Letters of Mary Stuart*	In full
Teulet, A.	*Papiers d'État*	*Pap. d'État*
,,	*Relations politiques de la France avec L'Écosse*	*Relations*
Thou, J. A. de	*Histoire Universelle*	de Thou
Tytler, P. F.	*History of Scotland*	Tytler
Villa	*Juana la Loca*	Villa
Whitaker	*Mary Queen of Scots vindicated.* 1778	Whitaker
Wilson, Dr Thos.	*The Oration.* 1570	*Oration*
Wright, Thomas	*Queen Elizabeth and her Times.* 1838	In full

PART I

Chapter I

A RECONSTRUCTION OF THE SCENE OF THE TRAGEDY

PRELIMINARY

TECHNICALLY, Mary Stuart was never tried; her case was heard before a Commission, empowered to hear both sides but not to give judgment. Every step taken was a negation of justice; the accusers not only received special favours not accorded to the defence, but their evidence was kept secret from those representing the Queen. The Commissioners themselves were sworn to silence, and no attempt was made to sift the evidence in relation to the scene of the murder. Two witnesses only were heard for the prosecution, and none for the defence. The two witnesses were heard in secret. Documentary evidence, procured under most suspicious circumstances, was accepted from the accusers, but kept hidden from the defence.

A letter dated 22nd October, 1568, from the Earl of Sussex to Cecil describes the situation so succinctly that I cannot do better than quote a part of it as a preliminary:

This matter must at length take end, either by finding the Scotch Queen guilty of the crimes that are objected against her, or, by some manner of composition, with a view of saving her honour. The first, I think, will hardly be attempted, for two causes: the one, for that if her adverse party accuse her of the murder by producing her letters, she will deny them, and accuse the most of them of manifest consent to the murder, hardly to be denied; so as upon a trial of both sides, her proofs will fall out best, as it is thought....

I think surely, no end can be made good for England, except the person of the Scotch Queen be detained by one means or other in England. Of the two ends before written, I think the first to be the best in all respects for the Queen's Majesty, if Murray will produce such matter as the Queen's Majesty may, by virtue of her superiority over Scotland, find judicially the Scotch Queen guilty of the murder of her husband, and therewith detain her in England....

If the Queen was not tried in England, she has certainly been on trial ever since; yet none of the numerous writers who have investigated the case has ever made a proper enquiry into the essential preliminary, the physical character of the scene in which the action took place. Without this the evidence cannot be weighed, nor can a conclusion be come to on the theory advanced by the Queen's accusers. There is sufficient material to enable a reconstruction of the surroundings of Kirk o' Field to be made; in the following pages I will attempt to bring this material together. The result will differ in many respects from what has been already written on the subject; but I will endeavour to prove the case as we go along, without delaying to touch on the numerous points which do not accord with other opinions.

In general it may be said that much of the confusion which appears in the descriptions of Kirk o' Field is due to two things: the first—a misconception of the real meaning of a curious rectangular structure which, in the reproductions of the early pictorial map of Edinburgh by Gordon of Rothiemay, is shown a little to the east of the Provost's house. This has been taken, almost universally, to be the ruins of the house in which the explosion took place; and the various authors have coloured their stories accordingly. Whatever else this structure may be, it certainly has nothing to do with the original precincts of Kirk o' Field; I have dealt with it below. The second—a misreading of the pictorial representation of the scene of the explosion, drawn very shortly after the occurrence, presumably for Cecil's information. Many references to this "picture" will be made in what follows.

ECCLESIA SANCTAE MARIAE IN CAMPIS

The Church of St Mary, known to us as Kirk o' Field, dates from the latter half of the thirteenth century. The exact date is not known, but, at the time when the pious founders, believed to have been the Austin Friars of Holyrood, first conceived the idea of a church on the eminence overlooking what is now the Cowgate, there was little apparent reason for selecting the site. Already the large conventual establishment of the Dominicans, with their church, also dedicated to the Blessed Virgin, existed some 250 yards to the north-east, and a similar convent of the Franciscans or Grey Friars occupied the crown of the ridge some 300 yards to the west. One might suppose that the sparse population of the neighbourhood was more than sufficiently served. It may be that the open, healthy nature of the ground attracted the Austin Friars, whose own location at the low-lying Abbey of Holyrood was notoriously unhealthy; but I suggest that, from the first, the intention was to create an educational centre. If so, the magnificent design of the brothers Adam, which now occupies the site and forms the central establishment of the University of Edinburgh, is rather an evolution from a conception more than 500 years old than the outcome of the college which struggled into being after the Reformation.

At all events the church stood at first by itself, with, it must be supposed, some accommodation for the clergy, but without the more elaborate "Precincts" which will be referred to presently. That it was a foundation arising from and controlled by the royal Abbey of Holyrood does not admit of dispute; traces of the inter-connection are numerous. The charters of the original foundation are, however, lost.

As the Abbey of Holyrood was one of the richest in Scotland, flourishing under the patronage of successive monarchs, from David I, and endowed with properties of great and growing value, it is not much to assume that the Austin Friars of Holyrood aimed at making the new church worthy of the beauty of the parent foundation. It appears to have been of moderate dimensions, and, as I will claim later, is represented with fair accuracy in the coloured drawing or picture of 1567 which is preserved in the museum of the Public Record Office in London[1].

Far too little attention has been given to this remarkable piece of draughtsmanship. In what follows I shall make frequent use of it, and rely, for reasons given, on its general accuracy. It is obviously the work of an artist of considerable skill, and was undoubtedly prepared almost immediately after the tragedy at Kirk o' Field for the information of Cecil, though, unfortunately, the covering letter which must have accompanied it is not forthcoming.

But let us return to what has to be said about the Church of St Mary in the Fields. The design intended for ultimate completion was, I think, generally the same as that of the church at Dalkeith[2]. St Mary's, like several other churches of about the same period, was never finished, and the nave was still wanting when the troublous times after Flodden, continued with few bright intervals to that May of 1544 which brought the legions of Hertford, effectually destroyed any prospect of further expenditure. In the "picture"—let us call the 1567 representation by that name—the choir and the short transepts alone are to be seen. The apse, which certainly must have existed, does not appear; as the building is drawn from a north-western aspect, the apse may be hidden behind the buttress, or it may have been razed by the iconoclasts of 1559–60, whose destructive fury would have been more particularly directed against the east end. The tower or steeple is shown detached from the main building by a space of about 32 feet, but, connecting it with the body of the church is a low building having a wing projecting northward, which cannot have been part of the church proper or used in connection with worship therein. Below is a reproduction of that part of the "picture" which includes the church, and a ground plan of its probable dimensions. I have added in dotted lines the

[1] Reproduced in *The Early Views and Maps of Edinburgh*, 1544–1852, Royal Scottish Geographical Society, 1919, p. 318.

[2] See Dr David Laing's *Collegiate Churches of Midlothian*, Bannatyne Club, 1861.

PLATE I

A general aerial view of Kirk o' Field, looking at it from east to west, as it was in 1513, showing the church, undamaged; on the east, nearest the observer, is the quadrangle. The Flodden wall is not yet in existence.

outline of the nave, which I assume was required to complete the edifice[1].

It will be of value to our enquiry to speculate on the uses to which the low L-shaped building, shown shaded below, was put.

Although the services were carried on by monks sent from Holyrood, we may yet assume that some of them would be in permanent residence, both for religious exercises and for care of the hospital which stood 30 to 40 yards north of the church.

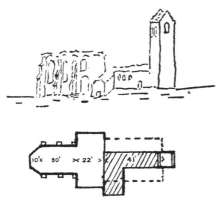

Elevation and plan of "Kirk o' Field."

(The term "hospital" does not connote a place for the sick in this case, but rather its proper signification of a place for entertaining travellers, a guest house.) For the resident "religieux" dwellings must have been provided; it is possible, but not very likely, that the low annexe to the church served this purpose; but, for reasons which will appear, I think that some of the

---

[1] It may perhaps avoid confusion if it is explained to those who have seen the original drawing in the Record Office, that the church and the town wall near it have been turned, counter-clockwise, through an angle of 90 degrees, in order to give greater freedom to the artist in depicting the movement of the groups of figures. To get the correct relation of the church to the other buildings, the movement must be reversed, until the steeple is westerly, and the town wall a continuous line facing to the south. The "picture" is reproduced in the Bannatyne Club volume of 1861, and less accurately in Chalmers, *Life of Mary*, 1.

houses which afterwards constituted the west side of the "pre-cincts" had been allocated to them.

In this view I suggest that the annexe to the church was set apart for the use of the *Collegium Sacerdotum* mentioned by Alesius[1]. The use which I ascribe to the building was that of a school where aspirants to the priesthood received instruction in the art of choral singing of the Mass, the canon law, theology, and other preliminary education for the sacred calling. The building was probably temporary only, intended some day to be replaced by the completion of the nave.

There is, however, reason to believe that the educational efforts of the friars who directed the activities of the new church at Kirk o' Field were not confined to religious teaching. When King David founded the Abbey of Holyrood, the first conven-tual establishment in Edinburgh, his object was to rescue the nation, not only from the depth of religious ignorance, but from the barbarous ignorance of learning and art of all kinds; and the Austin Friars, whose monastic rules permitted greater freedom as to worldly intercourse, were the chosen instruments in giving effect to his intention. It might be said that while the Domini-cans were the preaching friars and the Franciscans the healing friars, so the Augustinians were the teaching friars. It is, indeed, on record that the first named had no sympathy at all with the idea of secular education. They probably wished nothing to interfere with their primary vocation of preaching[2].

James Grant in his comprehensive work on *Old and New Edinburgh* says[3] that the first grammar school was "attached" to the Abbey of Holyrood. He does not quote his authority, but it would appear that, even before the Kirk o' Field was advanced to the higher status of a collegiate church, secular teaching in its neighbourhood was established. It is beyond question that there was a connection between the church and the first grammar

---

[1] *Miscellany of the Bannatyne Club*, I, p. 187. At the same time, it is as well to note that when Alesius wrote I believe the Collegium had removed to a new building which will be referred to presently.

[2] See W. Moir Bryce, *Black Friars of Edinburgh*, p. 53.

[3] II, p. 287.

school; an Instrument of 1503 refers to the school as being in the "Lane of St Mary in the Fields[1]," and this lane led from the Cowgate to the church, past the hospital, where afterwards the "Duke's House" was built. With the curious persistence of ancient rights of way, the northern entrance of the old college stood on the same line as the old track, and even to-day there is a postern door in the new buildings very near the same spot. Even more, the ancient trackways, both the one now referred to and the other from the Cowgate at Blackfriars Wynd, converged to the Potterrow, and here too is an exit in the new building, corresponding to one in the old college, and precisely on the

[1] I find difficulty in being precise on the question of the site of this grammar school. There is not, so far as I know, any reference to a "Wynd" or Lane to which the name of the Church in the Fields was attached, until the early years of the sixteenth century, though, during the fifteenth and fourteenth centuries, there are several references to the other approach to the church, this latter being then the principal road, which even to this day exists between the Cowgate at its junction with Blackfriars Wynd, and the Potterrow (see *Charters of St Giles*, Bannatyne Club, 1859, pp. 183, 281). It seems likely that the lane of the Blessed Virgin came into existence only when the school was opened. That the original school was adjacent to and connected with the "hospital" of Kirk o' Field seems certain, and, when the site of the latter was sold to the Hamiltons in 1554, we are told by Grant (*Old and New Edinburgh*, II, p. 287) that the school was temporarily removed to the house of the Archbishop of Glasgow in Blackfriars Wynd, showing, I think, that it stood on part of the land disposed of. It returned again to new buildings at the head of what was then to be definitely named "School House Wynd," probably only a short distance north of the original site, but outside the new Hamilton area. Twenty-four years later it was removed again to the new high school erected on the site of the Blackfriars convent. It is worth remembering that, though there were formerly other schools—one in the Canongate, for instance— these were apparently closed in favour of a single school at Kirk o' Field, of which the masters seem always to have been prebendaries. Until the opening of the school there would have been no great reason for a regular lane between the Cowgate and the hospital. The "Horse Wynd," some 40 yards to the west, would have served all purposes of persons passing to the church. Even a hundred years later, as shown by Gordon's map, the sloping ground south of the Cowgate was not thickly popu- lated, and before the erection of the Flodden wall it was probably almost bare.

spot where the little flight of steps shown in the picture indicates the ancient junction.

Later Instruments dated in 1508 and 1516[1] definitely connect the Master and Wardens[2] of the church with the school. In the former year one Thomas Russale resigns his rights to the school-house in favour of the Master, Matthew Ker, who in turn granted them to David Vocat. In the latter year, David Vocat conveyed to the use of the church his four houses, which were bounded on the north and west by the lane mentioned above, which connected the Cowgate-Blackfriars junction with the Potterrow. We know from the "picture" that the said lane did make a southward bend, where the four houses shown as forming the north range of the precincts stand, and it seems that these four were more ancient than the rest, and were perhaps the original dwellings of the permanent friars of the Kirk o' Field.

The matter is rather interesting than important to our subject; but it does indicate that the construction of the precincts of Kirk o' Field was rather a completion, by addition to a pre-existing state of things, than a creation *ab initio*; and this view supports other things that we come to later. Enough has been said to show that when, in 1583[3], the town gave a grant for the establishment of a college, and the "Duke's House" was taken over to form the main building for accommodating the schools, for at least a hundred years previously the same site had contained a seat of learning, which was dependent on the Church of St Mary in the Fields.

The construction or, as I have said, the extension of the precincts at St Mary's appears to have been taken seriously in hand about the year 1510, when a plot of land was conveyed on which the west side of the quadrangle was erected. Possibly the pressure at Holyrood Abbey, which was constantly in request as a residence for Royalty, and was finally curtailed by the building of the palace, caused the Canons to seek a fresh outlet. But there

[1] Society of Antiquaries, Scotland, v, p. 147; also Bannatyne Club, 1861, *Registrum domus de Soltre.*
[2] Afterwards called Provost and Prebendaries.
[3] Edinburgh Burgh Records of 14th June, 1583.

may have been also another reason—the success of the several foundations of education at Saint Andrews perhaps led to a desire to obtain for Edinburgh similar advantages. At the colleges of St Salvator and St Leonard teaching in both theological and secular subjects was combined[1].

The time was apparently propitious; James IV was securely seated on his throne, and his marriage with Margaret of England had, it might be hoped, laid the spectre of continual war with the "auld enemy." James was a patron of learning and would be likely to encourage such a scheme as I attribute to the Canons of Holyrood. At all events, at this time the Church of St Mary was advanced to the status of a collegiate church, and I suggest that now the Provost would turn his thoughts to completion of the church, involving the removal of the temporary structure occupying the site of the nave. This, in its turn, suggests that the new precincts would contain a building set apart for the same object. We should not forget that collegiate status connoted a degree of importance not less than that of a cathedral; thus, Pope Pius IV refers to "Cathedrals, both those that are metropolitan and collegiate[2]." It is a fair assumption that the buildings for the new foundation, under the ægis of the Sovereign, and aided by the resources of the richest religious community in Scotland, would be substantial and would include accommodation for instruction. It was probably not chance but tradition which led to the schools of the present University being on the same site as the old precincts of 1510.

Hardly were the buildings complete, and before the work on the church had commenced, than the disaster of Flodden (September 1513) checked all progress.

The frontispiece of this volume, giving a view of Kirk o' Field at this time, and a bird's-eye view, taken from the same model, will make the position clearer. This model was constructed as I felt that nothing less would keep me from falling into as many errors as I must ascribe to other writers.

[1] Sir A. Grant, *Story of the University of Edinburgh*, I, pp. 10 ff.
[2] Pollen, p. 36.

THE PRECINCTS OF KIRK O' FIELD

It is, as I have said, of the first importance that we should have an accurate notion of the scene of the tragedy of February 1567, the more so because successive writers on either side of the controversy have neglected or misinterpreted the data which enable an opinion to be formed.

I have already referred to the sketch or drawing, called by me the "picture," which is preserved in the Museum of the Public Record Office, and I have made use of it in connection with the Church of St Mary. I will now take it as the basis of a description of the precincts. I suppose that many thousands have looked at this curious example of art without seeing in it more than a fantastic illustration of the scene; but, if we set aside the fanciful character of the attempt to depict a series of events in a single phase, which was very common among early artists, the rest is, I believe, an accurate presentment of the surroundings. As we go on I will give reasons for my belief.

Below is a reproduction of that part of the original sketch which shows only the precincts. To avoid confusion the rest is left out. The numerals and explanatory memoranda are added by me.

We are looking at the picture from a westerly point (not actually true west), and we see in the foreground the two principal houses, which formed the west side of the quadrangle. The larger (1) is the new dwelling-house of the Provost, built about 1511/12, the smaller, on the left, I call the Precentor's house (2). The Precentor, as the next dignitary in rank to the Provost, would most likely be lodged here. On the right, the Provost's house is connected with the town wall by a blank wall (3) having a doorway, over which is something that looks like a shield. On the left of the Precentor's house is the gable end of the northerly range of buildings[1], and left again of the gable end is a flight of steps, "Our Lady's Stairs" (6) leading *up* to the level of the

---

[1] Which may perhaps be David Vocat's houses, referred to above, p. 8.

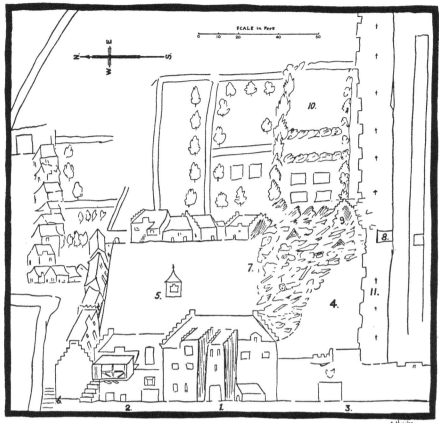

KIRK O' FIELD PRECINCTS

A bird's-eye view of the precincts taken from the contemporary picture
sent to Cecil shortly after the explosion. The original is in the Public
Record Office, London.

1. The New (Provost's) House, built about 1511/12.
2. The Precentor's house.
3. The enclosing wall added after the erection of the Flodden Town
   Wall, about 1514/15.
4. The "Little Court."
5. The quadrangle with well in the centre.
6. The flight of steps called "Our Lady's Stairs" leading from the
   Horse Wynd to the Cowgate and Blackfriars.
7. The confused heap of ruins caused by the explosion.
8. The postern in the wall.
9. The gable forming the end of the Old (Provost's) House, left
   standing after the explosion.
10. The East Gardens.   11. The Flodden wall.

eminence on which the church stood. The double line on the extreme left represents a wall and not a roadway, as might perhaps be thought. In the background, and forming the eastern side of the quadrangle, is a range of four smaller houses, and also the main entrance to the courtyard. Enclosing the southern side is the confused ruin (7) of the building blown up by the explosion of the night of the 9th/10th of February, 1567. In the farther background, behind the eastern range and the eastern end of the ruin, are gardens enclosed by walls (10). On the extreme right is the town wall, in which is the "postern gate" (8) which figures often in the evidence. The inner dimensions of the courtyard or quadrangle are approximately 86 feet from north to south and 73 feet from west to east.

The Provost's house has on the left (in all cases, left and right refer to the picture as seen by the observer) a projecting wing of two storeys, and a third storey which is, at least partly, an attic. Near by and projecting from the main building is a rectangular staircase tower, in which is also the main entrance to the house from the churchyard side. This type of stair tower was a common feature of the architecture of the period in the more important houses; we shall find later that there were two of them attached to the "Duke's House"; the house of Provand's Lordship in Glasgow, where Mary is said to have stayed, has one, and "Queen Mary's house" at Jedburgh and two old houses still standing in Candlemakers Row in Edinburgh are other examples. The stairs in them can hardly be described as spirals or turnpikes; I think it was Andrew Lang who dubbed them "spirals with corners," for in most cases they follow the walls with the usual central stone newel forming the inner end of the steps; in some cases the angles of the walls are rounded and the stair becomes a true spiral. It is evident from the "picture" that the lower storey with its small windows is more in the nature of a basement than providing living-rooms.

The Precentor's house is clearly on a lesser scale, and the upper storey is approached, as was so often the case, by an outside stair; but its special feature, to which I would call attention, is the projecting gallery, evidently constructed of timber filled in with rubble and mortar, and supported by two timber struts, a very common practice in Edinburgh. Another example of the same projecting gallery is to be seen on the house on the left of the eastern range on the far side of the quadrangle; this too is approached by an outside stair. It may be added that the rather large doorway shown to the right of the Precentor's house is probably a passage-way into the court and not a door into the house; we shall have occasion to refer to another such passage-way presently.

The remaining houses call for no special remark; they are mostly one-storeyed, except perhaps the one of the gable end, which seems rather larger than the others. For the moment I will not refer to the ruin on the south side. Altogether there seem to be ten houses besides the Provost's, that is, counting the gable house as two, which by the two doors seems to be correct; and this agrees with the establishment of ten Prebendaries which we know were allotted to the college.

Let us now turn to a very interesting confirmation of a great deal of the above description. It is well known that the house occupied by successive Principals of the University of Edinburgh, up to the date of the erection of the present buildings, was on the site of that of the Provost of Kirk o' Field. Thomas Crawford in his *History of the University*, written about the year 1640[1], refers to it as the "lodging of the Provost, where now the Principal hath his rooms," but it does not seem so clear that it was recognized that the Provost's house was not only "where" that of the Principal's was, but that it was the very *same house*. Dr Robertson himself wrote that, "The place prepared for his (the King's) reception was a house belonging to the Provost of a collegiate church called Kirk o' Field. It stood almost on the same spot where the house now belonging to the Principal of the University now stands[2]."

During the construction of the new University buildings, several sketches of parts of the fast disappearing old college were

[1] See the MS. copy in the National Library, or the printed copy in the British Museum.

[2] Robertson, IV, p. 193, ed. 1802.

made; one of these showing the south-eastern corner of the college quadrangle is reproduced below[1].

It is quite clear that in this sketch we have the *same building* as that shown in the "picture" of 1567, minus, however, the right wing. The projecting left wing is the same, with its attic window. The rectangular staircase tower remains, but the entrance door has been changed. The old crow-stepped gables have been cut down, and the roofing altered. A new wing has been added to the back, presumably in place of the old right wing. As to these alterations, we know from the Town Records dated 19th March, 1648, that the house, being in bad condition, was

S.E. corner of the old college quadrangle

vacated by Principal John Adamson until it was repaired. It is natural to suppose that it was at that date that the alterations were effected, and it may also be presumed that the right wing, which must have suffered in the explosion, was then finally condemned. Another confirmation of this important fact is the gable end of the old Precentor's house clearly seen in the sketch. Windows have been pierced in it, but it was presumably too intimately bonded into the end wall of the Provost's house to be entirely removed.

The blank wall on the right of the house, seen where it meets

[1] It is to be found in several books, *e.g.* Bannatyne Club of 1861; Dalzel, *History of the University*; Sir A. Grant, *History of the University*, etc.

the new outer wall of the college with the large entrance in it, is not the same as the blank wall shown in the 1567 "picture"; it covers the space left by the demolished right wing. It has a doorway in it which rather adds to the resemblance, but the wall of 1567 extended in the same line beyond the college wall. The large entrance mentioned above was made during the building of the present University, when the usual entrance on the town side was closed. It was of this that Andrew Dalzel wittily remarked that it is "professedly for the Professors but principally for the Principal," the fact being that the Professors had to walk a long way round to get to it! Almost needless to add that the wall on the left of the sketch and the range of houses on the right belong to the later period of the old college and did not exist in 1567.

THE QUESTION OF DIMENSIONS

Fortunately we are in a position to ascertain within narrow limits the dimensions of the Provost's house, or, what is the same thing, those of the Principal's house. There are several early maps of Edinburgh, as Edgar's of 1742 and 1765, also Ainslie's of about 1780, and on each of them the house is clearly shown, minus, of course, the demolished right wing. The left wing, the rectangular stair turret, and the new extension at the back are mapped and can be measured with fair accuracy. Thus we find the Provost's house, without the right wing, was 40 to 42 feet long on the front and 36 feet deep from front to back. From this as a basis we can build up the remaining dimensions. The original size of the house was 61 to 63 feet long, including the right wing, and the depth from front to back of the latter was about 26 feet. The frontage of the Precentor's house was about 36 to 38 feet, and the gable end 18 to 20 feet. All these and the approximate plan of the remaining buildings, as well as their relation to the old and the new University, are drawn to scale on the general plan below. It may be added that a gratifying proof of the correctness of the plan appeared *after* its completion, for the flight of steps, called "Our Lady's

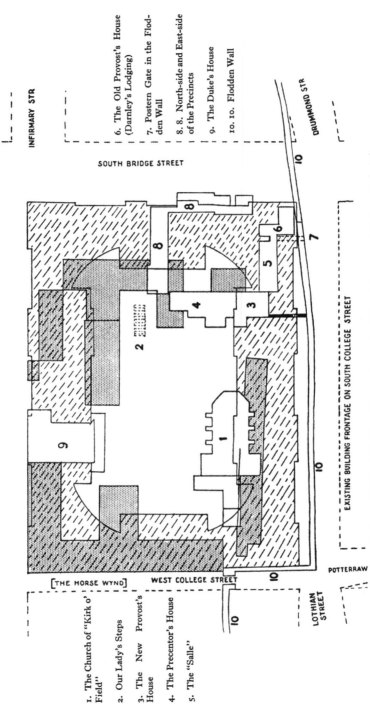

INFIRMARY STR

6. The Old Provost's House (Darnley's Lodging)
7. Postern Gate in the Flodden Wall
8. 8. North-side and East-side of the Precincts
9. The Duke's House
10. 10. Flodden Wall

DRUMMOND STR

SOUTH BRIDGE STREET

CHAMBERS STREET

EXISTING BUILDING FRONTAGE ON SOUTH COLLEGE STREET

POTTERRAW

[THE HORSE WYND]   WEST COLLEGE STREET

LOTHIAN STREET

Superimposed plans of Kirk o' Field and its precincts, the old and the present University buildings. Unshaded buildings are those which existed in 1567. Buildings dotted are those of the old University buildings. Buildings hatched are those of the present University.

1. The Church of "Kirk o' Field"
2. Our Lady's Steps
3. The New Provost's House
4. The Precentor's House
5. The "Salle"

Stairs" on the 1567 "picture" fell precisely in line with the flight of steps shown in Edgar's map and nearly in the same place, thus showing that the overall length of the precincts from south to north is not far wrong. This I did not notice until the two plans were superimposed. It also transpired at the same time that the lane shown in the 1567 "picture" and called "The Milk Row[1]" correctly hits off the entrance of what is now Infirmary Street, which is traditionally as it should be. This gives considerable assurance of the accuracy of the plan from west to east. For these reasons I think the reader may feel safe in taking the various deductions made in the following pages, at least as regards site and size, with confidence that they are not far from the truth.

From the above it will be seen that the Provost's house was certainly not a mean dwelling. It compares not unfavourably with the size of King James' Tower at Holyrood, which contains all the historical apartments and covers, excluding the turrets at each corner, about 74 by 37 feet. The "Great Lodging" of the Duke of Chatelherault, as deduced from the maps mentioned above, covered about 75 by 40 feet.

THE PHYSICAL FEATURES OF THE GROUND
AT KIRK O' FIELD

It is a curious fact that not one of the many writers who have published their views on the story of Mary has given any attention to the nature of the terrain at Kirk o' Field. Yet the slopes and contours of the ground have a close connection with the character of the buildings, and a bearing far from unimportant on what occurred on the night of the tragedy.

The natural fall of the ground from the south-west angle of the present University buildings is both northerly towards the Cowgate, and easterly towards Holyrood. It is beyond question that the levelling effect of four centuries of building and rebuilding has considerably altered the contours and reduced the height of the ridge now crowned by the McEwan Hall and the populous area of Bristo Place, Teviot Place, and Lothian Street.

---

[1] Not shown in the partial reproduction on p. 11.

Few of the many thousands who pass daily along the gentle ascent of South Bridge Street along the eastern front of the University are aware that the street is artificially levelled and carried over a series of arches or that, as they approach near the southern angle of the building, they are passing above the site of the garden in which Mary is said to have "sung and made pastime" in the bitter nights of an Edinburgh February, which garden sloped quite considerably to the east. A visit to the under-street basements of the houses on the east side of the street will no doubt help to convince any who are sceptical.

When planning the new University buildings, Robert Adam mentions that the difference in level between the south-west and the south-east corners, that is, along South College Street, was 15 feet in a length of 365 feet, and the greater part of this occurs in the eastern third of the distance, that is to say, in the area which included the precincts of Kirk o' Field. Anyone who enters the quadrangle of the University by the eastern or South Bridge entrance will be aware of the considerable ascent; yet the level of the court is lower by some 9 feet than it was originally[1]. It was on the southern side of this court that the Church of St Mary in the Field stood, and the "picture" of 1567 shows that it was on a little eminence rising a few feet higher than the general level of the immediate surroundings, necessitating a flight of steps *downward* to the Potterrow at very near the same place where now is the western entrance to the quadrangle with steps in the *reverse* sense to reach its level. One would not be far wrong in stating that the church stood on ground not less than 13 feet above the present level of the quadrangle and perhaps more than this. Let it be recalled, that, when the ruins of the church were finally cleared away in 1628–9, the "upper court" was "cast into three level walks[2]." The upper court of the old college covered a part of the present quadrangle, and we may assume that by "level walks," Crawford means three ter-

---

[1] Tracts relating to the rebuilding of the University, 1816. Brit. Mus. Press mark 8365. f. 16. 4.

[2] Thos. Crawford, *History of the University*, p. 150.

races, and this operation probably involved a good deal of paring away of the highest part of the original ground.

At the present day the fall of the ground from the eastern end of the site of the church to the Cowgate at its junction with Blackfriars Street is not less than 56 feet, and in those days it was about 70 feet. The distance is about 780 feet, so the slope was one in eleven on the average; it was not, however, even, and the greatest gradient occurred where the Provost's house, the ruined house and the garden shown beyond the latter were situated. Speaking generally of the precincts in 1567 as a whole, the quadrangle and the surrounding buildings stood on ground sloping eastwards, and, just beyond the northern side, the slope was so considerable that a flight of steps, already mentioned, was necessary. From south to north, that is, from the ruined side to the side opposite, the fall was less pronounced.

THE RUINED OR SOUTH SIDE OF THE QUADRANGLE

GENERAL REMARKS

Let us now take into consideration the southern side of the precincts, which so far we have omitted, that is the ruins shown in the "picture[1]." At the outset there is a certain obscurity as to the correct designation to give to the buildings which stood here. The earliest document which refers to the explosion is the letter addressed to the Archbishop of Glasgow, then in Paris, and purporting to be signed by Mary, dated 11th February, 1567, though written on the 10th; this letter merely mentions it as the house wherein the King was lodged[2]. The same is the case with another letter written at the same time and signed by fifteen of the Lords and Bishops in attendance[3]. Nor are the later official accounts of Buchanan or of Lennox more explicit. In two other unofficial statements we find a little more; the

[1] See p. 11, no. 7 on sketch.
[2] See the letter in Keith, I, Pref. p. ci.
[3] See for the letter, Laing, II, pp. 97–8.

'Diurnal,' written by an unknown person, refers to the house as the "Provost's Lodging"; and, in the Records of the Town Council of date 11th February, 1567, the day after the King's death, reference is made to "the back door of the Provost's Lodging of the Kirk o' Field," and again, on 2nd July in the same year, there is reference to "King Henry Stewart, being in his lodging, some time called the Lodging of the Provost of Kirk o' Field." There is also the descriptive lettering on the 1567 "picture" which refers to the "Provost's Place," but from the position of this, one remains uncertain which particular part is so designated.

In his history of the University written about 1640, Thomas Crawford puts the matter thus, "On the east thereof, (that is of the church) was the lodging of the Provost where now the Principal hath his rooms, and to the east from thence, (within the present college yards) was the Prebendaries' chamber, blown up with fire at the murder of King Henry." As Crawford had been connected with the college since 1626[1] and probably knew it well for years before that, his time was not very far removed from the date of the tragedy, and the ruins, certainly of the church and probably of the blown-up house, remained in his day, and he would have had opportunity of making sure of his facts.

Combining these statements, together with the proof of the identity of the Provost's house with that of the then Principal given above on p. 13, I think one can safely conclude that to describe the ruined house as the "Provost's Lodging," that is, "dwelling-house," is an error. But for many reasons I have come to the conclusion that a part of the ruin was, in fact, the *original* dwelling-house of the Provost or Master, before the new and larger house which faces us in the 1567 "picture" was built. Likely enough, the name stuck to it, as sometimes happens to-day.

Now, there is not a shadow of doubt that the ruined southern side of the precincts contained more than the building which may be called the "Old Provost's House" (for short, the "Old House"). The total length of the ruined buildings cannot have

[1] Sir A. Grant, *History of the University*, II, p. 279.

been less than 80 to 85 feet—much more than would suffice for the Old House alone. The "picture" (p. 11) shows the ruins to consist of a long narrow part extending from the "New Provost's House" (let us call it the "New House") in a west-east direction to meet a more confused part of the ruin which lies north-south, and extends towards the city wall. Of this part, I have not seen any notice taken of the fact that the *eastern gable end is left standing*, clearly indicating the direction of the roof ridge[1].

This eastern section of the ruins was the Old House, and between it and the New House was, I am convinced, another building, not less than 50 feet long, comparatively narrow, I judge about 18 feet wide, and probably consisting of a single storey, which certainly had a vaulted basement. This was what Crawford described as the "Prebendaries' chamber"; it is mentioned in the 'Book of Articles' as the "Chaplain's chamber," and the same authority says that, of the four entrances into the Old House, one was from the Chaplain's chamber. Thus, whereas the Old House was very likely, as described, small, dingy and not in very good repair, it was, I think, without a doubt, joined on by a passage to a newer building, which contained a single large room, which throughout this section I will call the "Salle."

Here, I suggest, was the place of assembly of the *Collegium Sacerdotum* referred to by Alesius[2]. It was built to replace the

---

[1] This statement may be disputed, but I have no hesitation in affirming it. If the "picture" in the Public Record Office Museum, or the reproduction in the Bannatyne volume of 1861, be carefully examined, it will be seen that the colouring and shading and the outline of the rather confused brown "blob" at the east end of the ruin, near the town wall, bears a close resemblance to the ruined gable end of the small house next on the left. The brown "blob" has, I suppose, hitherto been taken for a tree, but the trees are all coloured green. The remains of the "corbie steps" of the gable end are discernible. As this interpretation is of some importance in the reconstruction, I hope to have the reader's concurrence. See p. 11, no. 9 on sketch.

[2] Alexander Alesius was a Scot who communicated a description of Edinburgh for inclusion in the *Cosmographiæ Universalis* of Sebastian Münster which contains a record up to 1554; he says that the Church of St Mary in the Fields is situated between the monasteries of the Franciscan and Preaching friars, *where also* (*ubiquoque*) is the priest's college, Lib. II, p. 51.

earlier room or rooms at the church as mentioned on p. 4 above, and I think one is justified in saying it would be a structure of some architectural embellishment.

I deduce a certain confirmation that this building, intermediate between the old and the new houses of the Provosts, was an erection of later date than the year 1511, from the deed of conveyance of that year. These deeds, of which there are several, are extraordinarily confusing, and the land seems to have been split up into small plots, held by different owners. However, in 1511, two plots adjoining each other were gifted to the church for the purpose of constructing houses for the "Master" and Chaplains of the Church in the Fields. These plots were bounded on the west by the cemetery and on the east by land of the Bishop of Dunkeld. I believe that on them were erected the two houses of the Provost and the Precentor[1]. If I am so far right, it means that the land on which the Prebendaries' chamber was built was in possession of the Bishop of Dunkeld in 1511.

The Edinburgh dwelling-house of the Bishops of Dunkeld was in the Cowgate, and it appears to have been the common practice that each house should have a long narrow strip of land behind it. In this case the strip extended from the Cowgate as far south, or nearly so, as the lands of Bristo, which more or less made the boundary of the whole area beyond the southern confines of the town. Being adjacent to the new building site it follows that it included a large part, perhaps more than half, of what later became the quadrangle of the precincts, as well as the site on which the future "pædagogium," or Prebendaries' room, was to be, but not the site on which the Old House was, as I think, *already* standing.

Unfortunately I know of no record of the grant by which this

---

[1] It would be a most interesting study for anyone conversant with all the town records to map out the situation of the numerous plots to which reference is made, as for instance, Thomas Dickson, Archibald Kincaid, Nicholas de Toweris, Francis Inchtok (possibly Blakstok), George Walklot, William Rapperlaw, John Bewick, John Welch, etc. We might by such means arrive at definite conclusions as to the dates of the buildings that interest us.

strip of land passed to the church; could it be found, and if the nature of the eastern boundary were detailed, I feel sure that an important advance in our knowledge would be made. The Bishop of Dunkeld of the day was Gavin Douglas, and his reputation for piety, learning and charity is well known. It is a reasonable supposition that when the strip of land was handed over, it was for the uses I have suggested[1].

Let us now turn to the details of design of the two buildings which most interest us, that is, the Old (Provost's) House and the Salle. A number of items will be cited as we go along from the Depositions made by the men executed for the murder of Darnley; I do not suggest that these documents are trustworthy as evidence, but the details worked into them are evidently from the hand of some person well acquainted with the place. Let me add that, though I cannot guarantee my reconstruction to be absolutely accurate, yet it satisfies so many conditions that there cannot be room for serious error.

In addition to the "evidence" referred to above, we have two statements as to the accommodation afforded by the premises; and, as both agree and one is certainly untainted, they may be accepted as accurate. The one, contained in a letter from the Lords and others attending Mary at the time and addressed to the Queen-Mother of France (dated 10th February, 1567), mentions "Une salle, deux chambres, cabinet et garde-robe." The other, being the statement of one Servais de Condé, who had charge of the household effects in the royal palaces, or at least of Holyrood, mentions "Une chambre, salle et garde-robe." The word "salle" may safely be taken to imply "reception chamber." This room was, I think without doubt, the long room of the building mentioned above. The internal dimensions of this room were

---

[1] I have spent much time in trying to put together the various plots of which descriptions are to be found in the city records, but too many pieces of the puzzle are missing to make a successful result possible. Much information is available from Mr Boog-Watson's monograph on the *Closes and Wynds of Old Edinburgh*, Old Ed. Club, XII; also *Charters of the Collegiate Churches of Midlothian*, Bannatyne Club, 1861; also Grant, *Edinburgh Old and New*, I, pp. 250-1.

about 45 feet by 14 or 15 feet. If I am correct in believing that the foundation of the collegiate establishment included the idea of ultimate expansion to University status, and under the patronage of Gavin Douglas this was probable, we may suppose that the building was designed in a style fitted for the accommodation of the Senatus of the future. In this connection it is interesting to note that the building partly coincides with the chamber in the present University in which the Senate assembles. Some little confirmation that this Salle was out of the ordinary is given by the statement attributed to Mary in the Lennox manuscript[1], when, to induce Darnley to go to the house, she said the rooms were "easy and handsome." It is inconceivable that such words could be put in her mouth, in reference to the mean accommodation of the Old House. It would be preposterous to tell a lie that would be apparent on the instant; and, after all, there is no suggestion that the victim was under any compulsion to remain there if he did not like it.

It was not the custom in those days to stint light; we have record of the design of the new high school ordered to be built in 1578, which had eight windows on the south in a length of 110 feet and four on the north, each 7 by 5 feet[2]. It is reasonable to suppose that, in proportion, this educational building would be also liberally treated in this respect. Let us remember that when it was built the town (Flodden) wall was not built, and the outlook from the south windows would have been pleasant enough.

At this stage of our enquiry it is possible to obtain a fairly accurate idea of the relations to each other in 1567 of the ruined Kirk o' Field, enclosed in its own churchyard, the group of buildings, *i.e.* the Provost's New House, the Precentor's house to the north of it, and the remaining eight buildings enclosing the quadrangle, and the Flodden wall running roughly from east to west cutting across what were at one time the south gardens.

---

[1] Mahon, *Mary Queen of Scots*. Cambridge University Press. Lennox MS. p. 126.
[2] Town Records under date 10th May, 1578.

This has been done by building a model of the whole area to scale, showing all these features based on the "picture" referred to on p. 11 above, and to Edgar's maps. The model was then photographed as if from an aeroplane approaching from the south-east. It should be compared with the conditions existing in 1513, shown in the frontispiece.

THE UPPER FLOOR OF THE OLD HOUSE

The "cabinet" or *chambre* referred to above was certainly the room allotted as a sleeping-place for the King during his convalescence. It was, we know, situated in the eastern end of the ruin, in what I have called the Old House, with a window looking eastwards over the garden, which sloped sharply on the ground now covered by South Bridge Street, and some little distance beyond towards the Blackfriars monastery. The latter would be in view many feet below, with its stately church and the magnificent guest house, or "Great House," as it was called —the scene of many historical pageants, and the frequent residence of the Kings of Scotland before the building of Holyrood. The Great House had been the asylum of the imbecile King Henry VI of England when his masculine Queen brought him hither after Towton. Here, too, Perkin Warbeck had masqueraded and married. In Darnley's time the monastery was in ruins.

On its southern side the cabinet was provided with one of those projecting galleries or balconies of which two other examples have been noticed (p. 12) among the features of the buildings of the precincts. Like these it was, one can hardly doubt, constructed of timber and supported by the usual wooden struts, and of a width or out-hang of about 4 feet, by about 8 to 10 feet in length. Its height from the ground would be about 14 to 16 feet, as we shall presently see. At the time of its construction, and before the defensive wall partially spoiled its amenities, it would be a pleasant enough retreat in which to spend an hour or two in meditation, and to enjoy the "temperate invigorating airs" which the Popes of old considered a desideratum when choosing a site for scholastic establishments.

This site, with its southern aspect and its elevation, pre-eminently possessed it.

The room itself was about 16 feet by 12 internally, perhaps not very spacious, but large bedrooms were rather the exception than the rule. The Queen's bedroom at Holyrood is 22 feet by $18\frac{1}{2}$ feet, which is not on a grand scale; at Craigmillar the bedroom said to have been the Queen's is about 18 feet by 12; at Jedburgh the largest room is about 17 feet by 15, but the room said to have been occupied by the Queen, during her sickness there, is less than 12 feet square. At Glasgow, the whole house known as "Provand's Lordship," externally is but 50 feet by 24 feet, with thick walls, and there are three rooms on each floor, the largest about 14 feet by 17 excluding the "gallery" at the back, but this is not shown as the bedchamber. Thus the room at Kirk o' Field cannot be described as exceptionally mean, and it was certainly large enough for temporary use as a bedchamber.

Opening out of it was the antechamber, referred to as the *garde-robe*, which is confused by several writers with the gallery referred to above, and by others called the wardrobe. In fact, the small room about 7 feet by 12 was used for the purposes described by Boissière's dictionary as "Le lieu où est la chaise percée," and we know that in the equipment sent from Holyrood such a piece of furniture was included, together with a canopy of yellow taffeta to enclose it[1].

The entrance to the anteroom was from a passage which also gave on to the turret staircase by a doorway. It was from this latter entrance that the door was taken, which we are told was used to cover Darnley's bath, and the inference we are intended to draw is that the removal of the door by Mary's orders was designed to facilitate the entry of the murderers into his bedroom. The story of the door is worth a short notice, the more so because it helps us to reconstruct the plan of the upper floor on which the two rooms used by the King were situated. The only person who refers to the matter is Thomas Nelson, a servant

[1] *Inventaires*, pp. 33, 167.

who was present during the residence at Kirk o' Field; Nelson
says, "She (Mary) caused take down the outer door that closed
the passage towards both the chambers (that is, the anteroom
or *garde-robe* and the bedchamber), and caused use the same
door as a cover for the bath vat wherein he was bathed; and so
there was nothing left to stop the passage into the said chambers,
but only the portal doors." Joseph Robertson in his *Inventaires*
describes the interior of the bedroom and says, "A bath stood
beside the bed having for its lid a door...." Apparently he was
prepared to look upon the bath and the door as more or less
permanent additions to the bedroom furniture!

Surely the intention underlying this tale makes a large demand
on our credulity. The door, like all doors of the period, was hung
on hooks, and two minutes would be sufficient to rehang it when
the purpose of keeping the bath hot was accomplished. We must
suppose that a good many kettles full of hot water would be
necessary to fill the vat, and meanwhile the door was useful. A
bath in those days was a rare function, and there is no reason to
suppose that more than one was prescribed by the "Mediciner."
Once the bath was over it may be assumed that both vat and
door would be removed, for the latter, at all events, would be
an inconvenient adjunct to the furniture of a bedchamber already
described as small. Besides, why incur unnecessary suspicion by
not rehanging the door? The conspirators had, so we are told,
keys to fit all the doors, and "mair-attour," as they would have
said, there was a corresponding door into the turret from the
lower floor which Paris had taken the precaution to lock—at least,
so said John Hay in his "evidence"; thus, in any case, there was
no open communication between the two floors.

However, the useful side of the tale is that it assures us that
the staircase gave entrance through a door to a passage, from
which two doors led to the King's bedchamber. In the plan of
the house which I have drawn I have shown the two rooms opening one into the other, because this was usual, also because the
party-wall between the two rooms would be, almost certainly,
transverse to the roof ridge, and finally because of the consideration of parts of the official "evidence" to which we shall presently

come. The passage led also to the Salle, and, as there was a difference of level between the floors of the two buildings, a descent of two or three steps was necessary; a door closed this entrance. This last-mentioned door is presumably the one named in the 'Book of Articles' which Hosack published; in the 'Book,' four several entrances to the house are detailed, of which "the thrid (third) was throw the chaiplanis chalmer[1]." This is the

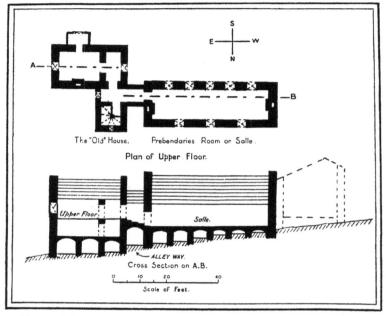

The "Old" House.   Prebendaries Room or Salle.

Plan of Upper Floor.

Upper Floor.   Salle.

ALLEY WAY.
Cross Section on A.B.

0   10   20   40
Scale of Feet.

Plan and Section of the "Old Provost's House" and the "Salle"

only place in the statements put forward by the prosecution where any mention is made of the Salle. It would seem, for reasons which I think are obvious, that the existence of this large room was suppressed as much as possible. As we shall see later, the movements of the actors were confined, by inference, if not by actual statement, to the small rooms of the Old House. The

[1] Hosack, I, p. 535.

reader's memory may be recalled to Crawford's designation of
the ruined building as the Prebendaries' chamber (*supra*, p. 20),
and a comparison made with the above name, the Chaplains'
chamber. One can hardly doubt but that they are the same.

I do not think that there were any other doors in the upper
storey than the four mentioned. The entrance to the gallery was
probably closed by a curtain.

THE LOWER FLOOR OF THE SAME

Let us now enter through the doorway on to the stone slab landing within the turret, and descend the "turnpike" to the next
landing about 8 feet below. We may assume with confidence
that the dimensions of the turret were similar to that shown in
the 1567 "picture," that is, externally about 12 feet square and
internally about 8½ feet; allowing 1½ feet for the newel and that
part of the step near to it which would have little width of tread,
the useful width of stairway would be, say, 3 feet, which is rather
above the average. I have allowed about 21 inches for the thickness of the walls; this may be an underestimate, and if so the
stairs were so much the narrower. From this landing a door
opened into the passage, the counterpart of that above except
that it had a door on the left opening to a flight of steps leading
to the ground level of the east garden[1].

The remainder of the lower floor was, we may confidently
believe, similar in the plan of its rooms to that of the upper floor,
except, of course, that there was no "gallery" projecting from
the larger of the two rooms, and this room—the one occupied
by the Queen on the occasion of her visits to Kirk o' Field—had,
so it is said, a window looking northward into the quadrangle,
which may have been absent in the King's chamber. The "evidence" of the persons condemned for the King's murder contain

---

[1] I have stressed the figures of the dimensions of the stairway,
because when we come later to the story that the murderers took the
trouble to carry the dead bodies of Darnley and his servant down the
turret steps, it will be seen that the physical difficulties were considerable, especially to men in a hurry.

several confirmatory details of the suggested arrangement of this floor. Thus, the servant, Paris, whose two depositions are confused and contradictory, speaks in the second of having taken "the *two* keys of the Queen's chamber," but in his first statement he refers to one key only. The witness, Nelson, refers to the key of the lower chamber where the Queen lay, *and* the key of the passage that passed toward the garden, but in another place he says, "the *keys* of her chamber as *also* of the passage that passed to the garden." John Hepburn deposed that, when he came forth from the Queen's chamber, after lighting the slow match, he closed *three* doors behind him, that would be, one leading into the anteroom, one from it to the passage, and one from the end of the passage towards the garden. It was this witness also who stated that there was a window in the Queen's room which looked into the "Close." John Hay, another of the condemned men, refers to the servant Paris as locking the door "which passes up the turnpike to the King's chamber[1]."

From these statements the reason why I have drawn the two rooms as opening one into the other will be apparent. As to the turret, I believe this was an addition to the Old House[2] when it was incorporated in the design of the south side of the quadrangle together with the scholastic building which we call the Salle. In all, four doors are mentioned on this floor.

THE BASEMENT AND SALLE

Let us now return to the turret and descend the turnpike to the ground entrance, called in the depositions the "Fore Entry." This was, following many other examples, in the front of the

[1] For all these depositions see Anderson, II.
[2] That the Old House was not part of the design of the new precincts when these were built between 1510 and 1512 is, I think, fairly obvious from its position and the way it juts out from the general line. This is partly borne out in the 'Detection' by Buchanan, who was fond of dwelling on its ruinous state. This may be discounted, but doubtless the period of the house went far back towards the beginnings of Kirk o' Field as a place of worship. Houses in those days were built to last,

turret, facing north, and giving entrance from the quadrangle. It is remarkable that in no single case of the many books dealing with the subject is it noticed that the level of the floor of the Queen's chamber must have been approached by a flight of steps both from the fore entry and from the east garden. From the former the rise would be about 6 feet, from the latter about 8 feet. The fact is of considerable importance and is proved by consideration of the levels of the ground already mentioned; but let us now be a little more particular.

We have already noticed the average slope of the ground from the Kirk o' Field towards the Cowgate, but there was, I might say *is*, a rather remarkable bank, of a steepness much exceeding the average which confronted the traveller on approaching the Kirk from the east and north-east. On this bank were situated the three sides of the quadrangle farthest from the spectator in the sketch on p. 11 (that is, the north, south and east sides).

From the front of the New House to the farther end of the ruins the fall of the ground was not less than 14 feet. We may suppose then, without fear of error, that the New House, the Salle, and the Old House, were stepped one below the other. From a sectional drawing I find that the floor of the Salle was not less than 5 feet higher than that of the Queen's chamber in the Old House, and the latter floor at its eastern end not less than 8 feet above ground level. This means that both these floors were on a series of groin-arched vaults, a practice very common among the old houses of Edinburgh. The vaults of the Old House, forming its basement, were comparatively lofty, varying from about 7 feet at the eastern end to nearly 6 feet at the western end, allowing a foot for thickness at the crown.

The vaulting under the Salle was much lower, varying from about 6 feet at the deep end to about 2 feet at the west end. Here we have the "Vaults, in low and darnit (hidden) parts and places," referred to in the indictment of the Earl of Morton many years

as witness the New (Provost's) House which endured, as we know, for more than 280 years. Buchanan was a discreet liar and would hardly refer in such terms to a house which would be only a few years older than himself had it been built with the others.

later[1]. It may be mentioned here, though an anticipation, that, when there was no longer any need to persecute Mary Stuart, there was no objection to stating the truth. For in this indictment it is clear that the gunpowder plot had relation to explosives placed under the Salle and not under the Old House, whereas, in the official story, the former is practically suppressed in the record altogether and the gunpowder is said to have been placed in the latter.

The vaults under the Old House could not have been referred to as low and hidden places, for here was the kitchen mentioned in the depositions, and, although it is not suggested in the *official* story that gunpowder was placed in these vaults, this is hinted at in other narratives, so that it is worth emphasizing that to do so would not have been possible. The confined kitchen space was occupied by the cook, one Bonkil, and we may be quite sure that he had a staff of assistants—in those days the "Cook, single-handed" was an unknown quantity.

Communicating between the quadrangle and the gardens lying to the south (we are talking now of the time previous to the building of the town or Flodden wall) was a narrow alley-way passing between the Old House and Salle and *under* the passage connecting the two buildings (see general plan, p. 28). Almost certainly this entrance would be provided with a door to close the quadrangle at night, though no specific mention of it is made in the depositions. Just beyond this door, and on the left of the alley-way leaving the quadrangle, was the door giving entrance to the kitchen which Paris mentions in his story. There does not seem to have been any other entrance to the kitchen, and it seems impossible to arrange space for a doorway at the base of the turret on account of the confined height available; besides, there is no mention of such. Even the door mentioned by Paris must have had two or three steps leading down to it, and the kitchen floor, at least part of it, must have been excavated below ground level. Finally, there must have been a door giving entrance to

---

[1] Arnot's *Criminal Trials*, p. 388. I do not mean to suggest that Morton was guilty of conniving at the gunpowder plot, for I am sure he was as innocent thereof as the Queen of Scots herself.

the basement of the Salle, and presumably situated on the right of the alley-way referred to above. Thus in all we have accounted for four doors in the basement—the fore entry, the alley-way, the kitchen, and the Salle basement.

In all, twelve doors, and twelve keys. The building of the town wall, to which we shall come in a moment, introduced another door, or at least a postern, and the thirteenth key. But in Hepburn's deposition fourteen keys are mentioned, and, as I have great faith in the accuracy of the details of this kind, woven into the alleged statements of the condemned men, I have been at pains to account for the last key[1]. There seem to be three choices, a doorway between the Salle and the New House, the door or gate shown in the 1567 "picture" on the right near the town wall, and a door leading from the quadrangle direct to the east garden. I am afraid I cannot solve the problem as to which was in question.

An outline sectional diagram through the Old House, the passage and the Salle is given on p. 28, as it may help to explain the above description.

THE TOWN WALL, OR FLODDEN WALL

A correct alignment of the town wall in the neighbourhood of Kirk o' Field is of considerable importance in our reconstruction and location of the precincts. I venture to think that local investigators are a little astray in their views, and I must disagree radically with those—W. Moir Bryce[2] and James Grant[3], for instance—who place the ruined house on the eastward side of South Bridge Street[4]. I must content myself here by referring

---

[1] Ormistoun, in his depositions, says only thirteen keys were made, so perhaps my search for the missing one is needless.

[2] *Book of the Old Edinburgh Club*, II.

[3] *Old and New Edinburgh*, III.

[4] Whitaker is even further astray, for, on the discovery of a closed postern in the then existing (1790) city wall, opposite the Royal Infirmary, he placed the house there, more than a hundred yards too far east. This postern, by the way, is clearly shown in Edgar's map of 1742, near the head of what I believe was known as Back Row, now Roxburgh

the reader to the plan on p. 16 above, which I believe to be as accurate as possible.

The reasons which guided the city engineers in their lay-out are fairly obvious—the intention to include the Kirk within the walls and after that to bend the wall northwards so that it should follow the line of the contour which ran almost parallel to what became in after years the line of Drummond Street.

Although it would appear that the friars of the collegiate church were favoured individuals, it is clear that military exigence required some sacrifice from them. The wall, while it certainly cut off practically the whole of their south gardens, also, as I think, cut off a part of the churchyard which extended over what is now South College Street and probably some little distance farther south; beyond this came a rough road or lane and then that somewhat nebulous area known as the "Lands of Bristo." The first northward bend of the wall was evidently designed so as just to save the Old House, for the trace shaves its easternmost corner and to all intents blocks up its southern aspect, at least as regards the lower storey. It is possible, and, I think, quite likely, that the Old House was slightly askew in relation to the Salle, and not exactly as I have drawn it. In that case the wall was in contact with its southern face all along.

At all events, it is certain that the exit to the south gardens was preserved and by some special ruling a postern gate was permitted in the wall, which continued the means of getting to and from the gardens. Based on the evidence of one Thomas Nelson, there is a certain confusion as to this postern gate. Nelson said that all the keys of the house had been delivered to him "except the key of that door which passed through the cellar [which above we have referred to as the kitchen] *and* the town wall." A little later he said, "Bonkil had the key of the cellar." Not unnaturally many writers regarded the postern gate as an access to the cellar or kitchen. I think this was certainly not the case. Apart from

Place. It was, I should say, very near where the present Drummond Street entrance to the University schools now is (Whitaker, III, p. 298), and, again marking the persistence of ancient rights of way, very near where the old trackway from the south passed through the city to Leith.

the obvious inconvenience of having the only means of getting to and from the gardens as a passage through the kitchen, there is the difficulty, already mentioned in another connection, of the kitchen floor being below the ground level. But a better evidence is Buchanan, who in the 'Detection' says, "There is a postern door *hard by* the house[1]," and this corresponds with what I have shown in the plan, in which the path to the postern is the direct continuation of the alley-way passing between the Old House and the Salle already described. Probably Nelson's statement was wrongly taken down. It may be added that, when the south garden was cut off by the town wall, what remained was enclosed by a new wall leaving a narrow lane between it and the defences, and in this new wall is also shown a gateway or door immediately opposite the postern, showing clearly the intention of the latter to provide access to the gardens. This is shown in the 1567 "picture," and can also be seen in the plan on p. 16.

The completion of the town wall created a small yard or court under the south windows of the Salle, which, perhaps for privacy or defence, was afterwards completely enclosed by a wall from the right wing of the New House joining on to the Flodden wall; this wall is the one in which was a door with what looks like a shield over it, as shown in the "picture" (p. 11, no. 3). This yard or court (*ib.*, no. 4) was about 80 feet long and of irregular width. It is of this place that Paris speaks in his deposition; he had just parted from Bothwell, he says, at the fore entry, and "I came to the Little Court, entered the kitchen and asked the

---

[1] The 'Oration,' a kind of companion document to the 'Detection,' but not written by Buchanan, says much the same: "A house...that stood *right over against* the door" (that is, the postern). It is a curious fact, that will be referred to again, that, in the document which I have called the 'Indictment' (see *The Indictment of Mary Queen of Scots*, published by the Cambridge University Press), which is a free translation of the Latin in which the 'Detection' was originally written and made by Buchanan himself after he was in communication with Cecil in 1568, this matter of the postern door is omitted altogether. Still later, in his *History of Scotland*, II, p. 321, Buchanan is still shy of this postern gate, and only mentions a gate which had been *made through* the town wall by the conspirators for the purpose of carrying through the King's body, which is very nearly, if not quite, nonsense.

cook for a candle[1]." From this quotation we gather confirmation both of the alley and the kitchen door already referred to.

The standard dimensions of the town wall are known; it was 7 ells in total height, or say 21¾ feet, 6 feet thick at the base, tapering to 5 feet at a height of 16½ feet; at this height was the "battling plane," or way, on which the defenders stood, commonly called the *banquette* in more modern parlance. From this point the wall was continued to its full height by a comparatively thin wall of say 1 foot thick, pierced with battlements. The wall, the record tells us, was to be "well pinnit and harlit" and to be provided with "murdreis" holes[2]. Though the wall was commenced shortly after Flodden, we may be sure that it was not completed for quite a long time, indeed the Burgh records show that parts of it were not complete even so late as the time we are dealing with; but there is reason to suppose that, at the date of Darnley's death, the particular part that interests us had been finished, though how long previously cannot be said.

Now the immediate connection of these details with our story is that the floor of the gallery projecting from the upper storey of the Old House would normally be about 15½ feet above the natural ground level. That is to say, it was very nearly on the same level as the "battling plane" referred to just now. We have seen that the wall passed close to or in contact with that side of the house, and nothing is more natural than to suppose that the gallery was converted into an extension, of which the floor was the aforesaid "battling plane"; a small alteration of the battlement wall made a gable end, a window is pierced through the same, two lath and plaster sides are added, and the projecting gallery has become the place where Thomas Nelson slept so soundly, at least he says so, that he heard nothing of all the commotion going on at his side on the night of the explosion. "This deponer," he says, "lay in the litill gallery, that went direct to

---

[1] Printed by Laing, II, p. 196.

[2] *Pinnit* means securely filled between the large stones; *harlit* is broadcast with gravel mortar; *murdreis* holes are loopholes for the type of cannons known as "murderers." See, for these details, *Burgh Records of Edinburgh*, 1567.

south out of the Kingis chalmer, havand ane window in the gavel (gable) throw (through) the town wall." And after the explosion, which woke him up, but miraculously did not harm him, "he stood upon the ruinous wall until the pepill convened." In other words, Nelson stood on the "battling plane" with a solid 5-foot wall under him.

We have nothing to do, at the moment, with this remarkable escape of Nelson except to point out how his story chimes in with the various facts that have been brought together. There is one point more. As we know, at this point the town wall was on rather steep ground, it was consequently stepped at every few yards, and this means that if the average height was maintained the plane was alternately above and below the average, and from this I deduce that the window "in the gavel" was very likely not more than say 14 feet from the ground, perhaps even less. We shall come to this again.

THE FURNITURE OF KIRK O' FIELD

With that curious exactness which characterizes the accounting of the period, we have a complete statement of the articles of household plenishing which were conveyed from Holyrood to Kirk o' Field for the use of the illustrious invalid. These are printed by Joseph Robertson from the inventories which still exist. An acquittance, purporting to be signed by Mary herself, is given to Servais de Condé, whose duty it was to account for the royal property, dated 20th May, 1567, that is, three months after the death of Darnley. In it Servais declares that the goods were delivered at Kirk o' Field in the month of February, a fact that I would ask readers to remember, for it is a confirmatory evidence not hitherto noticed, I think, that the coming of Darnley to Kirk o' Field was not premeditated so far as Mary was concerned. In fact, as Darnley arrived at Kirk o' Field on the 1st February, 1567, the furniture and he must have come almost together; this, however, is an anticipation, and will be referred to again.

The list of furniture is short; besides a few oddments it included a bed, a small table, and a "high" chair in the bedroom, a *chaise percée* or commode in the *garde-robe* or anteroom, a small carpet, a "high" chair and a "dais" or cloth of estate in the Salle, and a small bed in the Queen's chamber on the lower floor. It does not need much emphasis from me to indicate that this could not possibly have been the complete list of the furniture available; it merely represents the *articles de luxe* sent from Holyrood, and there must have been other chairs, stools or forms, besides tables large and small. Whether these came from the New (Provost's) House, then in occupation of Sir James Balfour, or whether they were permanent fittings in the house, is immaterial. But I want the reader to estimate mentally how much space this equipment would occupy, and then to remember that there were quite a number of people assembled at one time. We need only consider the last evening, the 9th of February.

This particular Sunday was one of high festival, Carnival Sunday, the day of masques and jollity. The Queen had been at a ceremonial supper in the town; at Kirk o' Field it was a great occasion, Darnley's last day of convalescence, and on the morrow he was to return to Holyrood and a new era of connubial confidence was to commence. It is not too much to suppose that all or most of the guests of the supper party would, as an ordinary matter of etiquette, accompany the Queen to felicitate the King on his recovery. Only a few names are mentioned—Bothwell, Huntly, Argyll, Cassillis, Lady Reres—but the contemporary accounts refer to the "Greater part of the nobility and gentlemen who were in her suite[1]." Buchanan himself in his history calls it a "numerous attendance[2]." The Queen in a letter attributed to her own hand says she was accompanied by "most part of the nobles then in this town[3]." Then there was Darnley himself, recovered from his sickness, and, we must suppose, some of the gentlemen in attendance on him, such as our sound sleeping friend Nelson, Sandy Durham perhaps, and others whose

[1] Letter of the Lords to the King of France, printed in Laing, II, p. 97.
[2] Buchanan, *History of Scotland*, XVIII.
[3] Printed in Keith, I, p. cii.

names are mentioned. Servants of sorts coming and going we must reckon on, for it may be doubted if an assembly of this kind on such an occasion would be long without the flowing bowl.

In all, how many will you say were in the room at one time? Fifteen? Twenty? I can count up to fifteen persons who almost certainly were there, and I am sure that is not all. Do not forget that some of the nobles were playing at dice, that the Queen was apart in amatory conversation with her husband, giving him a ring and so forth. Now I will leave the reader to decide for himself whether all this can be squeezed into a small room, say 16 feet by 12 feet.

And yet, every scrap of the evidence given or concocted for the persecution of the Queen of Scots was framed with the intention of confining the action of this drama to the room above that in which the Queen had slept. The reasons for this are obvious, because the story required a guilty knowledge on the Queen's part that gunpowder was placed in her room, and because any admission of the undermining of the Salle, where the King did *not* sleep, would weaken the allegation put forward that the sole object was to blow him up while asleep in bed.

I have strayed a little beyond the strict limits of this section, but I am at present only concerned to show that the place of assembly of the company referred to above was not in the small bedroom, as so many writers taking the "evidence" without much consideration have said, but in a much larger room which, as I have suggested, was the Salle.

THE TAPESTRIES

There is one point more, in connection with the Salle and its dimensions, which must be considered. Our useful Servais de Condé has several entries of the tapestries sent from Holyrood to cover the bare stone walls of the rooms at Kirk o' Field. The entries are not in complete agreement one with the other, but they are near enough for our purpose.

At p. 39 of Joseph Robertson's reproduction is an entry of seven pieces of tapestry representing "The Hunting of Coneys," of which set six pieces were lost at Kirk o' Field. At p. 51 occurs the entry of forty pieces, large and small, of which six pieces were lost in the King's chamber, and five pieces in the Salle; we are not concerned with the remaining twenty-nine pieces. At p. 167 is the entry of sixteen pieces, large and small, lost in the chamber, Salle and *garde-robe*. These include the eleven pieces just mentioned[1].

I should have thought that all six pieces of the "Coney" hunt would have been in the Salle, and perhaps Servais was mistaken as to this. Without venturing to estimate the length and width of "large" pieces of tapestry, there is enough to make it more than probable that they covered a very considerable area of wall, much exceeding what would be available in a "little" house such as Lennox in his Narrative tells us the Old House was; or, to take another account, "The house was so small, that it contained no more than two small apartments[2]."

THE EAST AND SOUTH GARDENS

In Mary's time the east garden was not an extensive plot, it could hardly have covered more than from 100 to 120 feet eastward from the Old House, over what is now South Bridge Street and a considerable part of the site of the existing houses on the east side thereof. Here a wall divided the garden from the enclosure of the Black Friars known as "Another West Garden[3]." In days before the Flodden wall, the east and south gardens of Kirk o' Field formed a continuous whole, but when Mary used

---

[1] Unfortunately for its veracity, the 'Book of Articles' mentions that "some tapistrie of valour" which was in the lodging was removed by the Queen, in order to save it from the explosion. Apparently the author did not foresee that Servais de Condé would give his "accompt." We can hardly suppose that other tapestries, besides those lost, were originally at the house; if so, then the wall space required for them must be still greater than I suppose.

[2] Clerneau's tale, see Pollen, p. 358.

[3] City Protocol Books, 9th January, 1568. Moir Bryce in his work, *The Black Friars of Edinburgh*, puts this dividing wall much too far to the east.

to sing and make pastime in the east garden, as the very improbable story tells us she did, its width was curtailed to about 40 feet at the widest part. Even part of this was taken up by an alleyway which I estimate was about 5 feet wide running along the town wall, and required for military purposes. The garden was shut off from the alley by a wall, not a very high one we may suppose, and a belt of trees, the latter being intended to block out the plain ugliness of the defences. Indeed, from the 1567 "picture" it appears that the plot was enclosed by trees, and the open space must have been very little. That part which was nearest to the house sloped sharply, becoming more gentle towards the eastern limit.

We can trace with almost complete certainty the alleged movements of the conspirators in the vicinity of the garden on the night of Darnley's death. It is not necessary to follow them from the gate of the Black Friars, whence it will be remembered they commenced to carry the gunpowder. The first witness says that the powder was carried to "the back wall of the yard *that is next the trees*." "Yard" is, of course, the equivalent term to *garden*, but "back wall" is not quite so clear; it means, I have very little doubt, the wall of the alley running along the town wall, referred to above. The word "back" seems to be almost equivalent of "south." Thus in Ainslie's 1780 map the town wall on the south is called the "back wall," there is also "back of the Canongate," meaning south of the same. Later in the same deposition the witness says he came "to the back wall and dyke, and Bothwell passed over the dyke." Now in this case "back wall" appears to mean the town wall, for "dyke" certainly means the garden wall.

The next witness says they came to a "slap" in the dyke, meaning a broken down place in the garden wall[1]. The same person says they came "to the back wall and dyke of the town wall, when Bothwell passed over the wall." Here it will be seen that "dyke" and "wall" are interchanged again; "back wall" is here the garden wall. I think, however, that we need go no further. It is clear that the conspirators came up the

---

[1] The word "slap" is still in use in Ireland and Scotland to indicate a gap or broken down piece of wall.

alley-way to a point not far from the house and, there finding a convenient "slap," passed over into the east garden with their burden of gunpowder. They were on their way, of course, to the back door, leading to the passage and the Queen's bedchamber, but this does not belong to this chapter. It was down the same alley that they ran away when the explosion was inevitable.

Little need be said as to the south garden; once, as I have said, a part of the gardens as a whole, it was cut off by the Flodden wall, and its dimensions further curtailed by a clear way which was maintained on the outer perimeter of the defences. Nominally this clear way was to be of 24 feet in width, but the order was not very religiously observed, and I think here it was less; at all events what was left of the south garden was enclosed by a fresh wall outside of and parallel to the town wall; in it, as has been said, was a doorway immediately facing the postern in the town wall. It was within this garden that the dead body of Darnley was found. The approximate spot would be about 30 feet from the corner (east end) of what is now South College Street and near the pavement on the south side thereof. Andrew Dalzel speaks of the ghost of Darnley as haunting a certain dark chamber in the house lived in by Dr Robertson, formerly the New House of Kirk o' Field, but I think one would be more likely to meet it on a moonless midnight of a 9th of February, fleeing across South College Street to the point indicated, to meet a fate he richly deserved.

THE "DUKE'S HOUSE" OR GREAT LODGING

Only a word need be said about this; it was, we know, built shortly after 1554, when the Friars of Kirk o' Field sold the site and remains of their old hospital or guest house to the Duke of Chatelherault, the head of the house of Hamilton. It evidences the decadence of the collegiate church that such a sale should be necessary (true the destruction wrought by Hertford, afterwards the Protector Somerset, in 1544, had rendered it useless for the time), but it also points to the lowering of the standard of charity and hospitality which in the olden time had been instrumental in maintaining the attachment of the people to the ancient

Church. The Cardinal of Lorraine had urged, at Trent, that this standard should be resumed.

The site of this building is precisely fixed by Andrew Dalzel in his *History of the University*[1]. "It stood in a transverse direction from north to south...in the very centre of the north side of the great *inner* quadrangle of the new College." But Dalzel was referring to the original design of the brothers Adam, and not to the design of W. H. Playfair which governed the University building as it stands to-day[2]. We have, however, the original drawings and can exactly place the required site. A space of approximately 30 yards separated it from the north porch of the church. The dimensions of the house can be taken from several of the old maps, as Edgar or Ainslie's, which show it to be a large building some 70 by 35 feet with square stair turrets at each southern corner. There is a wing at the north end, but I am not sure if it was a later addition made when the house was first taken over for use as a nucleus for the old, then the "new," college, in 1583 or thereabouts.

The house stood on a steepish slope and it is interesting to note that a passage-way is shown *under* it and through the vaulted basement.

It would appear that the original grammar school stood within the area sold to the Hamiltons, but how close to the old hospital I cannot say. At all events, after the sale, a new grammar school was built a little farther north and at the head of what now became School House Wynd, later College Wynd. There was, however, an earlier track, or vennel, over the same ground to which reference has already been made (p. 7).

THE "SECRET" WAY BETWEEN HOLYROOD AND KIRK O' FIELD

For reasons which will appear in due course, a short note on the "secret" way referred to in the story is desirable. It emerges several times, but only, I think, in narratives coming from the

[1] MS. in the Advocate's Library, also printed by Cosmo Innes.
[2] Sir A. Grant in his *Story of the University of Edinburgh*, i, p. 128, is mistaken on this point.

Earl of Lennox. In the first Narrative[1] it appears twice: "...more easy...for her, for that there passed a privy way between the palace and it, where she might always resort unto him...." And again, "Bothwell came the secret way she herself was wont to come to the King, her husband..." And in the third Lennox MS. "...There was a secret way for her to come to him there and not by the streets."

Andrew Lang, who was fond of such things, had some hopes of a tunnel, but really there is little in the matter. "Secret" does not mean more than private, in fact, as Lennox puts it, "not by the streets." A glance at de Wit's map (the same as Gordon of Rothiemay's) will show that what is meant was to follow the lane along the back wall of the south Canongate gardens to St Mary's Port, and thence without much hindrance from the town wall, which at that point was as yet unbuilt (*Town Records of Edinburgh*, III, p. 239), through the gardens and fields of the old Black Friars monastery to the east garden of Kirk o' Field; thence through the back door or garden door into the house.

On the famous occasion when Mary visited Darnley the evening before his death, she would not have come from or returned to Holyrood by this way, for, in fact, she had been supping in the Canongate, and therefore came by way of the Friars Wynd, and returning with so large a cavalcade she no doubt followed the same. But with small retinue on occasional visits the "secret" way may have been used.

It will be noted that the last stage of this approach was much the same as that used by the alleged carriers of the gunpowder in the official story.

---

[1] *Mary Queen of Scots*. Mahon. Cambridge University Press. Appendix A, pp. 126, 130.

Chapter II

THE PHYSICAL IMPOSSIBILITIES OF THE ACCEPTED NARRATIVES

THE UNOFFICIAL STORY

IT is, I think, a strong confirmation of the unexpectedness of the explosion at Kirk o' Field that those in authority in Mary's Government blurted out statements quite dissimilar from the allegations formulated at a later date. There are two letters, both written within a few hours after the occurrence, which contain almost the same matter; one is nominally signed by the Queen herself, though it is as certain as anything can well be that she had no hand in it; the other is signed by the Lords of Council. The former relates:

The house wherein the King was lodged, was in an instant blown in the air, he lying sleeping in his bed, with such a vehemency, that of the whole lodging, walls and other, there is nothing remaining, no, not one stone above another, but all either carried far away, or dung in dross to the very ground-stone. It must be done by force of powder, and appears to have been a mine.... Also whoever have taken this wicked enterprise in hand we assure ourselves it was dressed (intended) as well for us as for the King. For we lay the most part of all last week in that same lodging, and was there accompanied with the most part of the Lords that are in this town that same night at midnight, and of very chance tarried not all night, by reason of some masque at the Abbey...[1].

The other account says:

At about two hours after midnight, his lodging, he being abed, has been blown in the air by force of gunpowder...of such vehemency that of a *salle*, two chambers—*cabinet et garderobe*—there remains nothing, all being carried to a distance and reduced to dross, not only the roof and floor, but also the walls down to the foundations, so that

[1] Printed in Keith, I, p. cii. Addressed to the Archbishop of Glasgow in Paris.

there rested not one stone on another. Those who are the authors of this wickedness failed by but a very little in destroying the Queen with the greater part of the nobility and gentry at present in her suite, who were with the King in his chamber until almost midnight. And by chance only her Majesty did not remain there the whole night...[1].

At this stage no comment will be made on these two letters, which are of special value as being records of the first impressions. In point of date the next statement is found in a proclamation, dated two days later, offering reward to discover the perpetrators, the wording of which is practically the same, though it is added that the bodies of Darnley and his servant were found a short way from the house.

On the 16th February, 1566, one M. Clerneau, or Clarenault, of whom more later, arrived in London and reported the occurrence, adding, " It is clearly seen that this proceeds from a mine."

On 23rd February, a courier arrived in Paris[2] who reported that " Some scoundrels fired a mine, which they had already laid under the foundations of the said lodging. The house was reduced to ruins in an instant."

On 27th February, the above-named Clerneau arrived in Paris, and his report, as translated by the recipient (Bishop of Mondovi), stated:

At two o'clock or three, past midnight the mine was fired. It was laid under *that apartment only* where the King slept, and ruined entirely all *that* part of the house, the fall of which brought down the *other apartment* too....The conjecture has been made that he got up from bed because of the smell of the powder, before the mine exploded and was, along with his servant, afterwards suffocated by the smoke.

On 15th March, the Jesuit Father, Edmund Hay, and Moretta, the envoy from the Duke of Savoy, both of whom were in Edin-

[1] Sloane MS. No. 3199, f. 131. Sent by hand of M. de Clarenault, written by the Secretary Maitland and subscribed by Archbishop St Andrews, Bishops of Ross and Galloway, Earls of Argyll, Huntly, Atholl, Cassillis, Caithness, Sutherland, Bothwell, Lords Fleming, Livingston. Also the officials of the Council, as Richardson (Treasurer), Bellenden (Justice Clerk), Maitland (Secretary).

[2] Pollen, p. 354.

burgh at the time of the deed, arrived in Paris. What they said to the Bishop of Mondovi, as reported by him, though useful, does not affect us at the moment; but, at the same time, they told the Venetian Ambassador, Correr, that, the King having been assassinated *outside* the house, that part of the house, "where the King was accustomed to sleep," was destroyed. It is noteworthy that both the foreign emissaries, of whom it is alleged that their mission was to push Mary into extreme measures against the Protestant party, endeavour, rather pointedly, to confine the explosion to the King's lodging only.

The Earl of Moray left Scotland about 10th April[1], two months after the King's death. He passed through London on his return journey towards the end of July. At that time he told the Spanish Ambassador that he knew of a letter written by Mary to Bothwell, telling him that she would put her husband in the house where the explosion was arranged.

The Earl of Lennox left Scotland in April, a few days after Moray. Thirteen months later he drew up a document[2] in which he alleged that Darnley was brought to a place which was "already prepared with undermines and trains of powder."

Even the author of the 'Oration,' published as late as December 1571, was so careless as to neglect the official narrative in many respects and said that the Queen used the lower chamber lest, if it were left empty, "the noyes of the under-myneris wirking, and of the bringeris in of the powder" should create suspicion.

Fourteen years later, the Earl of Morton was executed for the murder of Darnley; his indictment included: "Powder had been a little of before, placed and put in by him and his accomplices, under the ground and angular stones and within the vaults, low and dern parts and places of the lodging."

I will call no more witnesses. Here is sufficient evidence that the first impressions, confirmed in the last three cases by subsequent consideration, were that the destruction at Kirk o' Field

---

[1] Simancas Records, Silva to Philip, 21st April, 1567.
[2] See Lennox MS. in *The Indictment of Mary Queen of Scots*, Mahon, p. 126.

was caused by underground mines, or at least powder placed in vaults below the building or buildings. I do not want to convince anyone against his will that these impressions were correct, but that they existed and persisted is evident. You may say, and, I think, say truly, that Morton's trial was a mere judicial pretext —he richly deserved what he got, but not exactly on the charge laid against him; but, even so, the wording of the charge is significant of the impressions.

THE OFFICIAL STORY

The official story, supported by the depositions of four persons executed for the fact, the statements of two witnesses, one of them actually involved, so he declared, in the explosion, the depositions of two others also executed at later dates, and finally the 'Book of Articles,' a summary of the accusation, is *radically at variance* with the first impressions.

Everybody knows the outline of the official story; that two or three hours before the deed, gunpowder was poured in a loose heap in the Queen's chamber, with her connivance, and exploded there at about 2 o'clock a.m., Darnley being asleep in the room above. That only a few men, headed by Bothwell, were concerned, that the victim was handled by none, but killed by being hurled by the explosion over the town wall into the south garden, where he was found lying, with the servant who slept in his room. There are variations forced on many writers by common sense, and by contemporary evidence, but the above is the story vouched for before the Commission held in England. As such, several writers, and notably Malcolm Laing, maintain its truth. If it is not true in its essential details, the whole fabric of the "evidence" falls to pieces, and we must seek some other explanation of Darnley's death. Let us examine it.

THE GUNPOWDER, ITS SOURCE AND
CONVEYANCE

Within a very few days after the explosion at Kirk o' Field, when those who reported on current events were without guidance as to what line to take, Sir William Drury, Commander at Berwick, wrote to Cecil, "There is one of Edinburgh that affirms how Mr James Balfour bought of him, powder, as much as he should have paid three score pounds Scottish[1]." But a month later, without any reference to his first report, he told a different story, viz. that the powder had been brought from Dunbar, of which place Bothwell was over-Lord.

The name of Sir James Balfour is so woven in the history of the case that I am inclined to believe that Drury's first story is more reliable than his second. Balfour, let us remember, had had full command of the premises at Kirk o' Field since the previous December[2]. Ample opportunity must have been available to collect and store gunpowder there in secret.

It is more difficult to believe that the powder was brought from Dunbar. This statement is of course an "official" one, and the intention, or at least the result, is to make Bothwell the culprit and, to that extent, to exonerate Balfour. We must not forget that, when the official tale was evolved, during the latter half of June (1567), Sir James was sitting in daily counsel with the Lords[3]. The powder on arrival in Edinburgh, several days

---

[1] *P.R.O. State Papers, Border*, XII, p. 207.

[2] A grant of the Provostry of Kirk o' Field was made to Robert Balfour, brother of the said James, on 9th December, 1566 (*Reg. Privy Seal*, xxxv, ff. 95/6, Edinburgh); the actual grant must go back considerably before this date, for it took time for a document to pass the stages before the affixing of the Privy Seal. The most confirmed Mary-hater can hardly think that the grant had anything to do with the plot that grew out of it.

[3] Melville to Cecil, dated 1st July, 1567, "The Earl of Morton and Athol with my Lord Hume and my Lord Lethington (are here), Sir James Balfour, Captain of the Castle, who is daily in counsel with them, also Master James Macgill and the Justice Clerk" (*State Papers, Scotland, Elizabeth*, XIV, p. 5). A terribly suggestive council. Every member

before the deed, how many days are not told, was stored—
where? In the nether hall, that is, the basement of Bothwell's
lodgings at Holyrood, we are told, though the tale is a little shaky
on this point; at all events it was taken there afterwards[1]. The
witness Powrie goes so far as to say that the powder and trunks
were only taken to Holyrood on the evening of Saturday. But
one asks why on earth they were taken there for twenty-four
hours only? Even more curious, the barrel, of which we shall
hear more, was, so says Hepburn, only obtained from the seller
on the very Sunday evening; yet it too was taken to Holyrood,
and could have hardly arrived there before it was taken to Kirk
o' Field. Can anything be more improbable? The palace was
closely guarded; we hear of the alert sentries in other parts of
the story. It seems impossible that horses conveying strange
equipment should pass in without enquiry, impossible that
nothing should subsequently transpire about it, but most impossible to suppose that Bothwell, intending to use the powder
at Kirk o' Field, and in league with Balfour, as parts of the story
tell us he was, should not send it direct to the place where it was
wanted. That course was quite simple and involved no necessity
to pass it through the town at all.

The conveyance of the powder from Holyrood to Kirk o' Field
is described in the deposition of William Powrie. Put in bald
language his story is this. On the evening of the 9th February
at or about 10 o'clock,

I, being at Ormistoun's lodging in the Black Friar's Wynd, received orders to go to Holyrood to bring on horseback two "mails,"
one being a trunk and the other a leather mail[2]. I knew that they
contained gunpowder. I was to take them to the gate of the Black-

except perhaps Athol was deeply concerned in the story. It cannot be
denied that Balfour had, at the least, opportunity of smoothing out the
traces of his connection with it.

[1] It was usual for the Lords in attendance to be lodged at Holyrood,
but which of the several blocks shown in Gordon's map was allotted
for the purpose, I am not sure.

[2] Fr. *malle*, a trunk or case, in this case one of those leather, shaped
receptacles which are made for being carried pannierwise on horses.
They are still used in the East when travelling away from beaten roads.

friars Monastery, and there hand them over to Earl Bothwell and others. This I did using two horses, belonging to "my lord," and then helped to carry the powder to the wall of the Kirk o' Field garden that is next the trees. The powder being in polks[1]. I was not permitted to pass beyond the wall, but returned to the Blackfriars gate, where, finding the horses gone, I and my companion shouldered the two mails and carried them to Holyrood. As we passed up the Blackfriars Wynd the Queen was a little in front of us, her company having lighted torches.

This was Powrie's statement of 23rd June; ten days later, he made another and different deposition.

He did not carry the powder on two horses belonging to "my Lord," making one journey of it. Only one horse was really employed, which belonged to a page, and two journeys were made to Holyrood and back. On the second journey as well as a mail he carried an empty powder barrel. He knew not how the barrel got to Bothwell's house.

Both of these depositions were put in as evidence before Elizabeth's Commissioners in the following year, and Malcolm Laing saw in the fact a convincing proof of the sincerity of the prosecution, and the truth of the story. Is it likely, he argued, that two such radically opposed statements would be put forward if the prosecution, with ample opportunity to destroy one or other, was not honestly convinced of their rectitude?[2]

Either story looks substantial enough on paper, but hold them up to the light and they become woefully thin. There was at least one good reason why, whether they desired it or not, Mary's unfriends could not suppress the first deposition, for the simple reason that it had already got into the hands of Sir William Drury, and was reported by him to Cecil in his letter of 27th June. But for this, I am inclined to think that we should never have heard of it. Yet this does not account for the making of the second story, for, so far as Cecil is concerned, either would have been good enough, and at that time none of the Lords contemplated a time when Cecil would be arbiter in the affair. There

[1] Scots. A "polk" is a bag; in this case it would be applicable to a leather bag used for carrying comparatively small quantities of powder between the reserves and the ordnance requiring it.
[2] Laing, II.

were other reasons, but it will be better to defer mention of them to another section; at the moment, we are only considering the method of conveying the powder.

CONSIDERATION OF TIME

Powrie started on his mission, he says, at 10 p.m. He had to travel a matter of three miles to complete his two journeys. The night was dark without moon (it was new moon at 6 a.m. that day); at Holyrood he had to find the horse, and, one must suppose, answer some questions as to his authority to take it; he then had to put some kind of saddle or pad on it, to take it to Bothwell's lodging, to carry out the first trunk, and to attach that, somehow, securely to the horse. Such a trunk containing, say, 100 lb. of gunpowder is an awkward load. He then had to proceed at a walking pace past sentries, past the inquisition of the keeper of the Netherbow Port, along thoroughfares still peopled on this festal night, to unload at Blackfriars. To do this all over again with the second load, to be subject to still more curiosity from the janitors, this time carrying in addition an empty barrel, perched, someway, on the horse. To unload again, to go on a message to buy six candles and, I suppose, to wake up Mrs George Burns from whom he bought them, to be back in time to help in transferring the powder, which other accounts say was loose in one of the trunks, into the polks, a horribly dangerous business with so many lighted candles about. How much time will you allow for all this? I wish a "pageant" could be staged to test the question, though I would strongly recommend dummy powder to be used. Surely not less than two hours must be allotted to this stage.

Then came the next stage. The conspirators, having escaped the danger of scooping up loose powder by candle light, and putting it into polks[1], took each a polk on his back or under his arm, and carried them to the wall of the east garden of Kirk o' Field. Two hundred yards uphill, some of it quite steep, in the dark, with at least two walls to negotiate. Somehow or other the

---

[1] One wonders where the spare polks came from.

barrel was carried too, as well as other smaller articles. We must suppose that lanterns[1], or at least one, were carried also. Next came the business at the garden wall, Powrie and one other were sent back to the Blackfriars Gate at this point, and apparently spent some time in looking for their horse. The remaining conspirators first carried the barrel to the passage door giving on to the east garden, across the garden, up the flight of steps, which, judging by many such flights still existing in old Edinburgh, would be none too easy to mount with an awkward load. Not a very light one either, for the handmade barrels of those days, especially if it was really a barrel made to carry gunpowder, were much more solid than the machine-made article of to-day.

However, the barrel which had passed comfortably into and out of the basement of Bothwell's lodging at Holyrood, refused to fit the door at Kirk o' Field. It had to be carried back to the wall and left there. The remaining three conspirators, perhaps four, then manhandled the polks, whether in one or two journeys is not stated, carried them up the steps to the door opened to them by the French page "Paris," along the few feet of passage to reach the door of the Queen's outer chamber, through this to her bedchamber, and there, by the light of the candle that Paris had borrowed from the cook, Bonkil[2], they proceeded to pour out the contents of the polks in a "bing," that is, a loose heap. It was apparently of cardinal importance that the bing should be exactly under the place where the King's bed was set up in the room above. Readers who have waded through all the depositions will remember that Paris made a great point of the Queen's annoyance at his stupidity in setting up her bed in that place where Bothwell wished the bing to be, and she even made him move the bed so that the bing area should be vacant. It was from this fact that Paris sapiently guessed that the Queen knew all about the scheme in hand.

---

[1] Among other things carried was a "towel." Now, a towel may be a mistranscription for "bowet," Fr. "bouget," which means lantern, but the word is given in Halliwell's dictionary of archaic words and means an oak cudgel. To get a "towelling" means, or used to mean, to get a thrashing.   [2] See p. 32 above.

It is a minor point that Paris' stupidity occurred on Wednesday, whereas Bothwell's decision to use the powder was not taken until Friday, but I want to set the reader wondering whether it made the least difference where the bing was put in the lower chamber, and what is the meaning of all the pother about the barrel. Whether the powder was in a barrel or in a heap on the floor would not have had the slightest effect on the result.

During the bing-making, Bothwell came down from the upper room where he was with the King and the royal party, and told the powder-men not to make so much noise[1]; evidently he could hear them at work. Strange nobody else did! It is remarkable too that, with only the short staircase between the two floors, the conspirators were so confident that nobody else would look in; no question *then* of the doors being locked. I suppose everybody was not a party to the plot. However, all went well and Paris, who had apparently been helping to pour out the polks, went upstairs to give the warning that all was ready. Certainly Paris would be in a filthy state from the powder dust, and there is an idea prevalent that Mary said to him, "Jesu! Paris, how begrimed you are." If she said so, it was really a most tactless remark, considering how well she knew why he was so dirty![2]

---

[1] Paris, deposition of 9th August, 1569.

[2] But, as a fact, the origin of that story is the fragmentary history, attributed to Claude Nau, and what Nau says is that as Mary was mounting her horse she made the remark. That is to say, Mary was already outside the house when she saw Paris, and one must deduce that Paris never went upstairs at all. Adam Blackwood and Anthony Herrera (see Jebb, *Vita...Mariae, etc.*, II), each using the same text, have a similar tale: "*In leaving the lodging...she met Paris...whom she asked where he had been, and said he smelt of powder.*" All three accounts date from about the year 1589, and to the extent that they are accepted are sufficient to destroy all the melodramatic scene of "the signal," the last kiss, and the hurried recollection of the wedding feast of Bastian, followed by the order, "to horse"—a story, let us remember, of which the Earl of Lennox, with all his means of knowing the truth, knew nothing. However, I do not wish to discourage the Mary-haters by this trifle. All three writers were probably detailing one of the many rumours of the time.

On the advent of begrimed Paris, Mary, suddenly recollecting her promise to attend Bastian's wedding party, announced her departure. We must suppose some little delay in the last fare-wells, and some little delay in cloaking, to face a ride on a February night, and then, "to horse." I suppose Mary did not keep her wraps in her bedroom knowing what was going on there[1]?

According to all the records Mary left Kirk o' Field at about or not much after 11 o'clock. The second stage of the proceed-ings cannot have taken less than three-quarters of an hour. Thus it must have been much nearer 8 o'clock than 10 when Powrie commenced his work. Yet, can we believe that all this nefarious coming and going into and out of the Blackfriars Gate was done between 8 and 10 o'clock on a night when hundreds of people were about?

Let us return for a moment to Powrie and his companion, left at the wall of the east garden, and told to go home. A very few minutes, empty handed, would have brought them back to the gate, where they had left their horse and portmanteaux; the horse was gone. Perhaps a loose horse finding his way home was not very noteworthy, but one might suppose that many witnesses would have recollected the fact afterwards; anyhow, I suppose Powrie spent the next halfhour or so in looking for it, for evidently he did not start back to Holyrood until the Queen and her train of nobles were well on their way up the Blackfriars Wynd, with Bothwell in her company. When we remember that the Royal party passed the monastery gate within a yard or so, on their way, inside of which Powrie was in the act of collecting the portmanteaux to carry home, it is more than odd that he confines his remarks to having seen the Queen and her attendants after he himself reached the Wynd. Surely he would not have run the risk of being seen bearing his unusual burden by some straggler of the party, to say nothing of the ordinary passers-by?

---

[1] In the Lennox MS. a totally different account is given and there is nothing about Paris or a signal.

THE QUANTITY OF GUNPOWDER USED

I admit at the outset that only an approximate estimate can be made, it can better be said what quantity is likely to be a maximum. The story is, that in one of the two receptacles the powder was loose, in the other it was already in polks—at least, that is the *average* of three stories, all different. Now a polk was a leather bag designed to carry comparatively small quantities of powder from the main store or magazine for use of the ordnance or to replenish the pouches of the hackbuteers. There is, or was, in our Army until comparatively recently, a trace of the polk still in use for the service of mortars, called a "budge barrel," which held 25 lb. of powder and had a loose leather top or funnel which, pressed in, prevented sparks getting at the explosive. If we assume a polk as being considerably more capacious than the budge[1], it would still be limited both for reasons of safety and convenience of manipulation. I should say that 30 lb., perhaps at the outside 35 lb., would be the capacity. There were five persons (in another account, six), each of whom "tuck yane (took one) upon his back or under his arm"; so at most there were 210 lb. of powder.

Roughly, we can get at it another way, the "barrel" often mentioned was expected to contain all, or nearly all, the powder. It was to be put, said Bothwell, "in an barril, gyf it may be gottin within the barril." Now a cask of the size we call a kilderkin—and sizes in this trade have been fairly constant from very old times—would hold about 180 lb. of powder of normal density, and fine grain. Incidentally, such a cask would weigh, empty, about 45 lb. and would be an awkward load to carry up a steep flight of steps and try to fit into a door at the top, if the latter were so narrow as to make it difficult. True, it would be simple to carry it in slings, but there is no mention of these being used.

Lastly, from practical considerations of what could be securely placed on horseback, I think a barrel of the weight and capacity

---

[1] "Budge" is corrupted from "bouget," a leather bag, whence, "budget."

mentioned, plus a trunk containing about 100 lb. of gunpowder in, or not in, polks, would be near the limit. Thus we come to say a maximum of two hundredweight of powder.

THE QUALITY OF THE GUNPOWDER

Perhaps it is time to offer another apology for polixity! I can only repeat that the dead weight of nearly four centuries of slander takes a "long" pull to shift.

Gunpowder in those days contained nominally nearly the same ingredients as to-day, but the methods of manufacture were vastly different. The saltpetre was villainous in more ways than Shakespeare dreamt of, the sulphur indifferently refined, the carbon impure. But the main defect must have been the lack of complete incorporation of the "blend," which would greatly reduce the efficiency. The grain would certainly be uneven, and it may safely be said that the explosive power was, even in the best makes, not so much as 75 per cent. of the modern article. But, from our point of view, there was another blemish which might, if our story had been true, have had an important effect on history. The powder was not glazed. Glazing is effected by introducing a small quantity of graphite into the "corned" or grained powder, with the double object of avoiding dust—the bugbear of the powder maker—and of rendering it more or less damp-proof.

The resulting mixture which we have to consider was a soft friable grain full of dust, and very liable to go "dank," as they called it. I can remember, when a boy, making what we called "spitting devils," that is, a little heap—a small "bing" in fact— of damped powder which burnt with a profusion of sparks and no other result, unless the bing was too big, and then an explosion might be expected at the end. Sixteenth-century powder tended towards spitting devil quality, and for a really good explosion a biggish bing was necessary. What the state of Bothwell's powder was, after being carried loose in a portmanteau from Dunbar to Holyrood, and thence to Kirk o' Field, one shudders to think.

The point of this reflection is this; neglecting the dangers run by the conspirators at the Blackfriars Gate when they scooped the powder up and put it into polks by the light of Powrie's six halfpenny dips, I want the reader to think of what went on in Mary's bedroom a little later. Pouring five or six polks each of thirty odd pounds of powder into a heap on the floor would have raised enough explosive dust to fill every cranny of the apartment. Whether the candle which Paris had borrowed from the cook was enclosed in a lantern or not, the result would certainly have been a premature explosion which would have saved Paris and his friends a great deal of subsequent trouble, and would have killed the King and the Queen and their nobles if they had been, as I am sure they were *not*, in the upper room[1]. I do not believe that even a magazine lamp of the present day would stand such a test. I am quite sure that no lantern supplied to the conspirators would have been of any use at all.

THE EFFECT OF THE GUNPOWDER

A positive statement, such as the last paragraph contains, might well end that part of the indictment against the Queen of Scots which includes her connivance in the placing of gunpowder in the room under her husband's sleeping-chamber. To my way of thinking it is as certain as anything can be that no such thing was done; still it is better to complete the investigation.

When Guy Fawkes undertook the practical part of the proposed destruction of the House of Lords, he applied or was supposed to apply the knowledge of mining he had gained in warfare in the Low Countries. To accomplish the end in view, he and his conspirators accumulated a quantity of gunpowder contained in thirty-six casks (the number varies from thirty-two upwards), of which thirty-four were small and two said to be hogsheads. Now, a *powder barrel* of full size, from at least the period of the Armada and probably long before, up to our day, contains about 100 lb., depending on the fineness of the grain,

[1] See p. 39 *supra*, where it is shown that so large a party could not fit in so small a room.

and it may be taken that, if it is literally true that hogsheads were used, it was only because they happened to be on the spot, for a cask of this size *full* of powder could not be man-handled. It may be said that the quantity collected by Guy Fawkes and his friends did not exceed 4000 lb., and was probably rather less.

Nor must it be supposed that the objective in that case differed in any remarkable degree from that of Kirk o' Field. In 1605 the explosive was placed in a basement below the south end only of the Lords' chamber, where the throne was situated, and the destruction of this part only was aimed at; a floor supported on wooden beams, as in our case, separated the upper from the lower storey. So that, to accomplish much about the same effect, something like eighteen times as much explosive was provided.

True, the official narrative avoids any reference to the destruction of the King's lodging—the Old House of our description—to the very foundations, but the contemporary evidence already quoted, together with the 1567 "picture," are overwhelming proofs of the fact. Yet it can be said quite definitely that 250 lb. of indifferent gunpowder, exploded on a floor over arched masonry vaults, would, in the first place, not crush these arches downwards, and, in the second place, would probably not destroy the walls, if, that is to say, the line of least resistance—the dividing floor—was not exceptionally solid. There is no reason to suppose that either the floor or the roof of the Old House were exceptionally solid; but, in any case, the effect would have been far less complete than was actually the event.

Though of this there is no doubt, it is yet certain that any person in the upper room would have been mangled beyond recognition, whereas we are told that the King's body was found in the south garden entirely uninjured. Mr Malcolm Laing, who is nothing if not consistent and had declared for the official story, rejected *in toto* any of the contemporary suggestions that the murder had been done in the house and the body then carried outside. In his view, "as the question of gunpowder is now (1819) better understood, it is admitted that, from the intervention of the floor and bedding, their (Darnley and Taylor his

servant) bodies were thrown out untouched by the explosion...
if they had fallen upon water, their lives might have been preserved[1]." If by some miracle Darnley's body had been deposited
uninjured in the garden, it would require a super miracle to do
the same for Taylor; but when a pair of slippers and some clothes
were found lying conveniently beside their owner, there is no
adjective sufficiently eloquent to describe that miracle.

In short, the official narrative falls to pieces in every direction,
down to the very "grundstane" as the story says. *It is absolutely
impossible that the effect could have been produced by placing a
comparatively small quantity of bad gunpowder in the Queen's room.*
We must seek some other explanation.

THE TALE OF A BARREL

The importance of the barrel, as affording a clue to the mystery
of Kirk o' Field, has been overlooked. Yet, as I think, he who
offers an unimpeachable solution of this side mystery will have
gone far, if not all the way, to solve the whole problem. I cannot,
I regret, claim to be that person, but, by bringing together the
facts, it is possible to show that the barrel never went to or came
from Holyrood, and that the whole story attributed to Powrie is
false.

In the official narrative, notwithstanding the haze cast by
innumerable contradictions, there is a certain thread of con-
sistency, which gives the impression that, with other names, a
story might emerge more satisfying to one's reason. As it is, the
fabric is so distorted, by being stretched to cover circumstances
which did not originally enter its design, that the pattern is
almost lost.

We have seen that one reason for the continued existence of
the first deposition of Powrie was that it had by some means
found its way into Sir William Drury's hands and had been
reported by him to Cecil on 27th June. It could therefore be

---

[1] Laing, II, p. 21. It is not quite fair to give Laing all the credit for
this discovery; David Hume and Whitaker had much the same story
before his time.

corrected, but not suppressed. There were two other reasons for making the corrections, and one was the omission of any mention of the barrel in the original. The other reason we shall come to later.

It is convenient here to step aside for a moment to mention that the first half of Powrie's deposition, that part which deals with the conveyance of the powder from Holyrood to Kirk o' Field, was in all probability not originally attributed to Powrie at all, but to some other person, whose name was suppressed. Powrie and Dalgleish, both servants of Bothwell, accompanied the latter to the scene of action, and, with sundry adornments, the story they tell of this second phase is approximately true, but there was nothing in it to merit death, for they merely obeyed their orders to accompany their master. However, we are at the moment only interested in the powder and its conveyance.

The barrel first comes into view in Hepburn's deposition, in what looks very like an interpolation, "On Sunday, in the *gloaming before night*, the deponer sent John Hay's man for an empty powder barrel, to the man from whom the said Hay had bought the same, who lives above Sandy Bruce's Close Head[1]." This is the effect of the statement. To me, it has an air of parade not compatible with serious facts. The barrel, as we shall see, was a big one. The decision to use gunpowder had been taken on the preceding Friday; "in the gloaming" would be about 5.15 o'clock p.m.; it is almost too strange to be true, except for the express purpose of exposing the barrel to the public view, that it should be carried to Holyrood through the streets on a Sunday evening before dark, and should then, within three hours or so, be paraded again between Holyrood and Kirk o' Field. But, if the barrel was in fact only a *parade* intended to divert suspicion to a wrong quarter in a certain event, then one can understand the action taken, or rather the suggestion that such an action was taken.

---

[1] I am not sure of the whereabouts of the Close referred to. Ainslie (1780) mentions a Close of that name leading south out of the Grassmarket, in any case it would be a Close within the town.

We have already seen (p. 51 above) that the barrel was introduced into the corrected edition of Powrie's deposition, and we have heard that, after dragging it up the steep slope to the steps leading to the door of the passage to the Queen's chamber, it was found too big to pass in. I want the reader to reflect for a moment what this involves.

It will be found that an ordinary doorway, such as exists in most houses, is about 35 inches wide in the clear, and it would be a very narrow entrance that would measure less than 28 inches. But, though this figure represents a narrow doorway, it means, applied to the large diameter, a very big barrel, of the class we know as a 54-gallon cask, and it would be quite impossible for John Hay's man to have carried such a cask, though empty, through the streets without assistance, unless on horseback, and there is no suggestion of this. A barrel of this kind could never, properly, have been described as a "powder barrel"; it would contain nearly 5 cwt. of powder, and, if full, would weigh close on 600 lb. In short, it would have been far too heavy to make it even remotely possible that such a size was ever used for the purpose. A cask of the next smaller size would weigh, filled with powder, about 4 cwt., and would be almost equally out of question as a "powder barrel"; its diameter would be a little over 25 inches, and it is hard to believe any door would be so narrow as not to admit it. An ordinary full-sized powder barrel, such as has been in use, as I have said, since the Armada and before, contains 100 lb. and is 17 inches in diameter at the "pitch," so that any door would easily admit it.

Thus one is driven to the conclusion that all the story of the barrel, too big for the door, was merely a cloak for some other design, and what that design was is suggested below. I will also repeat that a barrel of any kind was an entirely useless adjunct to the alleged plot, a fact which lends emphasis to the obviously forced nature of the repeated reference to it.

John Hepburn thus describes what was done, "they essayed to have taken in the said barrel, and it would not go in at the door, and then *they lifted the same and brought it back to the yard* (garden)." That is to say, they carried the barrel back to the garden wall where the powder had, in the meantime, been left in the polks. Now, reader, do you think that is natural? Please remember that there was reason for haste, ubiquitous Bothwell had already been down to tell them to hurry, the Queen, he said, might come forth at any time[1]. Is it likely that they would waste time in carrying the barrel back across the garden in the dark, when it could so much more easily have been left at the foot of the steps?

Well, there was a reason, and it appears in the narrative attributed to Bothwell and dated at Copenhagen in January 1568[2], which contains the following: "We were ordered by the Queen ...to make a diligent search for the said traitors....Coming to the house where the King lay a corpse we first put his body under a guard of honour, *and then we found a barrel, or cask, in which the powder had been, which we preserved, having taken note of the mark on it*[3]."

It is true that Bothwell's narrative is a pale shadow of the truth; he dissembles his own share of the affair, and adopts the official story that the King was blown up in his bed, presumably because this story obscures the inconvenient facts of what happened in the south garden. Yet it seems impossible to suppose that he would needlessly drag in the mention of the barrel had he been aware of the allegation that he had himself sent it to Kirk o' Field. But the whole purpose of the barrel—its conveyance to the scene of action, its "too bigness" for the door, and its reconveyance to the garden wall—seems only to have been that it should

[1] I do not want to flog a dead horse, but please note how utterly this statement disagrees with the story of the Queen awaiting the signal that all was ready.

[2] This manuscript is reproduced under the title, "Les Affaires du Conte de Boduel, l'an 1568," in the Maitland Club volume of 1829. The paper is unquestionably genuine, but in many respects leads to the supposition that the Danish scribe in taking down the Narrative failed in representing accurately some parts of the story. The extract quoted above gains its value from the fact that it could have had no other source than Bothwell himself.

[3] I think we may fairly deduce that the barrel was intended to be found, and that its finding should indicate the participation of somebody.

be discovered there next morning, as it was. The circumstances were, however, very different to what was anticipated, for neither the Queen nor the nobles with her had been the victims; the biter had been bit, and the tale of the barrel, originally intended to throw suspicion on some other party (I suggest Morton and the Protestant party, whose natural animus against Darnley was very well known), was, in the altered circumstances, utilized to inculpate the Queen and Bothwell. Of this intention to inculpate the Protestants, more will be said in the next chapter. "We preserved the barrel and examined its mark," says Bothwell, and adds not a word to what was discovered. It seems such a trifle to mention if there was nothing more to come. One can understand that Sir James Balfour, when he returned to Edinburgh after establishing his nominal *alibi*, might find means to quash any further enquiry, as he had apparently a strange power over the whole case; but that does not account for Bothwell deeming it worth inclusion. At least it seems unlikely that the barrel was traced to Holyrood, for in that case it is hard to believe that Bothwell would have brought it into prominence. If, however, it was traced to Morton, or to Archibald Douglas who represented him in Edinburgh at the moment, or to the Protestant party in general, it would not be difficult to understand why Bothwell should suppress what he knew, for in January 1568 he had probably not relinquished hope of composition with Morton, whose friend he had been. Perhaps he knew that the barrel was but a false trail, and that Morton or his party had had nothing to do with it.

There is a final reappearance of the barrel, which, though not a complete solution of the problem, is illuminating. It occurs in a letter from Sir John Forster dated June 1581, fourteen years after the event[1]. He says, "Mr Archibald Douglas' man is the accuser of him that bare a barrel of powder to the blowing up of the King." The construction of this sentence is peculiar, as often happens; there should be a comma after "him" and, put

---

[1] Not Sir John Seton as stated in the Calendar of State Papers, see Harleian MS. Brit. Mus. 6999, f. 187.

II] OF THE ACCEPTED NARRATIVES 65

into modern style, it should read, "Mr Archibald's man is his accuser, he that bare a barrel, etc." For "barrel of powder," I think, powder barrel would be more correct. The man in question was John Binning, who, under torture, confessed his master's share in the affair. It is common knowledge that the trial of Archibald Douglas was collusive, as we shall see later, for he was in possession of information which led to his receiving strong support from the government in England, but that took place in 1586, when James had been bribed[1] to an English alliance. In 1581 it was different; the Duke of Lennox and the Continental faction were paramount in Scotland. The execution of Morton had been decided on; Archibald Douglas, principal representative under Morton at the murder of Darnley, had fled, and Binning must be thumb-screwed into telling enough to condemn Morton[2].

Binning's indictment has, as I have said, disappeared, and was probably destroyed; but, combining Bothwell's remark of the finding of a barrel having certain marks with that of Sir John Forster quoted above, it is not too much to say that the barrel was in the first place traced to Archibald Douglas. I again express the opinion that those who purposely left it where it would be found intended that it should be so traced, with the object of inculpating the Earl of Morton and the Protestant party; this is tantamount to saying that those who laid the trail were *not* of that party. At all events, the story of the carriage of the barrel from Holyrood is discredited.

It is a fact which may have a bearing on our investigation that

[1] There is not, I am afraid, a shadow of a doubt that James, King of Scotland, accepted a bribe of £1000 to connive at the false trial of the man whom all the world knew was closely concerned in the killing of his father. Read this letter from the Master of Gray to Walsingham, dated 17th May, 1586: "Mr Archibald Douglas shall shortly be put to trial....The King has condescended to all things. I pray you...if the £1000 can be had, that it be, for I had enough ado to cause the King receive it." Printed in Caird, App. xx.

[2] Most of the record of the trial of Binning, especially the dittay or indictment, has disappeared; for what is left consult Pitcairn, *Criminal Trials*, p. 95. Further information also to be had from the trial of Douglas, *ib*. pp. 144 ff.

MKF   5

John Binning mentions meeting with certain conspirators, including, it is said, a brother of Sir James Balfour, at a house in "Throplowis Wynd foot." Now Throplow is undoubtedly the same as Thraples, which is also called Rapperlaw[1]. It would be a place admirably suited for a rendezvous, distant little more than a hundred yards from the scene, and connected with it by several of the narrow passages which ran between the various walled enclosures. If, indeed, we transferred the whole scene of Powrie and the polks from the gate of the Blackfriars to the gate of the Kirk o' Field demesne, we should get a more readable narrative. The gate in question was close to the head of Thraples Wynd, or at least near the several passages coming from Thraples Close. I am not suggesting this at the moment, there is not enough light.

THE UBIQUITY OF BOTHWELL

I have mentioned above that, if names other than those used in the depositions were substituted, a more intelligible story would result. Let us examine the statements as to the presence of Bothwell, and judge if his name can have been the original.

If we reduce the hour of the various happenings of Sunday, 9th February, 1567, to what may be called a standard mean time, we find the following. John Hay's story:

4 p.m.   Bothwell in consultation with the conspirators in his house at Holyrood, "until it was mirk"—say until about 5.15 p.m.

5.30 p.m. (or thereabouts). Bothwell walks from Holyrood to Blackfriars Wynd to Ormistoun's house, where he remained in consultation for, apparently, some two and a half hours.

8 p.m.   Bothwell walks down Blackfriars Wynd to the monastery gate, and strolled up and down the Cowgate during the two hours or so that Powrie was bringing the powder from Holyrood.

10.15 p.m. Bothwell in the King's lodging.

11 p.m.   Bothwell in company with the Queen passed to the Abbey.

[1] See Boog-Watson, *Closes and Wynds of Old Edinburgh*, Old Ed. Club, XII, p. 146.

So far so good, Hay has accounted for every minute of Bothwell's time. Now take John Hepburn:

6 p.m. to 7.45 p.m. or thereabouts. Bothwell is at supper in company with the Queen and many others, at a house in the Canongate.

8 p.m.   Bothwell having left the Queen and her party went to Ormistoun's house.

8.30 p.m. Bothwell left Ormistoun's and did not walk down the Wynd or stroll in the Cowgate as above. He went, Hepburn knew not whither; presumably he means to infer that Bothwell went to rejoin the Queen, who by this time had arrived at Kirk o' Field.

10 p.m.   Bothwell came down to the monastery gate (from the King's lodging?) to hurry the conspirators.

This will suffice as to this enquiry. It is quite obvious that in Hay's story, "My Lord," a term he uses almost invariably, without name, when referring to the doings of the Sunday evening, cannot relate to Bothwell. It is quite certain that Bothwell could not, for instance, have walked up and down the Cowgate during all the long time that must be allotted to the alleged bringing of the powder from Holyrood. But, if we substitute the name of Balfour for that of Bothwell, remembering that he would be styled "My Lord" as a Lord of Session, we have something at least in accordance with possibility. Malcolm Laing, who generally faced his difficulties courageously, and invented an "outgait" if none existed, is in this case driven to cover his dilemma by a bald mis-statement—the depositions coincide, he says[1], in the most minute circumstances!

If we neglect the "corrected" deposition of Powrie, and revert to the story that the powder was carried in one journey on *two* horses, the period of perambulating the Cowgate is reduced by more than half; and, if we go further and suppose that, in the original story, some place nearer than Holyrood was the alleged source whence the two "mails" containing powder were brought, then the time of waiting is reduced to something quite small. For instance, it might well be, as the tale of the barrel suggests,

[1] Laing, II, p. 7.

that Morton and not Bothwell was the original scapegoat; it is true he was not in Edinburgh, but to indicate his house in the Blackfriars Wynd, or alternatively Archibald Douglas and his house, would be all that was necessary; and to carry something from either place to the Friar Gate would take a very few minutes.

This brings us to the third reason for the "correction" of the original evidence attributed to Powrie; the transport was effected on "two horses of my Lord's, the one being his *own horse*," said the deponent. But that would be a dangerous statement to leave on the record uncorrected; it could hardly apply to Bothwell, who was employing his own horse, and probably all his horses, in attendance on the Queen, who was certainly mounted when she went to Kirk o' Field. Now, Hay and Hepburn were certainly two of the real culprits (I distinguish between those who were *real* and those who were merely scapegoats, see below), and they would assuredly have made "depositions," but we have no guarantee whatever that we have the very words they uttered (on the contrary, we know of omissions), and one of these makes very free with Sir James Balfour's name. It is as certain as can be that all the body of both Hay's and Hepburn's story is untrue. If this chapter has any weight, this must be admitted; yet it is equally certain that these two persons did in all probability describe the gunpowder plot *as far as they were concerned in it,* unless, under torture, they merely acquiesced to leading questions. As it seems to me, Bothwell's name is *forced* into the tale, and originally some other name must have been prominent— that of Balfour, I believe.

The reader may enquire why such glaring discrepancies as exist among the several depositions were not the subject of enquiry at the time; the answer is that the documents were never open to unbiased examination. They were kept secret in Scotland, shown in secret in England, and never printed until unearthed from Cecil's records two hundred years later; and the only attestation they have is the certificate of Sir John Bellenden that they are true copies of a record which itself has been destroyed. That certificate is worth nothing, for we have in the case of Hepburn's deposition two such guarantees that the copies are "true," the one of which omits much matter included by the other.

THE STORY AND THE REALITY

I suppose that the picture of the happenings of the night of 9th February which has presented itself to the mind's eye of the many thousands who have interested themselves in the story of Kirk o' Field has been formed from the tales told in the depositions, the 'Detection' and the 'Book of Articles.' From these, what we are intended to see is the stealthy approach of a gang of ruffians, burdened with the paraphernalia described, across the western gardens of the Blackfriars monastery, stumbling in the darkness over the broken-down walls until they arrive at the gloomy mass of the town wall, and thence still westwards until the wall of the east garden of the doomed house is reached. All around is silence, the lower storey of the house is dark, from the upper room comes the sound of voices and laughter. The nobles are playing at dice, the Queen is completing the last touches to her infamy by fondling her husband and giving renewed promise of a recommencement of conjugal harmony at Holyrood on the morrow. No friendly eye sees the garden door open and the furtive Paris peer out into the night ready to receive the expected murderers. None hears the subdued whispers, the muffled curses on the "too big" barrel, the shuffling down the stone-floored passage as the powder is borne within, the groan of the locks as the chief actors are locked in the Queen's room with their deadly charge, or the final retreat of the conspirators whose good fortune it was to retire. There is not a soul about to warn the victims of what is afoot.

That or something like it may be the picture, but what is the reality? The courtyard of the precincts must have been crowded with humanity from the moment of the Queen's arrival. No Scottish Sovereign nor any Scottish noble ever went abroad without a following of retainers. John Stewart of Traquair, captain of the Queen's guard and responsible for her person, would be there, and, as the merest matter of military routine, would have placed a guard on each approach to the house. With Argyll were Campbells, with Huntly there were Gordons, with Cassillis came Kennedies, with every other Peer and great Laird was a following of his own men. If there were twenty in the Queen's train, there were one hundred and fifty to two hundred people about the house; torch-bearers, horse-keepers, and a motley of general hangers-on, besides the gentlemen's gentlemen. And Bonkil, in the kitchen, had with his assistants a busy time. The occasion was not only a festival by the calendar but also, so to speak, by accident. The last day of the convalescence, an opportunity for wine; we may be sure that the "fore entry," the only way, as I think, of passing from the back premises to the reception chamber, was buzzing with attendants, and the staircase and passages as well.

In all this there was mighty little room for the Guy Fawkes business with the gunpowder; in fact, none at all. It would have been as easy for a stranger to enter the house as for a foreign bee to get unobserved into a healthy hive.

THE CHOICE OF STORIES

There is no choice! Perhaps I should apologize for wasting a dozen or so pages in demolishing a story—the official story—which had been already demolished by contemporary writers. Darnley was not murdered in the house at Kirk o' Field by an explosion. Neither was he murdered in the house and carried outside prior to the explosion; that would be too idiotic a proceeding. He was in fact murdered outside the house, in the south garden; how he got there is dealt with in the next chapter. The *unofficial* story must be so far credited, that gunpowder was placed under the building, in the basement. The demolition of the whole structure of the Old House and the Salle, covering not less than 80 feet in length, could only have been effected by a much larger quantity of powder than is represented, placed, not under the dwelling-house but under the adjoining Prebendaries' chamber, or Salle as we call it. The Old House, very likely in a state of decay as alleged, suffered in the catastrophe

to a greater extent than might have happened to a newer building, but even so the only part of the whole left standing is its
end wall (see p. 21 above). If the centre of the disruptive force
had been in the Old House, this wall—the tallest part of the
building—is the last we should expect to find intact.

Nor, in the unofficial story, is it necessary to accept the whole.
Mines and extensive preparation involving considerable time
were not essential. The proximity of the New House, in possession of the Balfours, gave all the opportunity requisite to collect
powder in secret; an underground passage breaking into the
basement of the Salle may have been the only work, and this not
of any difficulty. The conveyance of a dozen or more barrels of
gunpowder would not take an hour. The transfer was made, this
is my view, after the Queen left for the wedding supper at Holyrood. As in the case of the Gunpowder Plot of 1605, it was
massed, as to the greater part, under that end of the Salle where
was the Cloth of Estate, probably in this case at the end nearer
the Old House. Collective murder of this kind was not unknown;
an attempt to blow up the Duke of Florence as he sat in church
had occurred[1]; there was an attempt on Elizabeth some time
later[2]; there was the great plot against Mary's son. The fact that
a general holocaust was involved was no deterrent. In the present case I imagine that the absence of Moray and Morton was
cause for disappointment. Still, as I hope to show in the next
chapter, sufficient confusion would result from the death of the
Queen and such nobles as were expected to be present.

BIOGRAPHIA

A very brief sketch of what we know of some of the persons
concerned in the murder will end this chapter.

GEORGE DALGLEISH. Certainly a servant of Bothwell. Even
in the deposition attributed to him, and this document is less
garbled than the others, there is nothing on which he should have
been condemned. He merely obeyed his master's orders to accom-

---

[1] *Granville Papers*, VI, p. 255.
[2] von Ranke, *Geschichte*, I, p. 587.

pany him to Kirk o' Field after midnight, but took no active part; the reason for taking him is not clear, unless, as I have said elsewhere, he was part of the train collected by Bothwell to simulate the Queen's coming. But Dalgleish had to be put out of the way, because it was he who had been selected as the carrier of the famous Casket; on that piece of treachery I do not propose to waste time. Obviously, Dalgleish could not be left at liberty to tell the truth.

WILLIAM POWRIE. Also without doubt a servant of Bothwell. The evidence he gave is clearly divisible into two parts. The second, describing the midnight visit to Kirk o' Field, is couched in language so similar to that of Dalgleish that, as has been noticed by others, one mind must have worded both. It is only the first part that is interesting, i.e. that relating to the carrying of the powder from Holyrood. The statement as it stands must be false, and the double story made at the two examinations, one contradicting the other in such plain matters of fact, fails to impress me as a sign of good faith in those who permitted both to remain extant. I have already given my reasons for this opinion. But what is most to the point is that some person did in all probability, under torture, give an account of the conveyance of powder from somewhere to Kirk o' Field, and the words attributed to Powrie may bear a distant resemblance, names and places being altered, to what was told. Let it be noted that neither Dalgleish nor Powrie figure in any of the placards, nor was their evidence brought up at the trial of the Earl of Morton, as was the case with that of the others, though in fact Powrie's tale of a person cloaked with "mulis" [slippers] on his feet would have been particularly useful. I believe that both were perfectly innocent victims.

JAMES CULLEN. A soldier of fortune, experienced in foreign service under Henri II, and later (1565) in Denmark under Frederick; also, it is said, in Poland. An officer of the garrison of Edinburgh Castle in 1560, in the time of Marie of Lorraine. Captain of a "band" of hackbuteers[1] at the time of Darnley's death; described as a servitor of Bothwell[2], but without any clear reason for the statement, he was one of several captains commanding "bands," all of whom would be in general under Bothwell as Lieutenant-General, but, I should think, more directly under Stewart of Traquair who commanded the Queen's guard. Said to have been on guard at Seton during Mary's residence there after the murder. Named in the "not yet set up" placards as one of twelve other "murderers with the hands."

[1] That is, I believe, a company of fifty men.
[2] Bain, II, p. 325.

But the most interesting part of his story began after Carberry Hill. In a letter dated at Carlisle 16th June, Lord Scrope says: "The Lords have taken Captain Cullen, who, after some strict dealing, hath uttered and revealed the murder with the whole manner and circumstance thereof[1]." In this there is food for reflection, as Scrope had not yet had news of Carberry Hill when he wrote. His information deals with the 13th or 14th June. We know from John Beton's letter[2] that Cullen was taken on the 11th; clearly, then, he was not following Bothwell's fortunes at Dunbar. Scrope in the same letters says that Sir James Balfour is already negotiating with the Lords to betray the Castle to them. I may be wrong, but it looks as if Cullen was then a captain in the garrison of the Castle held at the time by Balfour.

The next item comes from the "Report of the Captain of Inchkeith[3]." It mentions the taking of "Captain Edington (probably Edmiston), and *another who is suspected made the train of gunpowder*." Almost certainly the person referred to is Cullen. Now, the very strange thing is that Cullen was released, no action taken against him, no copy of his revelations made under "strict dealing" (which means torture) was retained. We hear of him in Drury's letter of 20th June as still in custody, and then, in this connection, nothing more. We know that a companion in misfortune, one Blacatter, was hanged on 24th June, but Cullen turns up again later and was evidently let off on this occasion, even though he had uttered the whole manner of the murder![4]

No one can suggest that Cullen got off through any influence of Bothwell, who was at the moment proscribed and in flight; we are driven to suppose that he owed his life to Balfour, who, at that time, was using his secret power over the Lords to make terms for himself. Am I unduly suspicious if I suggest that Cullen's confession, if we could see it, told the story of the accumulation of gunpowder at the New Provost's House of Kirk o' Field, and all the other details which we would wish to know? If Cullen had involved Bothwell, his fate was

---

[1] *Border State Papers*, XIII.   [2] Printed in Laing, II, pp. 109 ff.
[3] Printed by Teulet, *Relations*, II, pp. 300 ff.
[4] In the long list of the Summons of Forfeiture (*Supplementary Parliamentary Papers*, XVII) for the King's murder, dated 1st October, 1567, James Cullen is not mentioned. It is interesting also to note that the names of Powrie and Dalgleish are omitted, nor does Ker of Fawdonside, nor any Douglas nor John Binning nor Thomas Gardner appear. The first two omissions indicate, as I have said, that these unfortunates were merely victims, the remainder point to connivance on someone's part —probably that of Balfour.

sealed; if he involved Balfour, we have already seen the power the latter had to suppress mention of his name. Why Cullen was not hanged out of hand, on the ground that dead men tell no tales, I cannot say; possibly, like Balfour himself, he had taken precaution to place his knowledge in other hands, to publish if harm came to him.

Cullen was still in durance on the 20th June, as said above; on or about that date Powrie was taken, and was examined on the 23rd, and the whole plot of the casket and the letters was boiling in the cauldron; the general plan, much altered as time went on, was sketched out. I suggest that all the stupidities put into poor Powrie's mouth about the carriage of powder was based on some ingenious twisting of Cullen's story.

But that is not all. The circumstances and date of Cullen's release are unknown; presumably he was free by the end of June. His next appearance is in a letter from the Earl of Moray, dated 15th September[1]. "Tullibardine and Grange are returned (from their fruitless chase after Bothwell). There is notwithstanding divers of his company taken, but few notable men, excepting Callen (Cullen) who chanced by God's provision in our hands, and being his chamberchild, and one of the very executors, he may make us clear in the whole action as it proceeded." Here again is food for reflection. Moray was of course out of Scotland when Cullen was previously taken and examined, but it may be thought strange that so important a matter as the alleged complete confession had not been made known to him. But it must have been explained later, for again Cullen went free!

The suggestion in the last quotation that Cullen was "chamberchild" to Bothwell is, I think, without foundation. He was a soldier and unlikely to be in such a position, but more dubious is the question if he was in Bothwell's company when captured by Tullibardine. It is clear, as I have said, that he escaped death on the first occasion by another influence than that of Bothwell—that of Sir James Balfour, I suggest. It is more likely that, when Cullen went north, he was about to seek asylum with Gilbert Balfour, who may justly be regarded as a fellow-conspirator. It is said that Gilbert was in charge of the castle "of Orkney," presumably Kirkwall, but it is not so generally known that his wife was one Margaret Bothwell, a sister, I believe, of Adam Bothwell, Bishop of Orkney, and that, since 1564, Gilbert had possessed lands there[2]. Having the favour of Sir James, at the moment in power, it is more probable that Cullen, after his

---

[1] *State Papers, Scotland, Elizabeth*, XIV, No. 81 a.
[2] *Accounts of High Treasurer*, 1564, p. 321.

late experience, would lie low in the Orkneys rather than follow the broken fortunes of Bothwell.

Cullen's last appearance was as an officer of the garrison of Edinburgh during the time of its defence against the Regent Lennox. Let us not forget that Sir James Balfour was then also in the castle. Cullen was captured by Morton in a sortie in June of 1571, and incontinently hanged. There is a little scandal mentioned in the *History of King James Sext*, to the effect that Morton took the part of David, and Cullen of Uriah, and that a pretty wife was in the background. But I conceive it more likely that Sir James' influence being then at zero, Morton was willing to stop an inconvenient tongue for ever.

It may be safely asserted that Cullen bore a more important part than has been hitherto given him, and that he was a henchman of Sir James Balfour, and not of Bothwell.

WILLIAM GEDDES. A person we know nothing about. He made a deposition, as stated in the examination of Powrie, but for some reason the record was destroyed, and the man liberated.

JOHN HAY OF TALLO (or TALLA) and JOHN HEPBURN OF BOLTON (or BOWTON). Both are consistently named, from the date of the "placards" onwards to Morton's and Archibald Douglas' trials many years later, as principals in the deed. Possibly they were cousins, for Hay's mother was a Hepburn. In general—with a wide margin—the Hays of Locherworth and Yester, to which family John Hay belonged, as also the Hepburns, may be classed as inclining to the side of the reformers. John of Bolton is described as a cousin and dependant of Bothwell. Neither of them would, I judge, side with Sir James Balfour.

Hay was captured in September 1567, and Hepburn in December (no detail or exact date available). At those dates, although Balfour had already, on terms, vacated the Castle of Edinburgh, he was still in intimate relation with the Regent Moray; and, that he took no interest in the fate of the two prisoners, other than to see to it that his own name was suppressed in what was put into their mouths in the depositions, is sufficient proof that they were Bothwell's men. What part they took in the affair, and in what way their action differed from that of Powrie and Dalgleish, is a question that cannot be answered with any confidence. As a conjecture I put it that Bothwell did in fact open his knowledge of the plot to these two, and placed them on guard to watch the house while he conducted the Queen back to Holyrood. Whether outside or inside the town wall, that is, whether they were "murderers with the hands" or merely agents to ensure that no escape should take place from the inner egresses, I will not guess.

I have already said enough on the subject of the impossibility of the depositions as a whole being true, the suppressed part of Hepburn's deposition is a strong evidence that the remainder is untrustworthy.

THE TWO ORMISTOUNS. James Ormistoun of that ilk and his uncle Robert. Both Bothwell's men. The fate of Robert is unknown to me, but both took refuge in their border fastnesses and were for the time safe from capture. James had thereafter a chequered career, not untainted with the apprehension of the Earl of Northumberland in December of 1569, and we find Cecil and Randolph in amicable correspondence with him in April 1571. It would appear that his pardon was promised as a bribe for his action in the affair of the English Earl, but later we find him harrying the attackers at the siege of the Castle. At last in November 1573 he fell into the hands of Morton, who hanged him at once. If any judicial deposition was made by Ormistoun before his death, and at the trial of Archibald Douglas a "deposition" was said to have been produced, it has disappeared. All that is available is a confession taken down by a minister, one John Brand. Although every item of Ormistoun's confession disagrees with what had been said before, there is yet a tangled similarity which seems to indicate that, though John Brand knew roughly what had to be said, he was so imperfect in his brief as to mix the two periods of the separate visits to Kirk o' Field, that is, the powder-carrying business *before* the Queen's departure and the subsequent midnight return of Bothwell.

As to the latter, if we take part of the story away from its context, Ormistoun said that when Bothwell called for him he was out, which agrees with Powrie and Dalgleish, but applies to the midnight visit, and not, as written, to the powder-carrying visit. In short, I imagine that part only is fact and that the two Ormistouns did in the end accompany Bothwell when he went to Kirk o' Field the second time at or after midnight.

When Ormistoun was captured, the secretary Maitland was dead and Sir James Balfour's star was in eclipse, at least with the ministers. Small wonder that both found a place in the confession.

NICHOLAS HUBERT (called "PARIS"). All that we read of this person bristles with so many queries that it would take a volume to consider them. Drury reported[1] him as drowned by Bothwell on

---

[1] Letter of 27th June, 1567.

PLATE II

This illustration shows clearly the "Salle" between the Old House and the new Provost's house, the gallery on the Flodden wall which was part of the Old House, and the postern gate in the wall between the Old House and the Salle. The large building on the north of the church is what was once the old "hospital" (see p. 6) which later became the Duke's House. At the time we are dealing with it was occupied by Sir James Balfour. The church of St Mary, Kirk o' Field, is shown in the ruinous condition in which it had been left by the enthusiasts of the Reformation in 1558.

15th June (1567), and four days later he confirmed this, "Paris, the French page to the Duke (Bothwell) of 20 years is *for certain* slain, he knew many things." Yet Paris, or *a* person who answered for him, appears again in Denmark. There was a good deal of correspondence regarding the extradition of Bothwell, commencing from November of 1567, and carried on through the following years, but I cannot trace any official demand for the person of Paris. In July of 1568, shortly after Mary's escape from Lochleven, the Regent Moray sent to Denmark for the return of one Captain Clarke on a matter of urgent importance. The case against Mary was then being worked up, and Clarke's assistance was required. A little later (21st August) the King of Denmark was requested to permit the Captain to execute Bothwell and send his head to Scotland. Which gentle demand was refused.

Clarke, however, did come to Scotland, for we find mention of his returning to Denmark in October (1568). He took back with him a commission to take the person of "Paris, Frenchman." Curious that in a document purporting to be at least semi-official, the nickname alone should be employed. Still more strange, on 30th October—suspicious expedition—Captain Clarke signs a receipt for the persons of two men, William Murray and "Paris, Frenchman," handed to him by one Peter Oxe, an official of Denmark. Again there is no mention of the man's proper name. The French Ambassador in Denmark, M. de Dançay, who had been there many years, and, under instructions from his government, had consistently opposed the extradition of Bothwell, would it must be thought never agree to the deportation of one of his own nationals. Yet we hear no word of any question arising. Remarkable, too, that if "Paris, Frenchman," arrived in Denmark in September of 1567, he would not long before have found his way home; if his own account is true, he could have had no love for Bothwell. Mr Froude puts it bluntly that Paris was kidnapped by Clarke, but that means that the Peter Oxe paper is a forgery[1], and it does not explain the absence of protest from Denmark at such a proceeding.

"Frenchman Paris" in the hands of Clarke on 30th October could very easily have been produced in London on, say, 15th November, in the nick of time to appear before the English Commissioners at Hampton Court and Westminster, at the very moment when Moray and his colleagues were pretending reluctance to produce the Casket Letters (having, by the way, already produced them secretly). Can a more telling *catastrophe* be imagined? The other witnesses unfortunately executed, before knowledge of this Commission came, but

---

[1] Froude, IX, p. 65.

now, heaven sent, the very man who carried the letters and knew every detail of the Queen's guilt. Would you not suppose that the fastest ship and the most minute precautions would have ensured the presence of Paris? Not a bit of it!

Paris came to Leith, "about the middis of June," unheralded and unsung, that is, seven months and more after the date of his handing over by Peter Oxe, his arrival unknown even to Cecil (so he says, at least). Nothing done about it, nothing said about it, until Moray returned from his tour of the north in the early days of August (1569). Then you would expect the contract between Clarke and Peter Oxe to be fulfilled, Paris was to have an open legal trial with full opportunity to call his friends. But no! He was haled off on 5th August to St Andrews, where dwelt George Buchanan, who had already expressed his desire to deal with him[1]; there he was examined secretly under torture on 9th and 10th, and hanged on 16th August. Elizabeth wrote 22nd August, the draft being in Cecil's hand, requesting that Paris may be preserved for examination, in England I suppose. Can anyone really believe that Cecil only heard of the arrival of Paris on that date? Why, even the diarist of the 'Diurnal' knew about it on the 5th or earlier! I am afraid that the letter was *timed* to arrive too late. It is a dreadful story. Can any Mary-hater read it and believe in Paris?

Of the stuff squeezed out of the victim, I will only use Andrew Lang's words: "The most bungling witness who ever perjured himself, could not have brought more impossible inconsistencies than Paris brings into a few sentences...." I think Andrew was moderate. The stuff was so incongruous that even Cecil could not use it when he got it.

It must be remembered that the precise period between the alleged arrival of Paris and his death coincided with negotiations, genuine or not, to effect the restoration of the Scottish Queen. It was in June that Moray received Elizabeth's demand to reply on this question, and in June Paris was found. The method has extraordinary similarity to that used on other occasions, a threatened action producing and intended to produce matter which would permit the abandonment of the threat. Mr Froude has, unwittingly, touched the truth very nearly: "He (Paris) mentioned circumstances which would have aggravated, had aggravation been possible, the hatefulness of Mary Stuart's treachery, and *made the thought of her return more vividly intolerable*." Was Elizabeth a dupe led by a knave, or a willing tool? It is not my business to answer.

---

[1] See Mahon, *Indictment of Mary Queen of Scots*, pp. 53, 54.

Chapter III

THE RATIONALE OF THE PLOT

THE CHOICE OF KIRK O' FIELD

I N the preceding chapter I sought to show that the official story of blowing up of the King by means of gunpowder placed within the Queen's chamber, and with her connivance, is false. But of the official story there are two readings. One was that Mary cajoled her husband to accompany her to Kirk o' Field intending his murder there; the other that she desired to take him to Craigmillar. In a previous volume[1] I have given the reason for discarding the former as depending on the discovery of the almost perfectly genuine Casket Letter, known as the "Short" Glasgow Letter. I will not repeat all that is said there. But, as the latter story is the one exhibited before Elizabeth's Commissioners, it is what ought to be believed by all good anti-Marians, even though many smears of the original concept are not quite wiped off.

The story told in London is vouched for by Thomas Nelson, a servant of Darnley, and later in the service of the Earl of Lennox, who says: "The deponer remembers it was devised in Glasgow that the King should have lain first at Craigmillar, but, because he had no will thereof, the purpose was altered and conclusion taken that he should lie beside the Kirk o' Field." Thomas Crawford, another witness, says the same thing[2].

Is there not also the "evidence" of the two Glasgow Letters? "I bring the man with me to Craigmillar on Monday," and again, "I answered that I would take him with me to Craigmillar, where the mediciner and I might help him[3]."

[1] Mahon, *Mary Queen of Scots*, p. 91.

[2] Camb. MS. DD. 3. 64, No. 36.

[3] Readers who have followed my little book on the *Lennox MS*. will be aware that one must accept these letters with certain reservations. The latter quotation is, I believe, quite genuine, the former is genuine too, but does not apply to Darnley. However, those who accept both letters at their face value must admit "Craigmillar" as well as the rest.

But there is other evidence, more trustworthy than the above, that the Kirk o' Field was not the Queen's choice. Within a few days after the event Guzman de Silva, the Spanish Ambassador in London, reported to his master, on the authority of Sir Robert Melville, who had just arrived from Edinburgh, that "the King had chosen" it. This statement, made immediately after his arrival, and before the cross-currents of other ideas had disturbed truth, has a particular value. In the *Memoirs* attributed to Claude Nau, we have it thus, "The King was lodged in a small house outside the town, *which he had chosen* on the report of Sir James Balfour and some others. This was against the Queen's wishes, who was anxious to take him to Craigmillar[1]." Again, we have in the *suppressed* part of Hepburn's deposition[2], "Enquired who devised that the King should lodge at Kirk o' Field? Answered Sir James Balfour can better tell nor he, and knew better and before the deponer, thereof." Why the part of the deposition containing this was omitted in the record sent to England in the following year, cannot be explained unless it be that the person for whom the extracts forming the Cambridge MSS. were made had means of insisting on a fuller "true copy" than was thought necessary for Elizabeth and her Commissioners. It would have been as easy to garble one part as another, and Sir John Bellenden's certificate that any part was a true extract was obviously worthless. However, the mere fact that the above survived in the Cambridge copy makes it a valuable evidence of the part taken by Balfour in selecting the house.

There is another evidence which to me is as convincing as any. It is contained in two letters of Sir William Drury dated 23rd and 26th January, 1567, and free therefore from suspicion of being written for a purpose. The first announced that the Queen "came yesterday" to Glasgow to visit her husband; the second, that she would return, if no danger to his health should arise from the cold weather, on the 27th[3]. Lest there be any question, let me say that, when Drury wrote they would return "Tomorrow," that is, the 27th, he obviously meant that the return

---

[1] Nau, *Memoir*, ed. 1883, p. 33.
[2] Camb. MS. Oo. 7. 47/4.   [3] *State Papers, Border*, XII.

journey would be commenced on that day. Equally it is clear that, writing on the 23rd, he did not *know* that the Queen had arrived on the previous day; he knew only that such was her programme.

Please reflect for a moment on what this involves. The itinerary of a Royal journey was as carefully mapped out then as now, perhaps more so then, on account of transport and food supply for a number of persons. The plan would be known to the court officials and reported to Drury. So it comes to this, Mary left Edinburgh on the 21st with the *previously* arranged programme of returning to Craigmillar with her husband, starting from Glasgow on the 27th. But I read more into it than that; it means that the correspondence between the pair had resulted in Darnley's promise to return if his wife came to escort him[1]. Whether he was honestly afraid to return alone, or had some other purpose in calling his wife to Glasgow at great inconvenience to her, I will not hazard an opinion.

If, then, the programme arranged many days beforehand was upset, and Kirk o' Field was chosen instead of Craigmillar, we are confirmed in attributing it to the advice of Balfour as stated by Nau, and hinted by others.

Nor must we ignore the several reports which reached Sir William Drury showing the early activity of Balfour. I have already mentioned the first report that it was Balfour who had purchased gunpowder, and in the same letter (28th February, 1567) Drury mentioned, "Balfour came to Edinburgh on Wednesday (26th February) at night accompanied to the town with thirty horsemen; when he was near unto the town he lighted and came in a secret way...he is hateful to the people." When did Balfour leave Edinburgh? Unfortunately we have no knowledge. It must be supposed that he was present during the days when the King lay at Kirk o' Field, the choice of which place appears to have depended on his advice; but I know of no mention of him during these days. One can only hazard the opinion that Balfour, having seen his plans put in operation, quitted the town on the night of Sunday (9th February). He

---

[1] Bishop Leslie definitely makes this statement in the *Defence*; see Anderson, I, p. 12.

returned seventeen days later, perhaps not without some secret understanding with the Lords then ruling the situation in Edinburgh.

It is not likely that Drury's report was literally true, for so marked a man as Balfour could hardly come into Edinburgh secretly, nor could he hide himself there. But we are on surer ground in saying that the absence of one who was a Lord of Session, Clerk Register of the Council and a Privy Councillor, at such a juncture is ample to confirm the statements that he was nearly concerned with the great event of the moment.

On a previous page[1] the careful accounts of Servais de Condé have been mentioned; and from them appears not only that the fitting up of Kirk o' Field was a late thought, but that the plenishings from Holyrood must have arrived there a very few hours before the invalid himself. Here we have a certain confirmation of Thomas Nelson's statement already referred to.

One other point is worth putting before the reader. When Darnley arrived in Edinburgh, he, no doubt, entered by the Potterrow Port, turning to the right up the short flight of steps to the level of the Kirk Yard. He would see on his left the big house of the Hamilton's some 40 yards away, in front of him; and, after he had passed the angle of the ruined kirk, appeared the "new" Provost's Lodging. Now it is a point alluded to several times in the contemporary accounts, that Darnley, being in front of the procession, made towards the Hamilton House, believing it to be the place set apart for him. I confess that, to me, the emphasis laid on this trifling incident seems to corroborate the statement that Kirk o' Field was Darnley's own choice, for otherwise it is unlikely that prominence would have been given to such a blunder as to suggest that he would make towards the Hamilton House. There was something to conceal and this was the clumsy method adopted.

I am a believer, as I think I have said, in the existence of a spark of truth in most, perhaps all the incidents which fill the pages of the 'Detection' and cognate documents. It was easy to adorn these tales by real happenings, twisted out of all recog-

[1] See p. 37.

nition, but it would be difficult to invent them as one went along. In the present case, the Hamilton House was as well known to Darnley as Holyrood itself. He must have passed it, and very likely been in it, scores of times, and it is quite inconceivable that, when he expressed his wish to go to Kirk o' Field, he had the remotest idea of using the "fort and garrison" of his enemies as a residence. Possibly what happened was that, arrived at the "new" Provost's Lodging, he thought his goal attained. The more so that, although this house was actually in the possession of Robert Balfour, it was popularly held to be a perquisite of his brother, Sir James. Bothwell in his narrative mentions it in this sense, so does John Knox[1]. This is another little filament to connect the move to Balfour's initiative.

In what has been stated above some confusion may appear to those not intimately acquainted with the facts by pointing out that the Queen had nothing to do with the selection of Kirk o' Field. As what I most desire is to be clear, let me explain that the final edition of the official story—we may call it the Craigmillar edition—superseded the earlier or Kirk o' Field edition, at about the time that Mary was incarcerated in Lochleven, that is mid-June 1567. The Kirk o' Field edition was simple and direct—Mary had gone to Glasgow to bring her husband to the house which, in consultation with Bothwell, had previously been decided on, Bothwell in the meantime taking the necessary steps to prepare the underground mines all ready for the appointed murder. There was no question of Craigmillar at all.

I have used the word "edition"; it is not a good one, for there was no regularly drawn up statement of the case, of which the copies could be called in and defaced. It was the story put about to cover the Queen with the maximum of obloquy. But when the inner circle "discovered" the Casket Letters, the new or Craigmillar conception was adopted in its stead. The transition was not a clear excision of the first idea, which still remained in the minds of several, and notably of Buchanan. The stain of the Kirk o' Field story clung to his writing of the 'Detection' a year later, and it appears still more clearly in the Hopetoun 'Book of

[1] Knox, *Hist.* p. 339.

Articles' which, as I have said in a previous volume, cannot be the final form of the document presented to Elizabeth's Commissioners[1]. In the Lennox Narrative it appears most clearly of all, for he knew nothing of Craigmillar, and retained the original notion in complete purity—or impurity.

In a word, what I want the reader to see and agree to is that, to arrange for committing murder at the house at Kirk o' Field, after the King had chosen it, is incompatible with the other story of a *previous* preparation of the same place selected by the Queen and Bothwell ten days or more before she decoyed her husband to Edinburgh. The former is unquestionably the final and official narrative.

THE LAST HOURS AT KIRK O' FIELD

When Mary and her gay train of lords and ladies clattered along the winding lane into the courtyard of the precincts at or about 8 o'clock on Sunday evening (9th February, 1567) and there dismounted to join Darnley for an evening's merrymaking, one of two things must have happened. The attendants must have been told that the horses of the Queen and her ladies[2] would be required again at about 11 o'clock, or they were told that the Queen would spend the night at Kirk o' Field. In the one case men and beasts would take such shelter as they could find; in the other, those belonging to the Queen's immediate circle would probably return to Holyrood, unless there were stables at Kirk o' Field[3], in which case they would be strawed down and the caparison taken off. The Queen's *écuyers* would see to all this.

---

[1] To suppose that Hosack's valuable discovery is a copy of the document put forward to the Commissioners infers too great a demand on their complacence, for it contains the Kirk o' Field conception almost naked with but a slight attempt to write in allusion to the new story.

[2] The notion that the Queen would sleep alone in the room under Darnley's is too absurd to make it worth discussing. Attendant ladies are not mentioned in the Narratives, but they must have been there all the same.

[3] There may have been a limited accommodation on the north side of the precincts.

Certainly it would not be left to chance, for Mary had the reputation of being a horse lover.

Thus, when begrimed Paris appeared in the reception Salle, and Mary affected to remember her forgotten promise to attend the masque at Holyrood, she would have found her horses " awa " as Powrie did at the Friar's Gate at about the same time. As this did not happen, and as, on her Majesty's call, " to horse," an immediate departure appears to have been made and the whole cavalcade was mounted and in motion, we must admit that the forgotten promise story loses its savour[1]. At all events it is clear that those without were expecting her, and Darnley and his servants would be very obtuse if they did not know all about it. We may suppose that Darnley would have been gallant enough to lead his lady down to the mounting step and to see her off. As all the gay crowd passed down the turret stair, none noticed the locked door leading to the Queen's bedroom, and none could tell that within a very few feet of it Hepburn and Hay are nursing the cook's candle in that deadly atmosphere. What an improbable story!

And so, Darnley, deserted at least for the time, returned to the Salle. Begrimed Paris and locked doors have awakened no suspicions in his mind. He is now quite recovered, able to be in the Salle with the company there, able on the previous day to confront the Lord Robert Stewart in a quarrel, in which both parties would have had recourse to their weapons had they not been parted, and able to return to Holyrood again on the following day, to resume normal life. Our most detailed account of this

---

[1] And of course we must not forget that Lennox, when he told his first story, had no knowledge of the forgotten promise, but gave quite a different and probably equally untrue account: " It seemed that she would have tarried all night with him, but both he and she were persuaded to the contrary by Bothwell and others, who seemed to bear a good countenance (that is, who seemed to be sincere), appointing for that she had appointed to have ridden the next day in the morning to Seton." That is, reminding her that she had arranged, etc. For some reason the editor of Keith says that Mary walked from Kirk o' Field to Holyrood; I do not know his authority, but it seems on the face of it very improbable.

last evening comes from his father, Lennox. Thomas Nelson, who was at Kirk o' Field throughout the affair, and was actually, so he says, involved in the explosion, remained in the service of Lennox after his retirement into England. From him there was every opportunity of hearing what occurred. The Lennox Narrative was unknown to the older writers, and but slightly examined by others. What follows comes from that source[1].

Darnley's first act was to give orders that his "great horses" should be ready for his use at 5 a.m. on the next morning. A strange order; surely Lennox would not mention it without some motive? Pitch dark then, and for a couple of hours after, a raw February morning, a convalescent going for his first outing! At least it serves to show that Darnley's external world was not entirely dead, his horses and his grooms were somewhere outside where a message would find them, yet the Lennox story would lead us to believe that, except for a very few indoor servants, he had been left alone. Then, after a melancholy reminiscence that Mary had mentioned the death of Riccio to him that evening, which his favourite servant begged him to think nothing of, "he and his well beloved servant" sang together the fifth psalm. The King then "called for his wine and drank to his servant, *bidding him farewell* for that night," and so "merrily" to bed. Wine, by the way, would presumably mean one of those warmed possets dear to the hearts of our ancestors, and this seems to imply some further connection with a waking world downstairs[2].

The King had not lain one hour and a half, being asleep, till 50 persons in number environed that house, whereof 16 of them, Both-

[1] See for fuller details the study of this document by the present writer. It is not suggested that the narrative is a truthful exposition of the case, but it represents what Lennox wished to be credited at the time he wrote.

[2] Here we have one of the minor mysteries, which, like the 'Tale of the Barrel,' would, if elucidated, go far to settle everything. The "beloved servant" was evidently Alexander Durham, known generally as Sandy. His name appears quite frequently in the case, but particularly in the 'Oration,' written towards the end of 1570, by an English-

well being chief, came the secret way she herself was wont to come to the King her husband, and with their double keys opened all the locks of the garden and house and so quietly entered his chamber, who, finding him in bed, finally did suffocate him with a wet napkin steeped in vinegar. After which being done, bare his body into the garden, his nightgown laid beside him and his servant William Taylour, who suffered death in like sort....All which being finished the house being blowed up with powder[1].

This is the story of the Earl of Lennox. It was written by him, partly in his own hand, between 22nd and 28th May, 1568[2].

Thomas Nelson adds a few details:

The Queen, being departed toward Holyrood House, the King within the space of an hour past (passed) to bed, and in the chamber with him lay the late William Taylor. This deponer and Edward Symons, lay in the little gallery that went direct south out of the King's chamber, having a window in the gable through the town wall, and beside them lay Taylor's boy[3], which persons never knew anything until the house (room) wherein they lay was fallen about them....

Although I hope that the official story of Hay and Hepburn with the "bing" in the room below, is sufficiently laid to rest,

man, Dr Thomas Wilson, a violent anti-Marian. Wilson represents Durham as making every possible excuse to get away from the fated house, and finally as being "thrust out by the Queen herself," to save him from the fate she had prepared for her husband. Lennox has a totally different story—Sandy and his master are on the best of terms, the Queen has left half an hour ago. Darnley drinks *farewell* to him for that night; apparently the story is so far true that Sandy has permission to be absent for the night. He was, according to Wilson, a spy and a talebearer; almost one gathers that Sandy told of things done by Darnley, rather than concealed from Darnley things about to be done to him. It is difficult to believe that Sandy would be coolly singing psalms if he was aware that he was standing over a magazine that might go up at any moment. Incidentally, let us ask why the explosion was delayed. If the Queen left near about 11 o'clock, what object was served by waiting say two and a half hours? Certainly, the impression I gather is that, whatever Sandy knew, it had no connection with Hay, Hepburn, and the "bing" in the Queen's chamber.

[1] Mahon, *Mary Queen of Scots*, pp. 130 f.   [2] *Ibid.* pp. 78 f.
[3] The term "boy" is more likely to mean "body servant" than "lad." It has survived in the former sense in the East to this day.

there remains the *fact* of the explosion. Gunpowder was ready or available somewhere; in the vaults under the Salle is what I suggest. At any moment within, say, half an hour after the Queen's departure it would have been possible to apply the match and retire. The alleged object of slaying the King would have been accomplished. Why did they delay? If it is true that Darnley was the only victim aimed at, I can imagine no answer that meets the question; if, on the other hand, the statement made in the letter sent to the Archbishop of Glasgow, already referred to (see p. 45), that the plot was "dressed (prepared) as well for us (the Queen) as for the King," is accepted, then a reasonable explanation is available. One is *forced* to believe that the conspirators were awaiting some event. The Queen's return from Holyrood, I think; but we are going too fast, let us get back to the subject of this section.

There are two distinct schools of allegation, apart, that is, from the official absurdity, as to Darnley's death; the one, of which Lennox, quoted above, is typical, viz. that he was strangled in his bed and carried outside; the other, that he escaped from the house and was strangled outside and then carried to the south garden. There are a dozen practical reasons for saying that the first is quite untenable. Murderers who had made immense preparations to blow him up would not bother about going inside. But if that is not agreed to, on the ground given, so it is said, by Captain Cullen, that it would make *sure*, then there are other stumbling blocks. How did the murderers get in? False keys, you say! False keys are no use when doors are locked on the inside with the keys in the door, and it would be the precaution even of half a century ago to do that. But if you suppose it was neglected, if you suppose that no servitor was sleeping across the doorway, as would be likely, can you believe that the deed was done so noiselessly as not to awaken the sleepers in the little gallery a few feet away from the victims? Is it possible that the two bodies were carried out into the passage, down the stairs, through the fore entry, across the "little court," through the postern in the wall, across the "Thief's Row," into the south garden, over to the tree and, with infinite compassion, the clothes

and slippers as well?[1] Think of the physical difficulties, think of
the utter uselessness of it, not only that, but the foolishness of
it, and agree with me that the story is untenable.

It is certain, I say it without qualification, that Darnley *left
the house of his own motion*. One can afford to be positive, because it is the only alternative. But there are two aspects of that
alternative: did he leave at a moment chosen by himself, or did
he leave under the compulsion of some sudden emergency? In
the answer to these questions lies the root of the mystery of Kirk
o' Field.

Against the first of these two cases there is the immediate and
formidable reply that no one, then or since, who has set about
a reasoned statement of the events of 9th/10th February, 1567,
has hinted that Darnley was himself an actor and not merely a
victim. In itself this need not be considered conclusive, for of
contemporary authorities who published what may be cited as
histories, there are but two. On the Catholic side, John Leslie,
Bishop of Ross; for the Protestants, George Buchanan. Leslie
writes with the object of casting the guilt on the Earls of Moray
and Morton, in fact, on the Protestants; Buchanan condemns the
Queen and through her the Catholics. From the former, for
reasons which I hope will appear, the whole truth cannot be
expected; from the latter, even though his history contradicts
much of what he wrote to order at the time, the political necessity of maintaining the Queen's guilt veiled any desire to give a
different colour to the event. Besides, I doubt if Buchanan ever
did know the truth; he was not the sort of man to whom much
would be imparted. There is but one hint that Leslie knew more
than he wrote. He would answer, he said, all accusations, "So
far forth as the time present may yet permit to be published and
disclosed."[2] In after years he wrote his *Paralipomena ad His-*

---

[1] Buchanan in his *History*, having conveniently forgotten the story
to which he had previously given his authority, definitely says that all
who saw the body were agreed that he could never have been thrown
out of the house by the force of powder, for there was nothing black
or blue or bruised or broken about his body, nor were his clothes so
much as singed (*Hist.* ii, p. 321).

[2] *Defence*, in Anderson, i.

toriam, and, though then he was a free agent so far as Scotland is concerned, his tongue was tied from other considerations.

There remain the *Memoir* of Sir James Melville, the Lennox Narratives, the *Memoir* of Claude Nau and one or two others, anonymous papers. The first evidently knew very little, the second is valuable only because he wrote in his *first* story, quite different from the second and third, what he had carried away from Scotland when he left, as the recognized exposition of the case, plus a few items added out of his own knowledge; that story, however, was valueless from the point of view of getting the whole truth, since his only aim was to portray his son as the innocent victim. The third authority, very valuable in parts, because it is derived, as I have said in a previous volume[1], from the Queen's surgeon, was, in this particular matter of the catastrophe, very meagre.

Besides all these are the letters and rumours of the time, containing, I freely confess, little to confirm my thesis. But independent views are not to be expected, and all are written with a partisan or a political or a religious bias.

The maelstrom of controversy which belongs to later years has brought every line and word of the original indictment under dissection, an enormous amount of matter has been brought to light, but no departure from the beaten track has resulted. Buchanan, Leslie, the proceedings of Elizabeth's Commissioners, the written word of the letter writers, most insecure of supports without most careful consideration, still constitute the arsenal of both attacker and defender.

It is left for us to do what is possible to examine the two alternative explanations of Darnley's escape from Kirk o' Field, in the light of such circumstantial evidence as can be adduced. We can expect nothing better, no direct evidence is likely to exist.

The first point which strikes one is that the accounts of Darnley's escape from the house come from the three foreigners whose names are so closely connected with the affair—M. de Clerneau, M. du Croc, and Signor di Moretta. One might,

[1] Mahon, *Mary Queen of Scots*, p. 133.

indeed, leave out du Croc, for his reports were based on the hearsay of his special messenger, who had but a confused idea of what happened (see pp. 101, 102). Clerneau and Moretta made reports in London and Paris, and what they said seemed to grow in detail the farther they got from England (see pp. 46, 104).

In London Clerneau gave no information other than that the King was found dead at a distance of sixty to eighty paces from the house. Moretta was but little more explicit; what he said to Elizabeth or Cecil we do not know, but to the Spanish Ambassador, de Silva, he hinted that he knew more than he would tell, and in general conveyed the impression that the Queen was guilty of fore-knowledge of the plot. Arrived in Paris, both these persons opened their thoughts more generously. What we know of their stories comes from the letters of the Bishop of Mondovi and of the Venetian Ambassador, Giovanni Correr.

Clerneau's tale was that Darnley was awakened by the smell of the burning powder and was afterwards suffocated by the smoke—evidently a halting story which we may neglect, and if this was all that he told the Bishop of Mondovi[1], it is certain that he was concealing the truth. It is, however, to be noted that the Bishop had also sent a secret letter after du Croc's arrival, not preserved, in which he may have displayed greater knowledge than he allows to appear in his open correspondence. Clerneau said so little that it appears he was not free to speak, was, in fact, a minor character in the drama, with a small part.

It is from Moretta, the envoy from the Duke of Savoy, that we learn most. I confess to suspecting that he knew a great deal more than he spoke, but I will try not to let that prejudice a consideration of what it is alleged he said. Unfortunately, no document has yet come to light which gives his own statement; we have only the reports of third parties, hearsay evidence. Of these there are two, varying in an important degree. The one was communicated to the Bishop of Mondovi in Paris and reported by him on the 16th March, the other reported by Giovanni Correr to the Signory in Venice on the 20th idem.

[1] Pollen, p. 358.

In the first, the story was that the King, hearing the noise of people surrounding the house and trying to open the doors with false keys, wanted to go out by a gate that led into the garden to escape the danger. There he was strangled, and brought out of the garden into a little yard outside the town wall. Then the house was blown up to murder any others within. We can only bring the searchlight of common sense to bear on this, and in that light the story is weak.

If Darnley was awakened from innocent sleep as described, there was no reason why any idea of a gunpowder plot should come into his mind; indeed, so long as the house was surrounded and people were trying the locks, it might have occurred to him, if he thought of it at all, that he was safe from such an attack. What, then, would an ordinary man do? There were admittedly six serving-men in the house. Surely all would be called at once to the defence. I refuse to admit the possibility that they were unarmed—to be so would be too completely against the spirit of the times. Six men at the head of a narrow staircase would hold the fort indefinitely against almost any number. Cries for assistance from the windows, the firing off of a "dag" or two would awaken his grooms and certainly alarm the attackers. Instead, the victim, followed by one servant who has the time to snatch up clothes and slippers, rushes down the stairway, not out by the "fore entry" into the courtyard, but by the passage to the garden door (which, by the way, was not possible, if, as said in the official story, the door was locked by Paris), into the arms of the attackers, who were *surrounding* the house. There, not content with killing him, the conspirators go through all the "business" of carrying him, his servant, clothes and slippers, by the circuitous route already mentioned. Finally, for some totally inexplicable reason they attract the attention of the world by blowing up the house.

The other story is better, though it, too, has stumbling blocks. It runs thus: towards midnight the King heard a great disturbance, at least, so certain women who live in the neighbourhood declare, and from a window (the window in the King's bedchamber looking east towards the Blackfriars monastery must be meant) perceived many armed men were around the house. So he, suspecting what might befall him, *let himself down from another window* (that through the town wall, I suppose) looking on the garden. But he had not proceeded far before he was surrounded by certain persons, who strangled him with the sleeves of his own shirt, under the very window from which he had descended.

Before going any further, will the reader please look again at the account given by Lennox (p. 44): sixteen of the conspirators approached the house by the "secret" way the Queen was wont to come. Now the view from the east window of Darnley's bedroom would give an uninterrupted view of any party approaching by the "secret" way through the Friars' gardens, and if anyone had been watching for that event, plenty of warning would have been given. At the moment, however, we must not suppose that anyone *was* on the lookout, and the noise that woke Darnley must have been occasioned when the party entered the east garden, close to the house; this is strange, for one would suppose that the approaching party would be silent and Darnley's window would certainly be shut having regard to the season and the hour.

Just now, as we are accepting the tale at its face value, let us suppose that Darnley did hear a noise, did look out of his east window, did come to the conclusion that he was attacked on that side, did *not*, as the other story says, rush down the stairs and out by the garden door into the arms of the party he had seen approaching, did not decide to defend himself and call for help, but did decide to let himself down from the south window, thus putting the town wall between himself and his enemies. This is a story which hangs together, at all events in parts. We can easily assume that Darnley saw nothing out of his south window to alarm him—indeed, as will be shown later, we know that the men on this side were hidden in the three cottages (see p. 107 *infra*). We may be puzzled why he did not choose the "fore entry" and flee across the courtyard to his horses which were somewhere not far off, but possibly when he saw the attackers they were close, and he might suppose that entry would be also invested. We may also be puzzled as to how with such celerity he got out of the south window; but that point shall be dealt with later. We must also be definitely shaken in our credulity when we remember that Nelson, Symmons and another were sleeping in the "little gallery," through which Darnley and Taylor would have to pass to get to the south window, and yet were not awakened![1]

The rest of the story seems true; the south window did look on the south garden, though the narrow passage called Thieves Row, lay between. Still, the tree under which Darnley's dead body was found was less than 40 feet away. It remains remarkable that Moretta could have told, practically at the same moment, two stories so essentially different; Correr could not possibly have invented the additional information of his version. It looks as if Laureo (the Bishop of Mondovi) did not wish to admit the escape by the south window; Correr, on the other hand, innocent of any knowledge, saw no harm in repeating what he had been told.

In any case, Correr's description comes nearer to a full and true account, and we obtain considerable confirmation of it in the sections which will now follow. With this further information to aid us, I will suggest that the weight of evidence points to a chosen moment for the flight. In other words, I suggest, that between the stories of Lennox and Correr we can discern the truth—that the approach of the party by the "secret" way that the Queen was wont to use was watched for, and that, at the appropriate moment, Darnley left the building by way of the south window, not without having made previous preparation for doing so, as also for the next step, as witness the ordering of his "great horses."

Another matter must be mentioned, not conclusive in itself but significant. Father Edmund Hay of the Society of Jesus, whose full account of the whole affair was so eagerly awaited[2] by the Bishop of Mondovi, mentioned on his arrival in Paris

---

[1] It is true that Lennox says nothing of this last tarradiddle, which is *only* the official statement of Nelson's evidence.

[2] See several letters of Laureo, Pollen, pp. 352–71.

that Darnley had heard Mass on the Sunday morning[1]. One cannot but be reminded of the disclosures made under Sacramental confession to Fathers Garnet and Greenway, at the time of the Gunpowder Plot in 1605. The eagerly awaited account of Father Edmund, if it still exists, has never been made known; the Bishop of Mondovi mentions that he expects to receive a written statement, but said nothing of its contents when he received it.

WAS THE QUEEN'S RETURN TO KIRK O' FIELD EXPECTED?

The only satisfactory answer to this question must come from a witness without bias to any side in the controversy, and I know of none. As usual, we can only weigh the few chance indications which exist.

That the Queen had promised to remain all night at Kirk o' Field on the fatal Sunday is vouched for in many places. Most of them ascribe the change of intention to the forgotten promise to attend a marriage ceremony at the Abbey. Lennox does not mention this, but ascribes it to her intention to ride to Seton the next morning, presumably starting early. Thus, 'Book of Articles': "She said she would lie there all night." Nelson's evidence: "She promised also to have bidden there the Sunday at night." Lennox Narrative: "Seemed that she would have tarried all night with him." Letter of the Lords to Queen Regent of France: "It was a mere chance that Her Majesty did not remain there all night." Letter attributed to Mary addressed to Archbishop of Glasgow: "And of very chance tarried not all night, by reason of some masque in the Abbey." Bishop Leslie[2]: "She returned thanks to God for her preservation from so great a peril, for it looked as though the contrivers of the plot had expected that she would pass the night there with the King,

---

[1] He adds the words "according to his custom," but it is a little difficult to suppose that this was a daily practice, for, if so, John Knox would surely have had something to say about it.

[2] *Paralipomena*, translated in Forbes-Leith.

and they planned the destruction of them both[1]." Letter, Cockburn to Cecil, 19th March, 1567: "Bastian...showed the great hazard that our Queen's Grace escaped that night, for were (it) not for Secretary Lethington and Bastian that was married that day, her Grace would not fail to have lain in that same house, and been utterly destroyed...."

The Queen had passed the night of Friday at Kirk o' Field and also at least one other night, and, on the face of it, there was nothing unlikely in her promising to spend the Sunday night as well, except that, as this was the last night of the convalescence, it would seem that, unless pressed by Darnley, she would not have decided on another night of comparative discomfort.

Indeed, I think we must go further, and ask why Darnley remained at Kirk o' Field over the Sunday. A day of festivity, it would be apparently just the one to choose for a homecoming. He was quite recovered; his bed even had been taken back to Holyrood, he was to occupy it there on the following day. There is no suggestion anywhere that he agreed under persuasion to spend another night in the Old House. Considering the extreme simplicity of the "bing" arrangement and the alleged ease of carrying it out, one would suppose that any day from that of his arrival at Kirk o' Field would have met the Queen's requirements. But any day would not suit the converse case, in which the Queen would be victim and Darnley the escaping "innocent." That required the temporary absence of the victim.

As it seems to me, the story of the "forgotten" promise to attend the wedding is untenable; I have referred to this elsewhere (see p. 54), but there would be no very decisive reason why the Queen should not attend the masque and *return thereafter to Kirk o' Field*. Let us remember that she came "masqued" to pass the evening with her husband[2]. True, to be masked on Carnival Sunday was probably the common practice, yet it is also consonant with an intention to go to the wedding masque at Holyrood; and, for this and other reasons, I think Darnley

[1] This is valuable, written, as I have said, with partial independence.
[2] Clerneau's story to Laureo, in Pollen, p. 358.

knew perfectly well that she was going there. One of these reasons arises from a part of the Casket Letter, which is, I think, a genuine note of the Queen's. She is expressing her surprise at the intimate knowledge which Darnley, then lying sick at Glasgow, had of minor matters occurring at Edinburgh, "He spoke even of the marriage of Bastian." I can only read this to mean that he knew that the marriage was fixed for Carnival Sunday, a popular marrying day.

If Darnley's purpose was such as I believe it was, the temporary absence of the Queen would be a necessity; for, if once she was in residence, her guard would be around the place, and his chances of escape small. On the other hand, if her approach was known, to escape, while leaving the lighting of the slow match to an underling, was an expedient offering no insuperable difficulty. Let us remember that two of his servants were in fact caught in the explosion. A slow match could be arranged to burn for any reasonable time, and, if well devised, the Queen and her attendant Lords, the more the better from Darnley's point of view, would be taking a ceremonial farewell of their mistress, in the Salle, before leaving for the night.

The Lennox Narrative, which says so many things different from the discredited official story, states that the Queen would have spent the night at Kirk o' Field, but for "the persuasion of Bothwell." Now, we are told, and I think with perfect truth, that on reaching Holyrood, after spending a short time at the marriage feast (so says Clerneau, in his statement of 16th February), Mary went to her rooms in the palace and there entered into very earnest conversation, lasting till past midnight, with Bothwell, the only other person present being John Stewart of Traquair, the captain of her guard. After a time Traquair went out and the conversation was carried on for a short time, when Bothwell also left, and, having changed his clothes, went to Kirk o' Field[1].

Lennox would have it understood that Bothwell's *persuasion* was applied at Kirk o' Field to induce Mary not to spend the

---

[1] 'Detection,' 'Oration,' 'Indictment,' 'Book of Articles,' Buchanan's *History*, all repeat this fact.

night there, or at least to give her a good excuse for not doing so. I suggest that the suasion was applied at Holyrood to prevent her from returning. Those who condemn the Queen lay some stress on this midnight conversation, and look on it as the last infamy of a woman sending her lover hot foot to the murder of her husband. But, in taking this view, it seems to me that they overlook the essential continuity of their own story. At Kirk o' Field everything is ready; all this time Hay and Hepburn are standing by the "bing"; unsuspecting Darnley is by now fast asleep; what more could there be to occupy Bothwell for an hour, and that too in the presence of Traquair? Surely a guilty Mary would have sent her assassin off immediately to get the business over, if, that is, his presence was requisite—and I wonder why it was. According to one story, "She caused shoot a hagbut...that their complices might...know she was away," and yet, an hour and a half later, she is impeding Bothwell's start. Was there ever such a concatenation of irreconcilable falsehoods?

To me, and I hope to open-minded readers, the conversation has a different meaning. It has never been hinted, either then or later, that Traquair had any hand in a plot to murder the King, and yet it was well known that he was present at this last conversation. His duty was the safeguarding of the Sovereign, and one must conclude that some threatened danger to her person was the subject of discussion. It was after he left that Bothwell opened to his Queen the full extent of the villainy of her husband, and told her in plain terms of the fate intended for her should she return to Kirk o' Field. My conviction is this, that there was great difficulty in persuading her that the man who had fawned on her at Glasgow and promised repentance, on whom she had lavished her forgiveness an hour or two ago, could be guilty of such treachery. It would fit all the known facts as to the otherwise inexplicable delay in firing the mine, or the equally obscure question as to why, the King being already dead outside, the explosion should have been given effect to at all, if we suppose that the conspirators were awaiting the Queen's return and were deceived by the approach of a party which had been delayed by Bothwell's difficulty in obtaining the Queen's warrant to test his allegation.

Let us imagine his proposal; that the Queen should remain at Holyrood under the protection of her guard, he to return to Kirk o' Field simulating her own return; if the expected result occurred, he craved her warrant to take the fugitive dead or alive. Let us not forget a little aside which the blundering Lennox inserted in his first Narrative, "Some said she was present at the murder of the King, her faithful husband, in man's apparel, which apparel she love oftentimes to be in...[1]." No difficulty, then, in impersonation, especially on a day when all the world was fooling. We find this story nowhere else, and Lennox does not repeat it in his later Narratives, a fact which rather adds to than detracts from its value.

This concept of what passed between Mary and Bothwell covers the facts; no other solution that I know of does so. Some things remain to be fitted in to the story. I will endeavour to show that they find their places.

To this extent, then, Mary would have had foreknowledge. That she consented to anything but a capture of the fugitive, I doubt; it was not in her nature to wish for the shedding of blood, even in cases when any of her contemporary rulers would have turned the thumb down without a moment's compunction. Yet the result was almost inevitable, if, as appears to have been the case, the Douglases and Hamiltons were those who awaited the flight of Darnley. Dr Wilson, who gave more away in his 'Oration' than did Buchanan in the 'Detection,' tells us of an ambush "set before the door (that is, the postern in the city wall) so that none should escape." Probably Bothwell did not tell the Queen all he knew, or the extent to which, the event being expected, was prepared for.

[1] It is a small point worth noticing that the 'Diurnal' mentions the Queen and her Maries masquerading in man's clothing at a banquet given to the French Ambassador, Rambouillet, almost exactly a year previously. The present occasion was also a banquet to an Ambassador, Moretta, who was departing on the next day; it was from this banquet that Mary went to Kirk o' Field. It is quite possible, when Clerneau said she was "masked," that he merely means she was in "fancy dress."

She listened for the explosion, says Buchanan, full of hope for its success. Yes, she listened, I think, distraught as to whether the story told her was true or false, and when the sound reached her, and within a short time the news of what had happened, this woman, who for five months had been on the border-line, collapsed mentally and physically.

But we must go further before this thesis will be accepted.

A REMARKABLE FEAT

Of the several branches into which our enquiry must now separate, I am beginning with one which has been singularly neglected, that is, the conveyance of the news of Darnley's death to Paris, where it was known in the afternoon or evening of Wednesday, 19th February.

When the news of the birth of a son to the Queen of Scots was conveyed to London by Mr James Melville, a certain *éclat* was given to his performance, for he left Edinburgh at 12 o'clock mid-day of 19th June, 1566, and reached London in the evening of the 23rd, covering the 400 miles in something like four and a half riding days. But we may assume that he had fine weather, the roads at their best, and unlimited daylight. We might add that the posts were probably warned and the best horses in readiness to carry him forward. His average speed may be put at between nine and ten miles an hour. Dick Turpin is credited by Ainsworth with an average speed of nearly twenty miles for ten and a half hours, and though it seems rather outside probability, it was rather a test of poor Black Bess than of her rider.

In our present case the distance from Edinburgh via London, Dover, Calais to Paris is not less than 640 miles, excluding the channel crossing. The days were short, not more than nine and a half hours of light, the roads at their worst, the post-horses probably out of condition on account of the season, and it is unlikely that the weather was good. We must take the average speed at nine miles an hour for eight hours a day and nine consecutive days, and even that assumes that the channel was crossed with a favourable wind in the night time, when rest would have been imperative in any case. A fine performance and worth a little niche in history; and it has a good deal to do with us.

Buchanan, in the Latin summary called afterwards the 'Detection,' sets the keynote; and, though he wrote a year later, we may quote him first: "And, whereas the murder was committed after midnight, they had, *before daylight*, caused by special *fore appointed* messengers, rumours to be spread in England that the Earls of Moray and Morton were doers of that slaughter." Now, before going any further, I would like to recall what was said in the 'Tale of a Barrel,' viz. that that theatrical piece of property was specially placed where it would be found in the morning in order to direct suspicion in some desired direction. That direction, I suggest, was not likely, originally, to have been Holyrood, but rather leading towards Morton or Moray or even Archibald Douglas, their active agent.

This forthsetting, by these very early newsrunners, of the rumour that heretic hands were responsible for the tragedy seems to confirm this suggestion. Ordinarily I should set little store by what Buchanan said, but in this case other independent evidence corroborates him, and it is a curious fact that there was, it appears, something inconvenient in permitting the matter to remain on the record, for it is omitted when Buchanan himself put his Latin into English[1]. Nor is this rumour to be found in other contemporary narratives, though it plentifully besprinkles the reports of foreign letter writers[2].

That the messenger (I will assume there was but one) was "special" and "foreappointed" can hardly be doubted; but here is something of a mystery. How did he get so rapidly into England, without apparently touching Berwick or Carlisle, and thereafter use the English posts with such freedom? As to the first, I think, we must assume guidance and furtherance of the

---

[1] See 'Indictment.'
[2] The 'Oration' has a bare mention of the spreading of slanders, without mention of names.

Borderers, or some section of them, to whom the hidden byways were an open book. As to the rest, it looks as if the French Ambassador, du Croc, had smoothed the way. At least it is certain that the aim of this rapid traveller was to overtake the Frenchman, who, as we know, was making a leisurely journey towards France, *not ignorant*, as Drury wrote, on 14th February, of an impending event at Kirk o' Field[1].

The news carried by the messenger is very interesting; it appears first in a letter from Drury, who was at Berwick, to Cecil of 11th February, written early in the morning, Drury having had it from Dunbar; but it is clear that its source was not our man, although the story was very similar to his. *He*, as I have said, did not travel by Dunbar, and was already far south of Berwick when Drury got his message. It was, however, of such importance, that Drury sent off a courier at once to London; he says: "Even at this present there be advertisements come unto me *and sent from Dunbar* that the Lord Darnley was upon Sunday at night slain.... It is also reported that some evil is set or was meant at that present to his father." In the evening of the same day, writing at 10 o'clock, he sent another special courier to Cecil. "I have now further knowledge that he lies slain. His body was found in a field and strangled as it would seem.... *His father is also slain.*" Nor a word, be it noted, regarding du Croc's secret messenger, and we must conclude that Drury knew nothing of him.

At all events, on arrival in London, presumably on the 14th, the secret courier went at once to the French Ambassador, and was sent on by him to Dover; there (again I must say, presumably, for the exact dates are not recorded) he met du Croc on the 15th; on the 16th or night of the 15th, du Croc crossed, and

---

[1] It is necessary to note here that there is confusion among the historians regarding this special messenger. Even so careful a commentator as the late Father Pollen appears to mix him up with M. de Clerneau, who was officially despatched from Edinburgh on 11th February, more than twenty-four hours later. See Pollen, note on pp. 352 f. Our "special" messenger was certainly unofficial, and it was his information, and his alone, that reached du Croc at Dover on the eve of his crossing into France.

arrived in Paris on the 19th. His arrival and the news he bore are contained in a letter from the Bishop of Mondovi.

...On the 19th of the present month, M. du Croc, the French Ambassador in Scotland arrived here...while at Dover, before crossing into France (he) received an express messenger sent him by the French Ambassador (in London) with an urgent commission to use all speed to reach this court (Paris) and to be the first to communicate the news of the death of the King of Scotland *and of the Earl of Lennox, his father*....On the morning of the last Sunday of Carnival time, at an early hour, he and his father were found dead in the public street, both of them stripped[1].

Cecil had had the same news, whether from Drury or by communication from the French Ambassador, and, in his letter to Sir Henry Norris, in Paris, dated 20th February, he says, "His father was first said to have been slain, but it is not true, for he was in Glasgow at the time."

The Venetian Ambassador in Paris had the news from du Croc, and reports it in the same terms as quoted above and adds, "It is the work of heretics *who designed the same for the Queen*, intending to bring up the Prince in their religion[2]."

Nor can we omit to note here, though it must be referred to again, that, at the moment this messenger was speeding south, another messenger was speeding north carrying a warning to the Queen that "there be some enterprise to be trafficked to your contrary...and to advertise you to take heed to yourself[3]." The Archbishop of Glasgow, the sender of the message, had the information from the Spanish Ambassador in Paris, Don Frances de Alava, Darnley's friend, and he hints that he had also heard it from others; he does not, however, appear to have sent the news very urgently, for it took fifteen days in transit, reaching Edinburgh the day following the death of Darnley. I want the reader to mark that there is no mention of danger to the King, and this is the more necessary because Froude and other historians prefer to quote a version of this

[1] Pollen, p. 351.
[2] *Cal. V. State Papers*, Correr to Signory, dated 21st February, 1567.
[3] Quoted by Keith, I, p. ciii, from an original in the Scots College in Paris.

letter given by Drury (14th February) to the effect that Mary should be careful to whom she imparted her secrets, and that her husband would shortly be slain. As Drury could have had no knowledge of what the Archbishop's letter from Paris really contained, his imaginary report is only useful to show how willing he, and those who copy him, were to asperse the Queen. Rumours of this kind current in Paris may easily have been in the hands of M. du Croc, when that envoy left his special messenger behind in Edinburgh to carry the news of the expected event to him; but, I repeat, the event expected was dangerous to the Queen, not to her husband.

There is enough in the foregoing to enable a reconstruction of the events to be given with tolerable accuracy. Du Croc had left an agent, of more than usual capacity for getting about secretly, to watch for some occurrence which was anticipated. For a reason which we need not guess at present, du Croc suspected that the Earl of Lennox might be in the neighbourhood at the critical moment; the agent, in the vicinity of the scene of action, in the darkness and confusion jumped to the conclusion that the second dead body was that of the Earl; with this erroneous information he started on his strenuous journey to find his master, and spread the news which reached all or most of the capitals of Europe before it was contradicted. Du Croc was not apparently surprised at the news, though it is certain that he must have known that Lennox would ordinarily be still in Glasgow. Can it be supposed that, with the avidity he displayed for news of the dénouement, and with the special means he had, through his friend Moretta, who remained in Edinburgh throughout the crisis, of knowing all that was going forward, he would be ignorant of this elementary fact[1]?

---

[1] In saying this I do not overlook that the Bishop of Mondovi, in the letter quoted above, mentioned that Lennox had accompanied his son to Edinburgh. I am still convinced that du Croc knew better, though it does not follow that he told the Bishop all he knew.

WHERE WAS THE EARL OF LENNOX ON
THE NIGHT OF 9TH FEBRUARY?

The interesting and, to our enquiry, not unimportant question is, whether the Earl of Lennox *was* in Glasgow at the critical moment? We must not neglect the statement of M. Clerneau, repeated by the Bishop of Mondovi in a later letter[1], that late on Sunday evening, that is, the evening of the tragedy in Edinburgh, the Earl of Lennox was attacked in Glasgow, and, but for the bravery of Lord Sempill, might have been killed. Even if the story had some foundation, it would still not necessarily have prevented Lennox from riding towards Edinburgh, but I doubt the tale; it is entirely unconfirmed and would surely have been brought forward by Lennox himself when drawing up his various narratives relating his grievances against the Queen; yet he is silent on the subject. It gives the impression that Clerneau was anxious to establish an alibi for Lennox; and the comment of Mondovi, that this alleged occurrence at Glasgow accounted for the rumour of the Earl's death at Kirk o' Field, is clearly ill-founded. It would have been impossible for the special messenger, hurriedly leaving the scene of action at some early hour before dawn on Monday, to be in possession of news of an event that occurred in Glasgow late the previous evening.

We have, however, another source of information of a more reliable character. Robert Melville, who had been sent to London on important business, arrived there on 22nd February; on the 26th of the same he informed Cecil that he had received a letter from his brother James, and, among other pieces of information, was this: "Lennox was at Linlithgow, but had returned to Glasgow." This was Edinburgh news of the 16th, and, unfortunately, we are not told when Lennox came there nor the date of his departure; but it sounds as if his return had been a few days before.

Now it is, of course, perfectly conceivable that, on hearing of

---

[1] Pollen, p. 358.

the death of his son, which he presumably did on Monday evening, 10th February, Lennox would start either at once, or on the following morning, on his way to Edinburgh to see his body and attend his funeral; but, if that be the reason for his presence in Linlithgow, why did he not complete his journey by coming the remaining seventeen miles to Edinburgh? It cannot be supposed that he feared attack on himself, after the blatant publicity given to the murder of the son; it is beyond imagination that the father, come to weep over his body, would be massacred also. Even the Mary of Laing's or Froude's fancy could be neither so foolish nor so brutal as that! If his conscience was clear, he had nothing to dread. It is clear enough from the opening paragraphs of the "long" Glasgow Letter, which I do not doubt are genuine, though not complete, extracts from Mary's rough diary, that Lennox was at the time of the Glasgow visit under suspicion of some treason; but even that, in the present circumstances, would not account for his absence from Edinburgh.

It would seem that his conscience was oppressed with some further guilt connected with the matter now under enquiry; and, if we suppose that his coming to Linlithgow, and perhaps even farther towards Edinburgh, happened on the Sunday night, we shall find several pieces of the puzzle falling into place. In short, the solution I suggest is that Lennox, having received the necessary hint that a climax was approaching, marched towards Edinburgh to succour the triumphant Darnley, at last successful, as he hoped, in destroying the Queen. I say, *at last*, for this plot was but one of several which had failed. If the intention of Lennox was known, and I think it was, we can account for the first rumour that he too had been killed at Kirk o' Field. In this puzzling enquiry, one cannot be too careful not to mislead; I do not think that Lennox had any knowledge of the nature of the plot at Kirk o' Field, but merely that an important attempt was in hand.

WHAT THE WOMEN SAW

There is, I believe, a binary star system, of which one partner, being dark, alternately obscures or uncovers the light of the other, and so, in our investigation, we have two stories of what women saw on the night we are interested in. One of these stories is dark, inasmuch as it is certainly untrue, and it is used to obscure the other which is light, and probably true; but there are occasions when the rays of the latter escape and reach our vision.

The dark story relates the experiences of two women, Mistress Barbara Mertin and Mistress May Stirling (*née* Crockat), who resided in Blackfriars Wynd on opposite sides thereof, and not very near the Wynd foot. What they *saw* and heard, particularly Mrs Mertin, on this moonless February night, at a distance of not less than 60 yards, makes such a call on one's credulity that I do not think we need bother about it[1]. Our interest really commences from the account given by Buchanan in the 'Detection.' "They sent for a few poor, silly women who dwelt thereabouts...(who) when they had blabbed out something more than the judges looked for, were dismissed again as fools that had indiscreetly spoken. For their testimony, though they touched some folks shrewdly, yet they were such as they might easily set light by." Now, Buchanan, it is true, does not specifically mention the Blackfriars Wynd, but I hope I do him no wrong in thinking that he meant this locality to be understood; certainly he has been so understood.

Dr Thomas Wilson, in whose impetuous hands so fragile a web as that woven by Buchanan should never have been placed, composed the 'Oration' as a pendant to the 'Detection,' but in more than one place betrayed a knowledge of the truth which a more skilful advocate would have concealed. In this case he repeats the story we are dealing with, with a difference. "A few poor folks, the next dwelling neighbours to the King's lodging, being called, neither dared tell what they had seen or

---

[1] See Add. MS. Brit. Mus. No. 33531, f. 37, being a statement of depositions made on 11th February, 1567, during an enquiry into the King's murder. It seems almost certain that, whatever was said at that time, the record was subsequently garbled.

heard; either they were with fear put to silence or despised as of no credit." Here we have the ray of light which Buchanan's dark story denies to us. The women were the *next neighbours* to Kirk o' Field, and not the widest stretch of imagination could place them in the Blackfriars Wynd.

There is another and confirmatory fact in this connection. The picture of 1567 shows three cottages as situated close to the postern gate in the gardens outside the town wall; they are shown in Plate III. On them a strong ray of light is thrown, which, to continue our stellar metaphor, has only now reached earth after nearly 400 years of travel. In his letter addressed to Cecil, dated 20th June, 1567, Sir William Drury says: "Blackater, Cullen, neither any of the rest that are apprehended for the murder, have been yet arraigned. The stay is for that *the three hosts of the houses* (for "hosts" we may read "tenants") out either of the which houses there came out eight persons that were all at the murdering of the King, cannot yet be gotten[1]."

This short extract contains so much that I am astonished that it should have been so neglected. Its truth is guaranteed by the effortless simplicity of the statement. It fixes a blot on Cecil's honour which no greatness can efface; for clearly, when he not only permitted, but actively aided, the fabrication by Moray and Morton to pass through the farce of the judicial enquiry at Westminster a year later, he was in possession of reliable evidence of a different story. It brings understanding of a part of the 'Oration,' which the indiscreet Dr Wilson introduced out of his knowledge: "They thought it not enough to have set open the postern door...nor to have set an *ambushment before the door*, that none should escape...." It gives us additional confidence, if such is required, in the substantial accuracy of the 1567 "picture." It brings home to us how completely the true course of the enquiry undertaken on the Monday following Darnley's death has been suppressed, and how little the existing fragment of it, already referred to, can be trusted. Even the very avoidance of these details offers an argument of their truth. It

[1] *State Papers, Border*, XIII, ff. 174–5.

tells us things in connection with Captain Cullen and others which we will look at later.

But the chief instruction which it contains is the general verification of the account that Moretta imparted to the Venetian Ambassador: "Certain women who live in the neighbourhood declare, and from a window perceived, many armed men were round the house[1]. So he, suspecting what might befall him, let himself down from another window looking on the garden...." Moretta did not tell the whole truth, or the Ambassador perhaps did not take it in correctly; but here at least is something reasonably comprehensible. These women were naturally on the lookout—the invasion of the armed men in their houses would ensure this—they were close to the place, and, as any such action as descending from the window would require a light, it is not unlikely that the movements were visible to the watchers. The conclusion is almost unavoidable that the event was expected; the preparations were too extensive to make it possible to suppose that an unarmed, newly awakened Darnley, hurriedly flying from a danger just discovered, was the quarry awaited; rather, a fully prepared Darnley, not without protectors.

THE 1567 "PICTURE" AGAIN

I have often alluded to the "picture" of 1567 and based thereupon a great part of the reconstruction of Kirk o' Field. But there is something more in it than a mere representation of the buildings and their surroundings. It contains, I think, also a narrative, and if the explanatory letter which must have accompanied it were forthcoming, we should learn much. Those who have examined the picture will have noticed four features[2] which the artist must have introduced with a purpose. The first is Darnley's furred pelisse, mentioned several times in the story, and indicating in the picture that he did not escape from the house without thought for the next step; the next is a somewhat

---

[1] As to "round the house," the women could only know of what occurred on their side of the town wall.

[2] As shown in the sketch on p. 110, extracted from the original in the Public Record Office.

confused article, which though shaded netwise, is, I think, a rope, which seems to indicate the means of descent from the window in the town wall; the third is certainly a chair; the last is a dagger or a sword, to indicate, I assume, that the fugitive was not unarmed.

A portion of "The Picture" of 1567 showing personal effects of Darnley, chair, etc., found by his body.

The chair and the rope, if it is a rope, seem of particular interest. If the town wall, at the point where it was penetrated by the window, was of standard construction, the height from the ground of the "battling plane," which was also the floor of the "little gallery," would be, as we have seen, about 16 feet. At this point, however, the terrain sloped sharply to the east, and the wall must have been stepped at frequent intervals, as shown in Plate III; at the lowest point of any of these steps the height from the ground might easily be reduced by

2 or even 3 feet; there was also a slope northwards and the ground outside the wall would be slightly higher than that inside, but this difference would be small. It is, then, quite possible that the drop from the window was not actually more than 13 feet or thereabouts; if a chair was provided to shorten the distance, we can take off another 18 inches at least[1].

Thus to an active man the difficulty of lowering himself from a height of between 11 and 12 feet would be trifling. I do not want to indulge in too much speculation, but, as I have said, the "features" must have been introduced in the picture for a purpose, and the purpose I have described seems a reasonable explanation. At the least, it is a straw, showing with other straws the direction of the wind; at the most, it is a definite proof that the escape was not the consequence of a sudden overwhelming necessity, but the result of a plan carefully thought out.

One other point. There is in the picture a body of horsemen outside the town wall, standing in a kind of *cul-de-sac*, the sides of which are walls, or what might be walls, of a colouring different from the dividing walls of the other gardens. No such *cul-de-sac* could have existed in fact, and I read this riddle as indicating the secret presence of the horsemen in question. In a document[2] without date, but compiled during April and May, the probable solution is given: Ker of Fawdonside, Drury says, was seen close to Kirk o' Field with others on horseback. He adds that he was there to give aid in the cruel enterprise, if need had been.

---

[1] It is to be noted that the idea of a rope and a chair as aids to escape occurs elsewhere; in a letter dated 2nd April, 1566, preserved by Bishop Keith (II, pp. 411 ff.), Mary informs her Ambassador in Paris of the facts regarding the murder of Riccio. Part of the letter contains this: "The Earls of Huntly and Bothwell...devised that we should have come over the walls of our palace in the night upon towes (ropes) and chairs which they had in readiness to that effect."

[2] I use the word document to distinguish it from an ordinary letter. There are several such in Drury's hand, which contain collections of items, some of which he used in his letters. These seem to be memoranda collected for Cecil's information, which need not be shown to Elizabeth. Many authors refer to them as letters and quote extracts therefrom of an extravagant kind which Drury did not think fit for inclusion in his serious communications.

Hosack[1] enlarges on this and tells us that Ker, an unpardoned rebel, had a blood feud against the King, and infers, thus following Drury, that his presence was inimical to the King. But is this correct?

Strictly speaking it is not the case that Ker was an unpardoned rebel, but there are several reasons for saying that his treason at the Riccio murder had not been forgiven by the Queen. Six weeks or so previously a pardon had been wrung from Mary, in circumstances which virtually gave her no option, in favour of Morton and over seventy others delated for that murder, but neither Ker nor George Douglas had been included, and the Earl of Bedford, who had been closely connected with the pressure brought to bear to obtain the pardon, mentioned to Cecil that Mary had refused to include these two names. Yet there is in the *Register of the Privy Seal* a separate pardon to Fawdonside, bearing *the same date* as that to Morton and the rest. One remains guessing how it got there. Knowing as we now do that, on more than one occasion, Darnley used the Royal prerogative and authorized orders under the Signet which Mary knew nothing about, it is not unlikely that this pardon was his act.

There are several records which show unmistakably that Mary's sentiments towards Andrew Ker were of the most hostile kind—which is scarcely to be wondered at when we remember that it was he who threatened her with a "dag" at the time Riccio was murdered; for instance, the proclamation put out in her name after her escape from Lochleven described this Ker and also his cousin of Cessford as "hell hounds, bloody traitors," and other terms; again, in a letter to Elizabeth a little later, she says: "Cessford and his son have been my rebels from the beginning." In his third Narrative, the Earl of Lennox says: "Whithaugh keepeth...in his house, as prisoner, one Ker of Fawdonside by her (Mary's) command."

There is also the record of Claude Nau:

About this time[2] a person named John Shaw came to the Queen and told her that Andrew Ker of Fawdonside had returned into

---

[1] Hosack, I, p. 241.
[2] That is, at a time shortly before the murder of Darnley.

Scotland from England, to which he had been banished for having presented his dagger at the Queen, and having killed the late David (Riccio). He having boasted to certain persons...(that) within fifteen days, he assured them, there would be a change at Court, and he would be more than ever in credit; and then he enquired boldly how their Queen was.

These words may be ambiguous, but, coming from this source, and whether they can be relied on or not, the intention was to indicate that the change in question was to be to the Queen's detriment. It cannot be supposed, in all the circumstances, that we are intended to assume a rise to favour of Fawdonside through the medium of a guilty Queen and Bothwell. The context does not warrant it, and other matter makes it more probable, almost certain, that the rise in credit was to come through Darnley.

Andrew Ker and his first cousin, Walter of Cessford, were ever on the side contrary to their Queen; and it is not likely that either was a partisan of Bothwell. There is plenty of evidence that, in his capacity of Lieutenant of the Borders, the Earl was the object of hatred to all the Kers, and especially to those of Cessford. Only a few months previously he had been sent to apprehend the young Laird of Cessford, on the charge of murdering his own uncle and godfather, the Abbot of Kelso. A very few weeks later, at a time when Bothwell was in power, the Laird himself was warded in Edinburgh Castle, which does not indicate any friendship between Bothwell and Fawdonside. To this may be added that James Ormistoun of that ilk in Liddesdale was certainly present and inimical to Darnley at Kirk o' Field, and as between Ormistoun and Andrew Ker there was deadly feud, they would assuredly be on opposite sides.

Both Fawdonside and Cessford were, if not strong supporters of John Knox, at least tinged with the policy of reform; the former was a signatory of the first 'Book of Discipline[1],' in the end he married Knox's widow, Margaret Stewart of Ochiltree, and several times we come across Ochiltree and Fawdonside acting together, a further indication that he was no friend of Mary[2].

[1] Knox, *Hist.* p. 510.
[2] An inquisitive reader may ask why, if Ker was tinged with reform, he should take part in a plot of which the ultimate aim was to counter

On the other hand, the evidence is that Fawdonside was a Lennox partisan—"good Levenax" as the phrase went. Present, and taking a leading part at Riccio's murder on behalf of Darnley, which is very much the same as naming Lennox himself, we find Lennox complaining of Ker's imprisonment by Whithaugh, and still later we find the same Ker supporting the election of Lennox to succeed Moray in the Regency. At a much earlier date, shortly after Lennox came to Scotland, a former servant of his drew up for Cecil's information a list of his late master's friends and enemies, in the former category of which are the "Kers and Humes," and the conjunction of names indicates the Cessford Kers, which includes Ker of Fawdonside. When Lennox came to power, there is no indication that he regarded Fawdonside in an unfriendly spirit, and it is to be noted that the placards spread over Edinburgh at the time of Darnley's death, a matter in which Lennox was not ignorant, never suggested the name of Andrew Ker as a participant in the murder.

I will not dwell further on this point except to repeat that, while the group of hidden horsemen in the picture may, with reasonable certainty, be said to represent Fawdonside and his followers, the balance of probability—I might put it higher than that—is that they were there in the interest of Darnley.

If the reader is with me so far, I will ask him to consider how much is implied. Fawdonside could travel quickly to the scene by the secret tracks known only to the Borderers, but the message that brought him must have been sent not less than two days previously, perhaps on the Friday, the same day that Darnley wrote to his father[1]. Again, we have the almost unavoidable conclusion that foreknowledge of the event, and preparation for it, is, if not proven, at least clearly inferable.

the new faith. I can only say that I do not know what story Sir James Balfour told him, but in any case, to many of the Borderers personal feuds were more potent than religion. To destroy the Queen and Bothwell and then rise to "credit" in the new régime would be a powerful lever in a decision.

[1] See, as to this, p. 115 *infra*.

DARNLEY'S SERVANTS

It is a charge against the Queen that, in order to promote her design, she caused the removal of the greater number of the attendants on her husband, "that should have defended his life" ('Oration'). It certainly is a fact that we hear curiously little of what became of the retinue which it must be supposed would ordinarily surround the King; that Darnley, whose too numerous guard of "Lennox men" at Stirling barely six weeks previously had been the occasion of dispute between him and the Queen, could not now, with his consent, have been unguarded. On the other hand, is it possible to suppose that so overt a step would have been taken as to deprive him suddenly of all but a few indoor servants? To do so would surely have given the secret away; how could even the most trusting and innocent of men have failed to scent danger at the sight of powder-begrimed Paris, locked doors, and, above all, sudden desertion of servants? Darnley, too, was far from having an innocent consciousness of rectitude, for there is no question that he had been plotting against the Queen for months. He would, without fail, suspect from such indications that something unusual was going on, that the tables were now about to be turned.

I mentioned above the "sudden" removal of his people. On the 7th of February, that is on the Friday before his death, he had written to his father, and Lennox himself gives us a copy of his letter, in which he says he is full of rejoicing at the happy state of his affairs, "I have thought good to write unto you by this bearer of my good health, I thank God, which is the sooner come to, through the good treatment of such as hath *this good while concealed their good will*, I mean my love the Queen. Which (who) I assure you hath all this while and yet doth, use herself like a natural and loving wife...[1]." Up to that time, then, we

---

[1] That some such letter was written seems to have been generally known; Buchanan mentions it in his history; but that Darnley writing privately to his father, who, before any other, knew why there had been lack of "good will," should have used the phrase in italics above I greatly doubt. I must add that, whatever the letter did or did not con-

cannot suppose his retinue removed by the Queen's orders. On that Friday occurred the alleged incident of Lord Robert Stewart's disclosing to Darnley a plot against his life.

Those who know of it will remember that Darnley told the Queen of the statement made. Be it noted that the Queen spent that Friday night at Kirk o' Field; what opportunity she had of confidential talk with her husband I do not know, but a guilty woman would have thrown her victim off the scent and hushed the matter up. *Her* step was to send for the Lord Robert on the following morning (Saturday) to confront him with her husband, and to call in the Earl of Moray and Bothwell to hear the dispute! If the story were true, can one doubt that it would have formed Moray's strongest count in his subsequent indictment of his sister? Yet never at any time, so far as the published proceedings of the judicial enquiry in England are concerned, did he bring it forward. Having in mind that Buchanan usually possessed a shred of fact for his incidents, which he ingeniously turned inside out, I think we must agree that some incident of the kind occurred; but I suggest that it was not a plot against Darnley that was in dispute, but a plot against the Queen, and we have in the Claude Nau *Memoir* some confirmation of this. There it is said that someone had advised him, Darnley, to make an attempt against her, Mary's, life. This is much more probable, and would accord with the calling in of Moray, and his subsequent silence[1].

The Earl of Lennox, with all his special means of knowing what took place on the last days, does not mention it in his first or second Narrative. But, in his third Narrative, written after he had had opportunity to assimilate the niceties of the case, he does refer to it, rather half-heartedly; "As for the device which she and Bothwell found together in raising a quarrel betwixt him (Darnley) and my Lord of Holyrood House (Lord Robert

tain, it made Lennox aware of some part of the expected event of the following Sunday night. Lennox would receive the letter on Friday night, and the messenger could easily return with a reply by Saturday evening.

[1] See Nau, *Memoir*, p. 242.

Stewart) a little before his death, thinking that way to have despatched him if she could, my Lord Regent (Moray) can declare it, who was there present." Please note that Lennox avoids mention of the cause of the quarrel and places the onus on Moray, who avoided it also.

In his first Narrative, the only one which represents his own mind, Lennox not only does not mention this quarrel, which should be of first-class importance to his argument, but inferentially he gives cause for suspicion that he had no knowledge of it. For, when he related the reminiscences which Darnley discussed with his servant before retiring for the night, the only one to which he gave prominence was some alleged chance remark that the Queen had made concerning the death of Riccio. Yet it is inconceivable, if on the previous day a plot against his life had been the cause of a serious discussion, that this should not still be uppermost in his mind.

But, so far as this section is concerned, the main point is that up to Friday there was evidently no question of reducing Darnley's retinue; and if, subsequent to the alleged disclosure of a plot against him, his servants had been removed, can one reasonably believe that the most simple of Darnley's followers would not have known that there was truth in the story, and taken precautions accordingly?

Let us, however, take another angle. We know of at least six servants left in the house at the critical moment[1], and we know of the departure of Alexander Durham, and we know that at or about 10.30 o'clock, Bonkil, the cook, was still in the kitchen; we may guess, without fear of error, that he was not alone. We know that somebody was about to answer a call for wine, and that men were not far off to receive an order about horses, and that Anthony Standen, Junior, was in Edinburgh, and that others of Darnley's household, as Hudson and some musicians, also Henry Gwynn and John Stevenson, both Englishmen, were in the neighbourhood. Besides, there were some guards, for I

---

[1] Of whom two were killed in the explosion and one was strangled outside. Of the former, it is curious that only one was mentioned at the time; not until years after was the fact of a second victim disclosed.

refuse to believe that there could be so great a departure from custom, as that an important noble would be without any. What became of all these? We hear nothing of them, so far as escape from the disaster is concerned. Yet most of them must have been at Kirk o' Field on the Sunday in question.

In his *History* Buchanan gives more information than he did in his 'Detection'—the "most part" of the attendants, he says, were "gone out of the way, as foreknowing the danger at hand." Wilson, in the 'Oration,' is also illuminating: "Of his other servants I enquire not...why they went away, why they then specially forsook the King." There we have the answer, his servants "foreknew" and "forsook" the danger. Well, it is certain enough that they did not get their information from the Queen or Bothwell, for neither of them, in the circumstances alleged against them, would value Darnley's Englishmen as worth the giving away the secret; in fact, we are expressly told that the house was blown up *after* the King had been murdered, in order to kill any others within it.

But Darnley's entourage was not the only consideration. It can scarcely be questioned but that an explosion so violent as that at Kirk o' Field would have done great damage to the adjoining buildings. The 1567 "picture" shows its effect on the house nearby in the northern range, and, though not shown, there must have been still more destruction caused to the back part of the eastern wing of the "new" Provost's house. The house was in possession of Robert Balfour, and it cannot be supposed that it was uninhabited, yet no single casualty is reported. I think we must assume that the indwellers were absent and forewarned. By whom? By Bothwell and the Queen, acting together or singly? Not very likely, for they would not care, and the secret was the main consideration. By Darnley or his people acting without outside assistance? Again not likely for much the same reason. By Sir James Balfour? This is, I think, the answer; we shall have more to say about him presently. In the meantime, let us remember the fleeting glimpse of the presence of a Balfour in the house at the foot of Rapperlaw's Wynd (p. 67). We do not know which brother is referred to, Gilbert or Robert, but it looks as if one or other had found a refuge in this conveniently situated rendezvous while the danger was imminent.

I think we are again driven to conclude that those who had warning to be out of the way had it from Darnley's side, in which, for reasons that we will come to, Sir James Balfour was included.

CONSTRUCTION

It may be that in the foregoing pages I have pulled some things to pieces without replacing them by others. Very briefly I will try to rectify the omissions to consolidate, as it were, the position we have arrived at.

First, as to the explosion. It may be said that practically every house in Edinburgh had a basement storey; very many were built on slopes, and the basement was a vaulted structure deeper on one side than on the other. The new Provost's house at Kirk o' Field was built on slightly sloping ground, its basement, unless excavated, was probably not high. Here, in ordinary circumstances, was stored fuel and sundries, an admirable *cache* in which to accumulate gunpowder. Adjoining this, at the eastern end of the house, was the basement of the Salle, shallow at that end and deepening towards the other (see p. 31). Whether there was any opening from one to the other I will not guess, but the persistency of the story of mining and previous preparation leads one to think that some work was necessary to make a passage. A passage once available, we need not suppose that the powder barrels were placed in position at once—a short time, even after the Queen had left Kirk o' Field on the Sunday night, would suffice for that. I mention this because, even if the reader still prefers the old story to mine, it must puzzle him to understand how those of the company who were in the know could have played dice upstairs over such a dangerous situation.

The suggestion then, as I see it, is this, that Sir James Balfour formed the plot—how long before I will not, at the moment, hazard an opinion—accumulated the gunpowder, and provided the required Guy Fawkes to place it in position at the proper time. Several fragments of stewed truth which float in Buchanan's cauldron can be recognized as originally suitable to form part of this explanation.

It may be asked why Darnley, *choosing* the moment of escape, should get out of a window in his shirt, when a little earlier, and leaving his servants to carry out the details, he might have gone out booted for his ride. Certainly it would have been the wiser course, and by going early he might have escaped the ambush; but the subsequent story would have been marred. Paraphrasing the sentence in letter alleged to have been written by Mary to the Archbishop of Glasgow (p. 45), Darnley would have said, "We assure ourself it was dressit alsweill for us as for the *Queen*," and continued, "we providentially learning of the attempt, without time given to warn Her Grace, escaped, sark alane, by descending from a window." This would have made quite a good tale if affairs had turned out differently, and the "sark alane" part of it would be essential. The clues had been laid to ascribe all to the heretics. All the Catholic world would accept it, for the Queen's orthodoxy was questioned.

William Taylor with the fur-lined pelisse thoughtfully provided against a chill; the "great horses" ready—and this is the reason why Lennox mentioned them; Andrew Ker of Fawdonside was there to provide an escort. The Queen and her attendant nobles were killed, the whole town in complete confusion, the capture of the young Prince from Holyrood not a difficult enterprise[1]. Lest I be thought too imaginative, let me say, as will appear later, that to seize the Prince and assume the Government had been already a rumoured intention of Darnley.

And then—away for Glasgow and Dumbarton and assumption of a real Catholic Government, under the ægis of a foreign power. To that we come in due course.

---

[1] As to this, I see, in the calling in of John Stewart of Traquair to the interview at Holyrood on the Sunday night, steps ordered against surprise in this direction, for Traquair was captain of the guard.

THE EARL OF BOTHWELL

SUNDAY, THE 9TH FEBRUARY, 1567

When Bothwell left the Queen's presence on the night of Darnley's murder[1] after midnight, he went to his quarters, changed his clothes, collected his servants, including Powrie, Dalgleish, the page called Paris, Wilson and probably some others whose names appear very indistinctly, and walked (there is no indication now of riding) without attempt at secrecy up the Canongate to the Nether Bow Port. The statement of all this, given in the depositions of Powrie and Dalgleish, in almost identical words, is, in my opinion, a correct account of fact. They were challenged by the Queen's guards on leaving the palace, their identity was not concealed. The party probably arrived at the Port some time after 1 o'clock in the morning.

The gate was closed, and they did not hesitate to awaken the porter, one John Galloway, and call on him to open it. Here they were held up "a good while" until the gate-keeper appeared. Again, every man of the party must have been seen. They then went up the Highgate, turned down the Blackfriars Wynd and called for the Laird of Ormistoun, who was not at home[2].

Bothwell and his party then went on by way of the monastery gate to the place where the wall of the east garden adjoins the town wall. That is to say, they did not exactly follow Mary's "secret" or private way (p. 43), but cut into it, so to say, when nearing Kirk o' Field. Some few minutes before reaching this spot, the party, which I assume was carrying torches, would be in view of the east window of Darnley's chamber in the old

---

[1] See 'Detection': "After she was come into her chamber, after midnight, she was in long talk with Bothwell."

[2] There is here one of those curious similarities in the several narrations, which seems to show a foundation of truth, overlaid with spurious detail; Ormistoun in his statement, taken six years later, says he went to his friend Thomas Henderson's house, and not to his own chamber in the Friar Wynd, thus confirming the statement of Powrie and Dalgleish.

house. The wall would have been reached not much before 2 o'clock. According to the best accounts the explosion took place near about the same hour[1].

I have done my best in the above record of times not to beg the question; if the reader will go through the whole matter, the hour of starting, the delays met with and the distances to be travelled, I do not think he will disagree with me that an hour and a half must have passed between the time of leaving the Queen to the arrival at Kirk o' Field. Admittedly, the hour of the explosion varies in the several accounts, but I have taken that given by the most responsible persons, "environ les deux heures après minuit," and this was written within a few hours of the event, when knowledge was not only fresh but unlikely to be dissembled. It may be said that it is unnecessary to prove what is already alleged in contemporary papers, that Bothwell's arrival was the moment chosen by Hepburn and Hay[2], shut up in the room below the King, to fire the slow match. But this point requires a little thought.

It is a fact, not, I think, commented on, that neither Hepburn nor Hay in their depositions give any indication that Bothwell entered the house, whether for the purpose of strangling Darnley or any other. They could not possibly have been ignorant of the fact had he done so, but all Hepburn says is, "They tarried therein (that is, the house) until after two hours after midnight" and then fired the train, while Hay's statement is, "Thereafter the Earl Bothwell...came to the backyard," and then they fired the train. It is not said what signal they had to know of Bothwell's coming, or how Bothwell, from outside, could have indicated his presence. It looks to me as if their story coincides with what I have already suggested, viz. that the coming of Bothwell's party was awaited by some person other than these two, and that

---

[1] Lords of the Council to Queen Regent of France, Sloane MS. 3199, dated 10th February, 1567.

[2] I am retaining, for convenience, the allegation that it *was* Hepburn and Hay who fired the train; but, in fact, although it is pretty certain that these two persons were present at the slaughter of Darnley, it is to me a matter of conviction that they were without and not within the house. The firing of the train was in other hands.

the signal was given from inside. They say, I know, that on coming out after firing the train they found Bothwell and his companions in the garden, but that I discard as untrue. Convinced as I am, and have, I hope, shown, that the train was fired under the Salle and not under the King's chamber, the conspirators would escape through the postern outside the town wall, or possibly across the courtyard of the precincts, and would not come in contact with Bothwell until the explosion was over, or, as I think more likely, not at all.

The situation, then, as I see it, is that Bothwell arrived at the east garden, knowing that his coming would be the signal to fire the train, but not knowing how many minutes would elapse before the explosion. Do you think that in these circumstances he would go into the house, or even approach it very closely? At that moment Darnley was being done to death outside the walls, or at least but a few minutes before, if, as is likely, his evasion took place when Bothwell's coming was first noted at some distance away. The sound of the struggle must have reached the approaching party, and Bothwell, content that all was going as anticipated, would patiently await the explosion at a safe distance. It is improbable that Bothwell saw, on that occasion, the body of the man whose life he might have saved, if he had had any desire to do so. The deed was not his doing, even if the ambush outside the town wall was within his knowledge, possibly arranged by him. He is not, in fact, delated as a "murderer with the hands" but as a "deviser." His participation as a "deviser" is probably real enough, even if, perfunctorily, he had given orders for the capture and not the killing of the fugitive.

The story of Bothwell's return to Holyrood seems to me to be wildly improbable. Just picture the occasion; a tremendous booming roar from the explosion, a flash lighting up all Edinburgh; Kirk o' Field on its eminence visible from the greater part of the town; the whole populace awakened and the people "convening," as we are told they did, from all parts—those of the Friar Wynd and adjacent Closes and the Cowgate filling the approaches to the scene within a few minutes of the event; John Galloway and his fellow gate-keepers on the alert; every sentinel at Holyrood and the Castle aware of an extraordinary occurrence, and in all probability a body of soldiers sent from the latter place to ascertain the cause. Is it likely, in these circumstances, that Bothwell and his party would make their way by the Blackfriars Gate, cross the Cowgate, ascend the Friar Wynd, cross the High-gate, traverse some of the Closes north of the same and attempt to scale the wall at Leith Wynd, double back to the Nether Port, call up John Galloway again to let them through, and then, please mark, run down St Mary's Wynd to join the "Back o' Canongate" road to Holyrood?

Surely, unless they had lost their heads altogether, the line of retreat was simple and direct, and out of the ken of the assem-bling people, namely, to follow the town wall to the Cowgate Port, opening direct on to the Back o' Canongate; it was not even necessary to go so far, or to go through any Port, for the whole of the town wall about the east of the Blackfriars gardens was in a tumbledown condition, and there are several entries concerning it in the Town Records. However, perhaps it is not necessary to dispute on the matter that Bothwell certainly went to Kirk o' Field on the fateful night and certainly found his way back to Holyrood; whether it is true that, on arrival, he called for a drink, took off his clothes and went to bed for half an hour before a pretended awakening to hear the news, may well be questioned. If you will add up all the time taken for the alleged perambulation of the town, plus the alleged details after his return, I think it will be found that so important a piece of news would have found its way sooner to the palace. I suggest that Bothwell returned at once to Holyrood and reported to his Queen the truth of the plot about which he had already warned her.

But a more important problem is, when did Bothwell first know of the plot, or, for those who prefer the old story, when did he originate it? As to the latter, in the "story" everything is in confusion, many dates are given or inferred, from Craig-millar—three months before—to the night or nights that Mary spent at Kirk o' Field. But I think we can neglect them and endeavour to come to some conclusion on independent grounds.

FRIDAY, 7TH FEBRUARY, 1567

Friday, 7th of February, is marked out as a day of exceptional happenings. It was probably the day of Darnley's bath[1], and the bath may be accepted as the prescribed measure which signified the end of convalescence, and the return of the patient to society without danger of carrying infection. It is quite likely that the return to Holyrood was planned to be on Saturday, though this is not definitely said; but Lennox in his Narrative[2] seems to hover round such an idea, thus: "(She appointed) the day that he should remove from thence into the palace. Taking such pains about him, that being in his bath, would suffer none to handle him but herself." And a little later: "...the day before his death she caused the rich bed wherein he lay to be taken down, and a meaner set up in the place, saying to him, that that rich bed they should both lie in the next night in the palace...." It is true that the latter clause infers that the bed was taken down on Saturday and the removal to Holyrood intended for Sunday, which from many points of view is likely enough, yet does not agree with the story given elsewhere and referred to above. At all events the differences of statement indicate that some question of a return to Holyrood had been on the *tapis*, and it adds to one's wonderment why Darnley remained at Kirk o' Field over the Sunday. Indirectly, Lennox seems to give the impression that the delay came not from the Queen. Her intention, he would have us to believe, was to destroy her husband on the Saturday, but I think he really was thinking of Friday, and was a little confused in his "lines[3]."

[1] The 'Book of Articles,' which may be taken as a kind of *catalogue raisonné* of the alleged incidents, tells us that it was on Friday that the King's bed and some tapestries were removed to Holyrood; and Nelson in his evidence, though he does not confirm the date, says that these tapestries were removed, ostensibly at least, to prevent them being soiled by the bath.

[2] See Mahon, *Mary Queen of Scots*, p. 127.

[3] I am sure that by "day before" he meant Saturday, and did not mean to go into the nicety of the murder being *after* midnight on the Sunday.

It was on Friday, according to his deposition, that Hay was informed by Bothwell of the intention to kill Darnley by gunpowder. On this day, too, says Hepburn, Bothwell finally decided on the gunpowder plan and gave up his previously formed intention of killing the King "in the fields." The 'Book of Articles' tells us that Friday was the day originally chosen for the explosion, but it was postponed, partly because everything was not ready. Friday was the day on which Darnley wrote to his father, telling him of his good health. I have already said that I regard this letter as suspicious.

The incident already referred to[1] of the communication to Darnley, by the Lord Robert Stewart, of a plot against his life, took place on Friday. It was given so prominent a place in the *dossier* collected against the Queen that one is inclined to sense a false note in so much protestation. When we compare it with the moderate, almost colourless statement of Claude Nau, which puts the affair in a precisely opposite light, it is difficult not to think that the latter is the more trustworthy. Nau's version is that, in a conversation with the Queen at Kirk o' Field, Darnley referred to information he had of importance to their mutual quiet; he begged her to guard against persons who meddled between them, and added that he had even been advised to take her life[2]. Nau does not mention Lord Robert at all; but it is probably true that he was called in the next day to say what he knew about the matter, and that Darnley mentioned his name as his informant. On the Saturday morning Lord Robert denied any knowledge, in the presence of the Earl of Moray and Bothwell. The Casket Letter referred to below is supposed to have been written on the Friday night and to relate to this incident.

When Sir James Balfour was making his peace with the Lords, he admitted that he knew of the intended murder before it was committed, and mentions Friday as the date of his first knowledge[3]. Even the Earl of Morton, years later, in his published "confession" says that a "little before" he had received the information by Archibald Douglas, possibly on the Friday.

[1] p. 116.   [2] Nau, *Memoir*, p. 34.
[3] Drury's letter of 29th June.

Truly there is enough to make us believe that Friday was, in fact, the day of intended action; why was it abandoned? I do not pretend to answer this question without a peradventure, but, glad as I should be to avoid the vortex of the Casket Letters, I think some consideration of the one dedicated, so to say, to this day will help to a solution. The Letter commences, "J'ay veille plus tard la haut...." It is singled out as of special importance and had, with the two Glasgow Letters, the honour of a place in the appendix of the earliest printed copy of the 'Detection[1].' All the other Letters were omitted in this edition. Only these three Letters are commented on by the Commissioners at York[2]. Buchanan does not refer to the "Friday letter" in the text of his work, but Dr Wilson says of it, in the 'Oration,' "Call to mind that part of her letters to Bothwell, wherein she makes herself Medea." Even Bishop Leslie, though he betrayed very slight acquaintance with the Letters as a whole, when the 'Defence' was written, has heard of this one.

Hundreds of pages have been spent in ingenious argument about this Letter, but more recent critics have been content to set these efforts aside as based on wrong premises, because of the finding among the manuscripts at Hatfield of a copy in what is believed by some to be the *original* French as used by Mary. Certainly the 'new' French differs essentially from that hitherto worked upon, and what is more remarkable, its meaning differs in some rather important points from the Scottish translation attached to the 'Detection' hitherto deemed to be sacrosanct.

Of one thing I feel quite convinced—if this "new" copy is truly from the original, then the latter was *not written* by Mary. Its style, orthography, punctuation are altogether at variance with what we know of her writing, and the errors in grammar could not be from the hand of a Frenchwoman, which, in effect, she was. Yet, like the Glasgow Letters, it is not a forgery in the sense of being a completely false composition, it is a partly genuine letter, garbled. The body of the letter, expressing humble devotion to the addressee, presumed to be Bothwell, is genuine

[1] A copy is in the Brit. Mus., Press mark 600/b/24.
[2] Cf. Goodall, II, pp. 139, 149 ff.

enough, but from whose hand did it emanate and to whom was it addressed?

Towards the end of the letter in the "new" French there is a clause which is puzzling, and yet seems to have a bearing on our subject which cannot be neglected. Apparently it gave those who prepared the first calumnious brief against the Queen a great deal of trouble. The fact that so much of it was preserved seems to show, as in the case of the short Glasgow Letter, which I have dealt with in another volume, the value attached to genuine[1] letters, and leads to the belief that this letter did in fact contain the clause in question, which otherwise I should have regarded as an interpolation.

It ran as follows in the *original* Scottish translation sent to Elizabeth's Commissioners, which purported, of course, to be a literal rendering of the *original* French, "Make good watch if the bird escape out of the cage or without *her* mate, as the turtle *I* shall remain alone for to lament the absence how short that soever it be." When Dr Wilson put this into Latin for the purpose of calumniating Mary in France[2] he left out the first three words altogether, and commenced, "Si avis evaserit...." It looks as if he did not wish to encourage the idea that a watch was to be set against an expected evasion. His other alteration was to change "the absence" into "thy absence" (*absentiam tuam*), a neat little touch to bring Bothwell, the assumed addressee, into the picture. The spurious French, of course, is taken from and follows the Latin.

Then in quite recent years came the finding of the "new" French copy, quite different in its meaning from the above: "Faites bon guet si l'oseau sortira (*sic*) de sa cage ou sens (sans) son per (Old English *phere* = mate) comme la tourtre *demeurera* (3rd person) seulle a se lamenter de l'absence pour court (*sic*) quelle soit." Of this we have the translation prepared by or for Cecil, also found among the Hatfield papers: "Watch well if the

---

[1] I do not mean by "genuine" that it is necessarily "genuine" from Mary's hand, but as meaning a real letter found among somebody's papers.

[2] See Mahon, *Indictment of Mary Queen of Scots*, p. 26.

bird shall fly out of *his* cage or without *his* mate, (like?) as the turtle (she?) shall remain alone to lament and mourn for (his?) absence how short soever it be." (The interpolations in brackets are mine.) Cecil has followed the "new" French exactly, only assuming the masculine where the Scots has feminine, making it quite clear that he intended Darnley to be the escaping bird and Mary to be the "turtle-dove"—lamenting for a little while!

Yet I cannot grasp the connection of the words, "Or without his mate." From Cecil's point of view, I suppose there was never an idea of both escaping together from Kirk o' Field, and if this sense can be read into it, one might, dimly, connect the reference to some other date, as, for instance, when Riccio was murdered and there was question of both escaping together. Neglecting this there is another possible rendering. If we take the unaccented conjunction *ou* and assume in its place the accented *où* and use it in the sense of the place to which the escaping bird has flown, we might have something like this, "Take good heed lest the bird fly out of his cage, *where* he will remain solitary, without his mate, to mourn her absence like the turtle, for a little while." This would cover the idea of an escaping Darnley, leaving his mate to perish.

Now, whether the reader accepts my version or the Hatfield, or prepares a better one, it must be admitted that the *idea* introduced of an escape, and the pains taken to make it plain that Kirk o' Field was the "cage" and Darnley the person, indicates some analogy to the story suggested in the foregoing pages. And, since the letter is unmistakably, by an interpolation, dated as written on the Friday night, we must suppose that some plot was arranged for that night as already said, and Darnley was suspected of an intention to avoid the catastrophe by leaving the house.

In a remarkable contribution to the subject by Professor Karl Pearson, there is the suggestion that Darnley, warned by Lord Robert Stewart of his danger, "determined to spend the night outside" his lodging, in other words to escape from it, and actually did so, being then met by his murderers. Pleasant as it is to see the new searchers after the truth leaving the old ruts, it would appear that the Professor has not given sufficient weight to the fact that the alleged warning was given on Friday, whereas the actual evasion occurred on Sunday night or rather Monday morning; nevertheless this distinguished support to the fact, I think I may call it so, that Darnley left the "cage" of his own unforced will, is welcome[1].

But the circle brings us back to the first question, who wrote the letter—to whom was it addressed? The Lady Jean Gordon is a name that occurs to one—she at least might have some reason to describe herself as Medea. Her extraordinary freedom from persecution after Bothwell's fall; the fact that she retained her jointure undisturbed, though the estates were twice forfeited to the Crown during her lifetime, might be taken to indicate that she was the possessor of a secret not convenient to be disclosed. Yet I cannot imagine why she should write in French to Bothwell, nor use such terms of extravagant devotion, for there is no evidence that she was devoted—rather, indeed, the reverse. She was, we are told[2], a woman of wide learning and great prudence, but the warning about the "escape" could hardly have come from her; if she were "Medea" I suppose she would wish to preserve the Queen's husband.

A more likely name is the Lady Janet Beton—the "Auld Witch of Buccleuch"—widow of Walter Scott, who was slain in Edinburgh in 1552 by his bitter foes the Cessford Kers[3]. Whether the murder of her husband unhinged Lady Janet's brain or not, there is little doubt that she was *eccentric*, to put it mildly; her reputation as a witch is almost synonymous with a certain degree of mental instability. Her name lives in Border story as the heroine of many strange doings. She is immortalized by Sir Walter Scott in *The Lay of the Last Minstrel*.

The lady, when her husband died, was about 36, and Bothwell a lad of about 17, but in the next few years young Bothwell became something of a hero on the Borders and did much

---

[1] *Biometrika*, xx b, July 1928.

[2] Sir Robert Gordon, *Earldom of Sutherland*, 1813.

[3] Another reason, by the way, for believing that Andrew Ker of Fawdonside was not at Kirk o' Field as a "fautor" of the Queen of Scots. See p. 114.

service for Mary's mother, and there is nothing unlikely in supposing that the Lady of Branxholm developed an infatuation for him. According to the "enemy" stories, he promised her marriage and had had intimate relations with her. The half-witted character of the amatory phrases scattered through the Casket Letters may well have been gathered from some of the love-letters thrust on an unwilling swain who had come to regard "Medea" as a nuisance. Touching the use of French as the medium of communication, I have not much to advance, except that all the Betons were rather "French"; Robert Beton, a brother, was with Mary in France and had married a French lady; Mary Beton, a niece, was, of course, as much French as the Queen herself; the cousins of Balfour seemed to find their natural home in France; whether Janet had been there I do not know. The Lady Rires (Margaret Beton), Mary's intimate confidant, was a sister; she would know perhaps better than Mary herself the treacheries of Darnley, and perhaps impart them to Janet.

It is useless to continue speculation to whomsoever addressed, the warning may be supposed to have put on the alert those whose duty it was to safeguard the Queen. That was the reason for the postponement of the Friday plot, and, since the Queen, whether it is true that she had heard of a plot or not, persisted in sleeping at Kirk o' Field, it can hardly be said that she was a party to it, or even thought seriously of what she had heard. The exaggeration given to the alleged report of Lord Robert Stewart may be accounted for by assuming that to take the initiative is the surest defence against attack, the *attack* of those who knew that the truth was the exact reverse of the story.

BOTHWELL'S ATTITUDE IN THE CRISIS

The opinion I have formed is that Bothwell heard on that Friday of a plot against the Queen, that he took precautions to prevent it, but that he did not attempt to persuade the Queen there was any danger. Perhaps he knew by experience that it was useless to move her in her present attitude of belief in the protestations of a reformed Darnley. Do not let us forget two things; the Queen greatly desired a reconciliation to further her now rosy hopes of an agreement with Elizabeth, and, secondly, even the "enemy press" relates the wordy repentance of the sinning husband. If it is objected that this secret plot, known to Bothwell and doubtless to others, could not in such circumstances have been further prosecuted, since those in it must have known that the mischief was out, I would reply by pointing out that, though the Riccio murder plot was known to many and discussed by letters for days before it took place, it was yet unknown to those most nearly concerned, viz. to the Queen, to Riccio himself, to Bothwell and others. It is not impossible, nor even improbable, that Darnley and Sir James Balfour had no knowledge that they were watched. It was not Bothwell's cue to prevent the attempt, but only to turn it to his own advantage.

What had Bothwell in his mind? Except for the scandals alleged in impossible circumstances by the "wildly vituperative" Buchanan[1], and those extracted from the unfortunate Paris, all of it too obviously colouring for a *post facto* creation, there is no indication of undue forwardness on Bothwell's part prior to the tragedy. No letters of responsible persons testify to it; many infer the contrary. In fact, as I have already said, he evidently did not rule the roost up to the date, late in March, when the Prince was removed to Stirling. The Queen's state of health made it rather a question of her survival than one of matrimony.

I do not think it can justly be alleged that Bothwell's first thoughts went further than to pose as the saviour of his Sovereign, as he had done after the murder of Riccio. Acquiescent in the killing of Darnley he certainly was, and he might reasonably have expected the tacit approval of England, and the friendship of the nobles, both those more immediately concerned and the others who accepted the deed as well done.

It was not until a date in March, which I conceive was after the Prince was safely in Stirling, that Drury began to open the subject of a union between Bothwell and the Queen. It occurs in a collection of memoranda which was not a letter, though often quoted as such, endorsed 29th March, and contained such notes

[1] I quote Mr T. F. Henderson, who yet seems to adopt much of the said *wild* abuse.

as these: "The great misliking with the Earl of Huntly for his yielding that the Lady Bothwell, his sister, shall be divorced"; "the judgment of the people that the Queen will marry him (Bothwell)," and so forth. On 30th March Drury embodied some part of these notes in a regular letter and said definitely: "The Earl of Huntly has now condescended (agreed) to the divorce of his sister from the Earl Bothwell." From that date onwards through April he enlarged on the subject.

It would seem that the negotiations with Huntly, if not known to the "people" as suggested by Drury, were certainly known to the principal nobles whose names are connected with the case. They must have been opened at a date very shortly after the visit of Killigrew. They were known to Cecil not later than 3rd April. Can it be disputed that the whole proceeding from this time to the signing of the so-called Ainslie Bond, which bound certain of the nobles to support the marriage, was an arrangement known to Cecil from its inception, and communicated, as I think, by Killigrew? A letter sent by Maitland to the English Secretary will be dealt with hereafter, which may contain the outline of the plot. It is dated 13th March and was carried to London by Killigrew, and it acknowledges letters from Cecil of 25th and 26th February and refers to some secret suggestions from him.

I read Maitland's letter to infer: "Your meaning is one that we can approve of, to force the Queen into a Protestant marriage, and thus complete her breach with Rome already far advanced; she may not yield at first, but will do so in the end. We intend nothing that is not 'right and orderly.'" The last words meaning that the Protestant husband would be denounced "in due time."

Several writers have pointed out that the Earl of Moray was not in Scotland at the time of the Ainslie Bond, and therefrom infer that he was innocent of *that* treachery; but he *was* present in Scotland when the Earl of Huntly "condescended" to the divorce of his sister, and there must be few who can believe him ignorant of that fact, or that he moved a finger to prevent what it presaged. Moray arrived in London on 16th April, Cecil had the news already, yet from England came no endeavour to prevent the catastrophe, if we except "Instructions" given to Lord Grey de Wilton dated 25th April, containing a strong indictment of Bothwell, based on Cecil's tardy conception that "so monstrous an outrage must be prevented." Yet Lord Grey never left London, nor, I imagine, except to salve Elizabeth's conscience, was it ever intended that he should.

Let me call to mind a paragraph in the *Memoirs* of Claude Nau: "Their plan was this, to persuade her to marry the Earl Bothwell, so that they might charge her with being in the plot against her late husband...." The author of these *Memoirs* often showed insight, and never more so than in these words.

Bothwell was a sinner, let us not doubt it, but his sins were white compared with the treachery of those around him. He inherited the ambitions of his father and grandfather to mate with Royalty, and fell easily into the snare, perhaps not without suspecting that it was a snare. To make his position secure, he carried the Queen to Dunbar and there forced her to a position that made marriage the only alternative to shame. That the idea of seizing the person of the Sovereign, perhaps not without the accompaniment of rape, was not foreign to Bothwell's schemes is shown in the records of the trial of the affair of the Earl of Arran (March 1562)[1], wherein Bothwell is said to have uttered this incitement to Arran: "(You shall) have her to the castle of Dumbarton and keep her surely, or otherwise demayne (treat, also ill-treat) her person at your pleasure, until she agree to whatsoever thing you shall desire." Sir James Melville, closely in touch with the ravishing to Dunbar, does not mince his words: "The Queen could not but marry him, seeing he had ravished her and lain with her against her will." The recorded observations of Mary's demeanour after her marriage give confirmation to this statement. The testimony of Mr John Craig, the minister called on to publish the banns of marriage, confirms it; the rape of the Queen, he publicly stated, made it unlawful to marry them, and he discharged his conscience before the Lords of the Council, who seemed to him, "so many slaves, what by flattery, what by silence, to give way to this abomination[2]."

[1] Pitcairn, *Criminal Trials*, p. 463.   [2] Knox, p. 341.

SIR JAMES BALFOUR

HIS INTRIGUES WITH THE CATHOLIC PARTY

"Mr James Balfour, that ons dyd rowe in a gallye" with Mr John Knox, is described by his fellow-*forçat* as an apostate and traitor; if the reformer had had the gift of introspection more strongly developed, his condemnation might have been more indulgent, but of its truth there is, I am afraid, no doubt. We need not follow very closely his early career, or enquire whether he was concerned in the murder of Archbishop Beton in 1546; possibly he was too young, at least he does not appear among those rewarded by Henry VIII for the deed; but he was certainly one of the garrison of St Andrews after the deed was done. During the next fifteen years he was ostensibly Protestant, yet, under the rose, seems to have been useful in betraying the secrets of the Congregation to Marie of Lorraine during her Regency. Possibly as a reward for services rendered he received the parsonage or rectorship of Flisk, but, as he was never other than a layman, he presumably held the emoluments *in commendam*.

Of one thing, I think, we may be certain, he was a shrewd and capable lawyer, with an extraordinary knack of keeping his name out of the record, and of covering his retreat when hard pressed. I think also that the character bestowed on him by Knox (and, by the way, Knox was writing in or about the year 1566, when he knew his man better) was not recognized during the first years of Mary's active reign, for he was appointed an extra Lord of Session a few months after her arrival, at a time when the Protestant Earl of Moray, then the Lord James Stewart, ruled Scotland in her name. At the same time it is hard to believe that, during the three and a half years preceding the arrival on the scene of Lord Darnley (February 1565), James Balfour was innocent of plotting; the best that can be said is that his name does not appear.

It was not until after the coming of Darnley that we begin to come into closer touch with our subject. The defection of the

Earl of Moray from his allegiance had brought fresh life into the latent aspirations of the Catholic party. There is evidence of sufficient weight to show that Balfour, Riccio, Leslie (Bishop of Ross), and the Earl of Lennox were preparing to take advantage of the opportunity. The last named was reported by Randolph[1] as receiving money from Flanders, and the other three are frequently brought together as acting in common. The old story, current since the time of de Gouda's visit, that the murder of the Earl of Moray was sought as the only way to ruin the progress of the Reformation, was revived. That the story was not without foundation may be gathered from Father Edmund Hay's opinion, dated 13th September, 1562, shortly after his return from Scotland on the termination of de Gouda's mission: "All the plans hitherto suggested...will be premature, not to say absolutely useless, as long as the Queen's illegitimate brother is alive, or at any rate continues to govern the kingdom...[2]." Even if this be considered ambiguous by some, doubt as to what was meant is made impossible by subsequent events, as will be shown later.

However, for our present purpose it is sufficient to quote from the history attributed to Claude Nau, that the "Laird of Balfour" had promised the King to kill the Earl of Moray[3]. It is true that Nau seems to attach a somewhat later date to this story, but I think it must be referable to the occurrences at Perth in July, 1565[4], confirmed also by Paul de Foix: "Cecil says, that the Queen's husband had wished to kill the Earl of Moray[5] (Sept. 1565)." It is remarkable that in none of the references to this incident—and there are at least four from sources friendly and the reverse—is it suggested that Mary was a party to any such scheme. My present object in referring to it is to indicate, what both this and other matters point to, that the rise to importance of Sir James Balfour in this year, 1565, was due to the favour of

---

[1] Keith, II, p. 320; and see chap. IV.

[2] Forbes-Leith, p. 80.

[3] Nau, *Memoir*, p. 28. The designation used does not, correctly speaking, indicate Sir James, but there is little doubt from the general context that it is he who is intended.

[4] See Randolph's letter of 21st July, printed in Keith, II, p. 335.

[5] *Relations*, II, p. 219.

the King rather than to any effort on Mary's part. There is indeed some testimony, though indirect, of the influence exercised by Darnley; Randolph reported (20th September, 1565) that Balfour and John Leslie, who were "bruited" to hold the office of Joint Secretary, *vice* Lethington, were believed to be coldly looked on as two supporters of Moray. But in Nau's *Memoir* another complexion is given to the affair, namely that it was Darnley who desired the supersession of Lethington by the Bishop of Ross (Leslie), always a stout Catholic and, in the absence of the Queen, signed a resolution to that effect in Council, which Mary cancelled on hearing of it[1].

There are many evidences that, during the first five months or so after her marriage, Mary exhausted every means to associate her husband in the rule. "All honour that may be attributed unto any man by a wife, he hath it.... No man pleaseth her that contenteth not him... she hath given over to him her whole will, to be ruled and guided as himself best liketh[2]." Discount this writing of Thomas Randolph (31st July, 1565) as heavily as you will, enough remains to show that things done then were less Mary's acts than Darnley's. In other letters of November from the same writer, her travail to secure the recognition of Darnley as King is related; and, when Balfour was appointed a Privy Councillor at that time, we may take it that he owed his advancement to the King and not to the Queen. In December, Randolph writes that the exile of the Earl of Moray was a matter in which the Queen was less adamant than her husband, and there are other letters to show that the part contrary to the Protestant Lords was his rather than hers. Riccio, Balfour and Darnley were acting in concert to prevent the recall of Moray, and this too was insisted on in the strongest terms by the Catholic party on the Continent.

The missions of Yaxley to Spain and Rome were inspired more by Darnley than by Mary, and we read of the King's rejoicing and his confidences with him, when this envoy returned to Scotland in August (1565)[3]. It is a small point worth noting

[1] Nau, *Memoir*, p. 20.   [2] Wright, *Elizabeth*, I, p. 199.
[3] Bain, p. 209.

that, after Yaxley's death, his servant, one Henry Gwynn, found his way into Darnley's service, and was in it at the time of the murder[1].

Nor is there anything paradoxical in the fact that a very short time after the year 1565, during which Darnley and Riccio had been hand in glove, there should have been a complete shifting of ground.

Allured by the vision of the Crown, Darnley entered with childish vehemence into the plot, fostered if not contrived in England, to destroy Riccio and reinstate the Earl of Moray. To what extent Darnley, in his exuberance, supposed that, once in power, he could turn again and carry out the constant aim of the Catholic party—the destruction of Moray—and forswear his temporary allegiance to the reformers, one need not guess. Riccio was merely a pawn; and if, by the loss of a pawn, a King should emerge, bound by every tie to Rome, the experiment was worth support; without support Darnley would soon have been swept out of the path of the advancing reform.

The Earl of Lennox bore the reputation of being a man of slow wit, yet, we may be sure, on broad grounds, that his concurrence in the Riccio plot was not based on any hope that the guarantee of the Protestant Lords to recognize his son as King of Scotland was in the least likely to be fulfilled, nor that the

[1] Francis Yaxley was an Englishman, an ardent Catholic. He held some small office in the time of Mary Tudor, when Philip was in England, and was intimate with, if not a dependent of, Margaret Lennox. He was in trouble in 1562 and was sent to the Tower as plotting for the union of Mary and the Lord Darnley at the instigation of Margaret. I gather that he joined Darnley in Scotland in August, 1565 (Maitland Club, *Selections*, p. 144), shortly after the marriage. De Silva describes him as a good Catholic and "ardently devoted to your Majesty (Philip)"; he adds that Darnley has made him his secretary. He was sent to Spain to announce the marriage and beg support against the rebellion incited by England through the Earl of Moray. He returned with letters to Darnley from Philip, in which the latter refers to his affection for the Earl of Lennox, and his hope that the marriage will further religion. Yaxley is referred to as Darnley's servant. See Mignet, II, p. 432, for the letter in full. The correspondence seems to have been addressed only to Darnley. Yaxley was shipwrecked and drowned on the return journey in January 1566.

support of England would be continued, once the real object of the plot—the death of the Queen—had been attained. He was well aware that, before letting him or his son loose in Scotland, Elizabeth had collected all the information available to prove, if necessary, that Lady Margaret Lennox was not legitimate—one of the many perfidies of the affair. He was aware, too, that his position as a client of the King of Spain during the reign of Mary Tudor (at which time his wife had been encouraged to hope for the English succession, and had shown her hopes by offensive behaviour towards the Princess Elizabeth) made it impossible to suppose any hints conveyed to Darnley at the present time to be sincere. Most of all he knew that a plot, even if successful, depending on union with the Protestants of Scotland, would be fatal to a continuance of support from Spain or Catholic England; and from these two sources he derived his only strength. On these grounds it is certain that the adhesion of Lennox to the plot was not due to any ultimate intention to further the Reformation. But, whether he was drawn into it by the importunity and the precipitate action of his son, or whether he was aware that the end would justify the means, it is at least clear that he incurred no marked disfavour from his masters in consequence.

It is less easy to be certain of the attitude of Sir James Balfour towards the murder of Riccio. In the letter addressed by Mary to the Archbishop of Glasgow (2nd April, 1566[1]) we are told that the conspirators were bent on hanging Balfour as well as Riccio, both being regarded as working against the rehabilitation of the Earl of Moray—as of course Darnley had also been, up to the moment that the Crown was invitingly held out to him. But we may suspect that this letter was drafted by Balfour himself, for he was then acting as Secretary, and I think the most we can draw from the statement is that it was what he wished the Catholic powers to believe. The Ruthven Narrative[2], to a considerable extent trustworthy, does not indicate that he had been in any danger, but that he and others had sought and obtained the *King's permission* to depart peacefully from Holyrood. He was the kind of man to prepare for either fortune; but he was

---

[1] Keith, II, p. 411.   [2] Keith, III, p. 272.

far too astute to have openly supported a scheme so hazardous as the one in question, though he would have profited by it had it by chance succeeded. His name did not appear as a prompter of the King; that post was occupied by George Douglas, who was Darnley's illegitimate uncle, but no friend of the Lennox Stewarts.

On the other hand, there is no reason at all to suppose that Balfour and Darnley were estranged because the former had succeeded in avoiding inculpation. It is to be noted that, as the truth of the inner working of the conspiracy emerged, so Balfour's "credit" with the Queen "decayed," a fact vouched for by both Killigrew and Randolph in separate letters[1]. It was at this time, too, that John Knox was writing the first book of his *History* and recording that opinion of Sir James which shows pretty clearly that he was far from the fold of the "true religion"; this must be taken to indicate that he continued to plot against the Protestant lords, a course to which Darnley speedily returned with an exaggerated vehemence which seems to indicate a desire to wipe out any stain cast on his reputation with the Catholic party by his brief essay in the opposite direction. I do not conceal that during the remaining months of 1566, while Darnley was in the full career of his intrigues with Spain, Rome, and the Catholics in England, Sir James Balfour's name is scarcely mentioned; but I have no doubt that he, who intrigued all through the previous year with Darnley and Riccio, did not suddenly change his spots in 1566. One is reminded of a dictum passed in his regard some fifteen months later: "Sir James Balfour...lives in some darkness, not very openly seen at Court; yet his advices and counsel do most prevail."

The whole *action* of the year 1566 was counter-Reformation by violence, and, whether you believe Mary to have been a zealous "papist" or not, violence was not in her thoughts; to this we must return. Here, I will only express my conviction that throughout Balfour was a King's man, secretly egging him to a course which openly he would not avow, while ready always to enjoy the fruits of success.

[1] 24th and 7th June, 1566.

THE SOURCE OF HIS POWER IN SCOTLAND

And so we come to the gunpowder plot at Kirk o' Field; but, preceding it by some two months, came the Council at Craigmillar, held in the early days of December (1566), which cannot be neglected as forming part of the same series of events. The broad outline is well known; Darnley's conduct, morally and politically, had become intolerable, and certain of the nobles and the Secretary Maitland of Lethington approached the Queen to suggest a divorce; she refused the idea and added that no steps should be taken which would stain her honour. Writers inimical to the Queen read into this the knowledge on her part, or at least the suspicion, that violence to her husband was intended. So much intentional mystery surrounds the whole affair that it is certainly difficult to ascertain now what the exact truth is. Lennox in his Narrative naturally conceals the mention of divorce; but, apart from that, he is rather uncertain as to what his accusation is. In one case he is definite that at Craigmillar, and even shortly before that, "she and her complices invented and resolved the time and manner" of the murder—which indeed is nonsense, for none could foresee the events of the next ten weeks. But in another place he puts it differently, and perhaps, on the whole more probably, "the Queen and certain of her Council had concluded at Craigmillar an enterprise...which was that he should have been apprehended and *put in ward*," awaiting only the conclusion of the ceremony of the baptism of the infant James[1]. While it is fair to say that, notwithstanding the outrageous conduct of the King, there is no evidence that Mary intended to proceed against him, from political motives if you prefer to put it on the lowest ground, there is a mass of somewhat contradictory testimony that at or about this time conversations, possibly agreements, took place between some of the leading nobles of the realm to act together against him. Yet, following closely the lives and deeds of these men, admitting that they were

[1] Reminiscent of Mary's own statement in a genuine part of the "long" Glasgow Letter: "I trow he believed that I would send him away prisoner."

treacherous, they certainly had a degree of reasoning cunning. Can it be believed of them, knowing as they knew, the little confidence that each could place in the other, that they would put their names to a bald agreement to murder the King? Still more difficult, that, having done so, the document would be left in the hands of Bothwell, or would be drawn up, as it is alleged, by so shifty a character as Sir James Balfour, who was known to be connected with the Catholic interests.

The nobles more immediately concerned at Craigmillar were the Earls of Moray, Huntly, Argyll and Bothwell, together with Secretary Maitland; Balfour was perhaps not in residence, but his then position of Clerk Register would probably bring him over daily from Edinburgh. Of these names three—Moray, Argyll and Maitland—were definitely of the Protestant party; Huntly and Bothwell, less definitely from the point of view of religion, ostensibly adhered to the same; as to Balfour, his ingenuity was such that, though known to have intrigued with Riccio and to have been condemned by Knox, he may still have been able to insinuate himself into the confidences of the Protestants. Viewing the case broadly, I would ask those who are convinced that Mary was a violently intolerant Romanist whether it is likely that she would connive with a Protestant *junta* to murder one who was the acknowledged hope of a large section of the Catholic party in England? On all grounds, as it seems to me, the notion of a murder bond drawn up at Craigmillar must be abandoned[1].

---

[1] The evidence for a bond rests largely on the deposition and confession attributed to John Hepburn. In the former he says that Bothwell showed him a deed subscribed by Huntly, Argyll and Bothwell himself and also Maitland; but he does not mention Balfour. He saw the deed at Dunbar at the end of April, that is, some five months after the Craigmillar conference. He does not say that it originated at the latter place. In the confession he is made to say that he did not see Balfour's name, but he would warrant that Balfour was the principal deviser of the deed. Note that this part of Hepburn's deposition does not appear in the official copy, see Univ. Lib. Cambridge, Press mark Dd. 3. 64. The date of this was December 1567. In his *Defence*, the Bishop of Ross says: "You (Moray), Morton, Bothwell and others, at Craigmillar, consulted and devised this mischief.... Interchangeable

Nevertheless it seems almost certain that there was a confederacy against the King, and that it fortified itself by a mutual bond.

I have not set out the foregoing merely for the purpose of contradiction; my aim is to probe the truth, and to account for the extraordinary power possessed by Sir James Balfour during the months of 1567 after the King's death and onwards to a date in 1569, which was more or less synchronous with the return from England of the Earl of Moray with the assured knowledge that Elizabeth and her Council had no intention of permitting any investigation of the truth, bond or no bond.

The real bond, and, I think, the only one, had connection with the recall of the Earl of Morton, Lord Lindsay and others, exiled for the murder of Riccio. We have to rely to a great extent on the statement of Archibald Douglas, a most unreliable witness, in his letter written many years later to the Queen[1]. What he says, in effect, is, that he was chosen as the intermediary between Morton and the rest who were in exile in England for the murder of Riccio, and Moray, Atholl, Bothwell, Argyll and Secretary Lethington, remaining in Scotland[2], to make offers to procure clemency from the Queen. He, Douglas, was told that the Queen's husband was the source of all the evils, and that, if Darnley were allowed to follow the advice of those about him[3], worse would ensue. They, *i.e.* the party in Scotland, had confederated to obey the Queen only, and to proscribe her husband;

indentures were made and subscribed by you...." But he does not definitely say that the indentures were made at Craigmillar. Date about 1569/70. In the 'Confession' of James Ormistoun there is more definite matter; the writing, he said, was drawn up and signed by Balfour three months previous to the murder—that must mean at Craigmillar, during December 1573, at a time when anything that could be devised in Balfour's disfavour by the minister (John Brand), who arranged the wording, was eagerly sought. It does not, in my opinion, justify the alleged existence of a Craigmillar bond.

[1] Dated towards the end of 1583. See *Bannatyne Memorials.*

[2] Except for the substitution of Atholl for Huntly, who was by this time dead, the names are the same as in the Craigmillar affair.

[3] The agents, secret and otherwise, of the Catholic party, must be referred to.

if Morton and his party would join this confederacy, then Moray and his adherents would undertake to intercede with the Queen for the pardon of Morton and the other exiles. Morton agreed to these terms.

Now this statement of the case by Douglas is obviously untrue. It is as certain as daylight that Morton would require no ambassador to Moray to procure his assistance, which he well knew had already been many times exercised in his favour; still less that Moray would make the condition mentioned. The adhesion of Morton to any such project would go without saying. What, then, was the subject of the *pourparlers*, for we need not discard the statement that there was a going to and fro of messages between the Protestant party in Scotland and the section of the same exiled in England? Let me note most clearly that Mary Stuart was ignorant regarding the *ambassade* of Archibald Douglas. The approach made to her at Craigmillar for the pardon of Morton in return for a severance from her husband, even though it is improbable that we have an accurate version of all that was said at the time, was certainly a move in the Morton-Moray-Cecil scheme. To secure her consent to any plan detrimental to her husband, even if it did not involve his life, would have been an immense asset for subsequent use against her, or for mitigation of the treason of those concerned. Archibald Douglas' instructions seem almost apparent—secure a combination of the Protestant nobles to destroy Darnley, and England will be behind you; but first try to commit the Queen, so that her name only need be used.

As we know, she refused the suggestion, as she had previously refused the Catholic incitement to destroy the Protestant leaders. More than that, she had persistently declined to pardon Morton for months past, until, with difficulty, it was wrung from her by the Earl of Bedford at the baptism, in circumstances which virtually forced her hand. As Bedford himself said: "The Queen has granted to Morton, Ruthven and Lindsay, their relaxation and dresse (pardon), wherein Moray has done very friendly for them, as I have done *by your advice*...[1]." There are two letters

[1] Bedford to Cecil, 30th December, 1566.

from Morton to Cecil expressing his gratitude for the assistance given. Bedford's service in favour of the exiles was, I think it cannot be questioned, the fulfilment of England's part of the bond to "remove" Darnley. Mary had escaped, but not unwounded, and only for a time; her name was still dragged into the affair, even though she had no knowledge of it.

There is a curious parallelism between the circumstances preceding the murder of Riccio and the present case of the negotiations preceding the recall of Morton. The position of the sections of the Protestant party was precisely reversed, for *then* Moray was "out" and Morton was plotting for his return, *now* Morton was "out" and Moray was the plotter. But the principal matter is the similarity of the support which the exiles in either case received from England. It cannot be questioned that, in the former case, Bedford and Randolph were cognizant of the affair for many days before it was put in execution, and it can hardly be questioned that both these persons were parties to, I think, instigators of, the murder; on political grounds Riccio's removal was a necessity. It is a corollary that Cecil was equally involved[1]. In the latter case the "comfort" which Morton received in England during his exile is notorious. The efforts made by England to procure his pardon have been mentioned above, and the strenuous action taken to quash his condemnation fourteen years later, when he suffered for participation in Darnley's murder, are sufficient indication that important secrets were concerned. The same applies to Archibald Douglas—Elizabeth refused to deliver him to justice, and eventually saved his life only by bribing the King (James VI) himself. The clues here are too patent to mislead.

We cannot but deduce from the episode of Kirk o' Field that, *at the moment*, Darnley, with his Catholic interests in England and his Spanish support from Philip, together with his immediate endeavour to stir these interests to the point of revolution[2], and,

[1] Of Elizabeth I say nothing; as in the case of Mary, many things were done under the shadow of her name of which she was innocent, but to many people, where Cecil's authority appeared, hers was inferred.

[2] *Infra*, Chapter IV.

I think, the anticipated advent of Philip into the Netherlands, loomed in Cecil's eyes as an enemy of greater importance than Mary. That the present attack should be rather on him than on her, confirms my opinion that the intrigue then going forward was his work and not hers. Darnley and his father were recognized as the centre of the Counter-Reformation. Mary had failed to fill her part.

It seems hardly disputable that here we have the interpretation of that sentence in Morton's confession published by Hollinshed's *Continuator* in 1586:

> After his return out of England...he came out of Wedderburn to Whittinghame where the Earl of Bothwell was at the same time, with whom there was conversation about the King's murder, but he (Morton) would not consent thereto. *After which, opening a long discourse thereof, laying the cause, the contriving, and the execution of the same in great persons now living, and confessing that they understood thereof....*

The *Continuator* appears to have had the names of the persons referred to, and, notwithstanding some weak argument on the part of the historian, Laing[1], there seems no doubt that pressure was exercised to prevent their publication; the context regarding the meeting at Whittinghame, at which place Archibald Douglas was present, and the fact that this meeting came immediately after Morton's pardon, seem to put it beyond doubt that Morton was dealing, in his confession quoted above, with the events connected with Douglas' embassy to Moray already mentioned, and that one at least of the great personages was Cecil[2].

Mary herself, with fuller knowledge than we possess of the names mentioned, wrote to Elizabeth after Morton's death, and, referring to the agents, spies, and secret messengers employed to accomplish her downfall in Scotland, says: "I will not at present specify other proof than that which I have gained of it by the confession of one (Morton) who was afterwards amongst those that were most advanced for this good service."

I have referred above to the parallelism of the two cases con-

[1] Laing, II, pp. 62 ff.

[2] Whitaker, III, pp. 252 ff., has the same conclusion based on other premises.

cerning Riccio and Darnley, especially in regard to the concurrence of England. There is a third instance, that of Cardinal Beton. I cannot afford space to put this before the reader, but it is fully exhibited in an appendix to volume v of Tytler's *History*. There it is most clearly shown that the negotiations between Henry VIII, carried on through his Lieutenant in the North, Earl of Hertford, and the Scottish traitors, ebbed and flowed on the vital question whether the King's warrant would or would not be given to execute the deed. Alexander Crichton of Brunstoun was the principal negotiator on the Scottish side, and he would do nothing until assured under the King's hand both of protection and reward. The value of the Royal word could not have been so much the prospect of its honourable observance, as the possession of something to display which would involve serious political difficulty, should it remain unredeemed. In the present case Hertford, as representing the English Sovereign, was replaced by Bedford, but there was not much to choose between them; Archibald Douglas took the place of Brunstoun.

This, then, was the reason why the document resulting from the embassy of Archibald Douglas in November/December 1566 became of such importance and gave so powerful a lever to those who knew its contents or had a copy in possession. It was not so much the adhesion of a number of Scottish nobles to an act of high treason which perturbed the English Court, but the inclusion in some form or other of evidence that Cecil was not ignorant of the project, and that, perhaps without her knowledge, Elizabeth's name was used.

By means about which I think it is not possible to be definite, Balfour was in possession of this secret. One story, as we have seen, says he drew up the bond himself, another adds that he signed it as a participant in its terms, a third says that he found it in a "little coffer covered with green cloth" in Edinburgh Castle, out of which coffer it was taken by the Secretary Maitland in Balfour's presence[1]. As late as March 1580 in a letter from

[1] *State Papers, Foreign, Elizabeth*, Randolph to Cecil, 15th October, 1570. This occurred, so it is said, after the Queen's defeat at Carberry

Mary to the Archbishop of Glasgow (Labanoff, v, p. 137) she says: "Do what you can that Balfour should write to me amply of the bond which he saw signed for the murder of the late King."

HIS CONNECTION WITH THE GUNPOWDER PLOT

When, immediately after the explosion at Kirk o' Field and the discovery of Darnley's dead body, the nobles took counsel together on the situation, I think one may say that they recognized two phases in the affair. As regards the slaughter of the King, not many of them were guiltless of art and part in meeting, personally or by proxy, the escaping Darnley, outside the city walls, and satisfying their lust for revenge. It was an opportunity fulfilling every condition they could have wished for. If my diagnosis is correct, the victim was caught red-handed in another attempt to obtain the Crown by the murder of his Queen, she could be cited as having given some kind of warrant for his capture and, over and above all, there was the bond carrying the sanction of—let us call it—"great persons now living and confessing that they understood thereof."

Possibly there was but a dim perception of the gunpowder plot, its object and its authors. There was a conspiracy within a conspiracy; and, in all the circumstances, it was inevitable that the desire to prevent enquiry into the one led to little probing of the other. It is alleged as a charge against the Queen that she was lax in attempting to discover the culprits. In my opinion, and I shall endeavour to substantiate it, she took no steps at all. She was physically and mentally incapable of doing so; she was for that time a cipher, and anything done or left undone cannot be laid against her.

The one man who understood the whole story was, I suggest, Sir James Balfour. He had no accomplices among the Protestant nobles, and it is unlikely that, suspected as he was of secret correspondence with the Catholic party, he would be admitted

Hill, that is, in June 1567, at or about the same date that the coffer or casket containing the Casket Letters was taken from Bothwell's messenger.

to the secret of the bond. What he did not *know* he could guess, and certainty came to him afterwards.

I ascribe to him the contrivance, completion, and execution of the gunpowder plot. I differentiate him from those who took Darnley's life, for I think that was not his intention. He alone among the immediate conspirators left Edinburgh, as I believe, on the very eve of the affair, and probably did not know that his plans had miscarried until some hours later; but then he would guess precisely what had happened—that, through Darnley himself or some of his servants to whom warning had been given[1], the secret had reached the ears of the Protestant party, and that advantage had been taken of it.

Balfour returned to Edinburgh secretly, so Drury says, on the 26th February, that is, sixteen days after the event, accompanied by a body of horse for his protection. After a lapse of two months (19th April, see *Border Papers*, XIII, f. 37) Drury says of him that, "For some fear he conceives he keeps his house, especially in the night, with great watch and guard." The Lords whose names are principally associated with the affair, and said to be assisting in the killing of Darnley, came and went without evident sign of perturbation; why, if Balfour was a member of their confraternity, should he alone be afraid? It seems impossible not to recognize that in some way his case was on a different footing to that of the others. I picture the two parties, each with a share of guilt, unable for that reason to denounce one another. I do not forget that Sir John Forster reported from Alnwick, under date 3rd March, that the Earl of Moray had taken Balfour and warded him in Edinburgh Castle. This news

---

[1] It seems likely that Sandy Durham was the betrayer of Darnley's secret; the vituperation poured upon him by Dr Wilson indicates that he took some special part in the catastrophe. It is worth noting that there were two Alexander Durhams. The one, "young Sandy," was evidently Darnley's "beloved" servant, who betrayed him; the other was probably his father, whose position was that of "Agentier," that is, collector of the Queen's rents. He is mentioned several times as assignee of the "thirds" of the benefices, *Register of Privy Council* under dates 2nd January, 1567, and 5th April of that year. I gather that he was a respectable official, not in trouble with either party.

would emanate from Edinburgh on 28th February or 1st March; but I do not think that Moray came there so early, in any case both were at the Council Table, say, ten days after. If there is a shadow of truth in Forster's story, which, I am afraid, cannot be admitted, it would show that Balfour's power was exercised at an earlier date than I should suppose possible.

"Un vrai Traître," so he is described by the Frenchman du Croc. No three words could better express all we know about Sir James Balfour. In the previous attempt on the Queen's life, as we have said, George Douglas was he on whom Darnley chiefly relied to devise and execute; in the present attempt this Douglas was still in exile, and, except that he and all the house of Douglas had conceived an undying hatred of Darnley as the cause of their undoing, he had personally no hand in it. *Now*, since Darnley by himself was incapable of thinking out a subtle plot, it was James Balfour who guided his weak vicious nature. In both cases the glitter of the Crown was the lure.

It was Balfour who induced Darnley to refuse Craigmillar and go to Kirk o' Field; Balfour who had all the facilities to prepare the latter place for the gunpowder plot; Balfour who, in the first burst of candour, was said to have purchased gunpowder; he who, in all the depositions and confessions, is named as the deviser of all. It was Balfour whose servant was secretly killed, as Drury reports, "Supposed upon very lively presumptions for utterance of some matter either by remorse of conscience or other folly that might tend to the whole discovery of the King's death" (letter to Cecil, 19th April, 1567). He it was who before the death of Riccio was held to be in the secret councils of that person as to foreign machinations tending to the downfall of the Protestant lords. He again who, after the death of Riccio, was said to have "understood most of the secrets and proceedings between France and the Queen...(in which) will appear hard dealings of some against the Queen's Majesty my sovereign and her country[1]." It was Balfour who vanished from Edinburgh

---

[1] Drury to Cecil, 29th June, 1567. Having before us all that is now known as to the intrigues of Darnley with the English Catholics, with Rome and Spain, his friendship with the Spanish Ambassador in Paris,

on the night of the murder, and he who returned secretly, armed, and in fear, a fortnight or so later. Finally, it was he who, with his curious facility for subtlety, was at hand when the mesh which dragged his Queen from her throne was knotted. But this is an anticipation; we must leave him for a space.

HIS CONNECTION WITH BOTHWELL

It is, of course, the standard tradition, repeated by friends and enemies, that, both before and after the death of Darnley, Balfour and Bothwell were accomplices; but there is no reliable evidence to show that this was so. The tradition rests mainly on the placards, which brought their names together, but the authors of this attack were working in the dark, for they brought in several names which were not pursued. The *depositions* (not the 'Confessions') of the four chief witnesses contain no mention of Balfour, excepting only the suppressed part of Hepburn, and even this is scarcely conclusive: "My Lord Bothwell sent the deponer (Hepburn) to Sir James Balfour, desiring that he would come and meet my Lord at the Kirk o' Field. To whom Sir James answered, 'Will my Lord come then? If he come it were better he were quiet.' And yet they met not at that place, then or at no time thereafter, to the deponer's knowledge." This piece of evidence, which was unknown to practically all the writers, undermines the veracity of the ramblings of Paris[1]; it is not likely to be exactly true, but at least it does not seem to show that the two were working together.

and other things which more properly belong to the next chapter, we should be safe in amending Drury's letter to read, "Between the Papists and the King." When Drury wrote, the order was, "calumniate the Queen."

[1] Paris alleged that Bothwell and Balfour spent a night at Kirk o' Field, presumably that of the 23rd–24th January, and that he met them returning from there on, say, the 24th. But the main object of Paris' examination was to bring evidence as then required, not only against Balfour and Maitland, suspected of acting in the Queen's behalf, but also to quash a movement in her favour, which Elizabeth, sincerely or not, was supporting (date, August 1569). As evidence the deposition of Paris is worth nothing.

On the other hand, the 'Confessions' of the witnesses, made at the scaffold (and let us note that *in theory* confessions were the untrammelled statements of persons *in articulo mortis*), certainly did connect Balfour with Bothwell, but rather as *post facto* complices than as working together before it. In this case the genuineness or completeness of the confessions were widely questioned, and even Buchanan refers to one matter which was suppressed whether it belonged to the deposition or the confession[1]. After the event, as we have seen, Balfour absented himself for a fortnight, and, on his return, I know of nothing to show that he was more at one with Bothwell than with any other of the nobles participating in the killing of Darnley. He was not, so far as the record goes, in company with the Court when the Queen was at Seton.

A Council was held on 11th March, at which both Bothwell and Balfour were present, and we may conclude from this that Killigrew, then in Edinburgh, had opportunity to meet both these worthies. The *sederunt* of two later Councils is given in the *Register*, those of 21st and 28th March; Bothwell was at both, but not Balfour. It was during this period that the Prince was handed to the Earl of Mar, and the command of the castle of Edinburgh given to James Cockburn of Skirling, who held it until the end of April, or, as the 'Diurnal' says, until 8th May. Drury's story that Balfour was given the castle at an earlier date in order to receive the Prince therein when Mary on her return from Stirling, on the 24th April, was supposed to be bringing him with her, is probably entirely untrue[2].

The true date of Balfour's taking command of Edinburgh Castle is 8th May, as stated in the 'Diurnal,' for Drury, contradicting his former statement, says, dated 6th May, that Skirling still had the Castle, Balfour having a room there with authority equal to the Captain. At this time Skirling was appointed comptroller, and Balfour definitely got the keys. Bothwell brought the Queen, closely guarded, to the castle on the evening of the 6th[3]. She must have found both Balfour and Skirling there.

---

[1] Mahon, *Indictment of Mary Queen of Scots*, p. 50, n. 7.
[2] Letter of 27th April.   [3] Drury, letter of 6th May.

The interesting point is, by whose favour did Balfour obtain command in the castle? Historians, taking the line of least resistance, tell us that it was through Bothwell, who required this alleged accomplice for the furtherance of his designs. But there is no proof that it was so, and there is nothing to show that the Lords who were now confederated against Bothwell made any outcry at such an appointment, which would, if Balfour were his nominee, be so seriously against their interests. On the other hand, a certain amount of circumstantial evidence appears to show that Balfour's presence at the castle was never agreeable to Bothwell.

If we refer to Sir James Melville's *Memoir*, though I admit that he was more than usually confused at this point, we find:

I was intimately acquainted with Sir James Balfour.... I knew how matters stood between Bothwell and him, namely there were some jealousies arisen.... I told him (Balfour) that the Earl intended to have the castle out of his hands, for the Earl and he had been great companions, and he (Balfour) was also very great with the Queen, so that the custody of the castle was committed to him. But *afterwards* he would not consent to be present, nor take part with the murderers of the King, whereby he came in suspicion with the Earl of Bothwell who would no more credit him, so that he would have had the castle out of his hands, to have committed the charge thereof to the Laird of Beinston.... *I dealt with Sir James Balfour not to part with the castle* whereby he might be an instrument to save the prince and the Queen, who was so disdainfully handled....

Obviously time had dimmed Melville's memory; he was writing in old age, after the year 1604, when many circumstances had shown the intimate connection of Balfour with the death of Darnley. Whatever his reasons were for veiling the part taken by Balfour, we must admit foundation of a general kind for his narrative. It is clearly wrong to suggest that Balfour had anything to do with the castle before or near the time of the murder, but there is a remarkable confirmation of the latter part of the story in Drury's letter of 14th May. In it he says: "The Lord of Benyston, a Hepburn, as I take it, is made constable of the castle." This must be Edinburgh news of, at latest, the 13th, and probably the gossip of Hepburn's appointment refers to a few days earlier.

Hence we have the interesting situation, that Bothwell arrived with the captive Queen on the evening of the 6th, to find Skirling captain, with Balfour waiting to step into his shoes. His first act is to endeavour to get rid of his alleged nominee, and put in this Hepburn of Benyston. In this he did not succeed, for, perhaps under the advice of Melville, as that worthy says, Balfour refused to quit.

There is food for reflection in this; if Balfour was Bothwell's nominee, it is strange that he should wish to oust him within three or four days after he had assumed his charge. To me it seems more likely that, taking advantage of Bothwell's absence at Dunbar with the Queen, the Lords, with the consent of Skirling, had insinuated Balfour into the post[1]. If this view is correct it means that Balfour had already compounded, or let us say opened negotiations, with the Protestant party. We know, of course, that he did so openly, a short time after.

It is not likely that at so early a date as 6th May there was any open breach between Bothwell and Balfour, it was not the cue of the confederate Lords to take any course that would prevent the marriage. *That* they could have done when Bothwell with a small company conveyed the Queen from Dunbar; the date of her coming was known to Drury a day or two before, and, we must conclude, to them also, yet none raised a finger to rescue her.

But, if there was no breach, Bothwell had grounds enough to know that Balfour was not his friend, and I think we must connect a proposal to send Sir James in embassy to England with Bothwell's desire to get him out of the castle. This is mentioned by Drury in his letter of 20th May, reporting that Balfour was to carry letters to England to announce the Queen's marriage. In Drury's next letter, of 25th May, he says this intention is not

[1] I have used the word "insinuated" because Balfour's entry into the castle does not seem to have followed the ordinary procedure, as Drury put it: "Balfour shall have a chamber there with credit as much as the captain." Skirling, in fact, remained as captain with Balfour as a lodger.

persisted in, for Balfour "doubteth of his entertainment in passing and returning." The word *entertainment* may mean only his expenses, but it may also mean that he doubted his reception should he relinquish his hold on the castle.

At the least, it seems clear that even then, before his marriage, Bothwell had good reasons to suspect Balfour, and believers in the story of Dalgleish and the Casket Letters would be well advised to reconsider their views. One is reminded of Bishop Leslie's comment in the 'Defence,' "Is it to be thought that either the Earl (Bothwell) would send to the said Sir James, who had before assisted the faction against the Queen, with the force and strength of Edinburgh Castle, and driven from thence the very Earl himself, or that the said Sir James would send any such thing to the Earl?" Certainly it is not very likely, and the reader must judge for himself whether in these circumstances the precious casket containing incriminating letters would be left in Balfour's charge.

Although we know that, within six weeks after Bothwell's arrival at the castle, Sir James Balfour was sitting in council with the confederate Lords[1], yet we are not so sure how soon this *rapprochement* commenced. At all events we can shorten the gap of six weeks by a consideration of that strange incident, the flight of Bothwell, taking the Queen with him, to Borthwick Castle. This happened on the 6th or 7th June, just three weeks after their marriage.

THE LAIRDS OF BEANSTON AND BRUNSTANE

References appear at this period to persons, or a person, designated as of "Benistoun" and of "Brunstane." The question arises exactly who is meant.

One connects the names of Balfour and "Benistoun" as procurers of the false key or keys designed to make easy an entrance to the King's lodging; another connects the names of Bothwell and "Benyston" (p. 153) in connection with the

---

[1] See letter from du Croc, dated 21st June, in Bain, II; also letter from Drury of 25th June.

charge of Edinburgh Castle; and in this case the relationship of "Benyston" is rather antagonistic to Balfour than friendly. The point at issue is this, was Balfour's coadjutor, Benistoun, the same person as Bothwell's nominee, Benyston? At first view it will be said that the two spellings are but variations of the same name, but I am not so sure that this is so.

The Hepburns of Beanston (modern spelling) are described under a variety of forms as Beinston, Benstoun, Benystoun. In the *Scots Peerage* (II, p. 142) it is said that letters of legitimation were granted to one Patrick and six other sons of John Hepburn "of Beinstoun," and this Patrick, who is usually designated as of Quhytcastell (Whitcastle), was son-in-law to Cockburn of Langton. Now, when Drury reported that Hepburn of Benyston was made constable of the castle, he also said that he was son-in-law to Langton, so if Drury be accepted as right it is agreed that Patrick Hepburn of Whitcastle (Beanston) was the newly-created constable. There is, I think, no doubt that both Langton and Whitcastle were Bothwell's and also Queen's men[1].

The Crichtons of Brunstane are the other half of my puzzle. The designation is also spelt variously; in Pitcairn (II, p. 27) the name is "Creychton of Benestoune," which is not dissimilar to that discussed above. But let us get a little further back in the history of the Crichtons. At the time of the murder of Cardinal Beton one of the principal intermediaries for procuring the reward offered by Henry VIII for accomplishing the murder was Crichton of "Brunston"; Tytler in the fifth volume of his history, and especially in the Notes at the end thereof, gives a pretty full account of that affair. This person was Alexander Crichton, and he was dead before 1558 (*Acts of Parliament*, II, p. 520). Tytler is therefore in error in not distinguishing between this Alexander and his son, John, involved in the murder of Riccio in 1566. In this deed, John Crichton appears as Brimston,

[1] There is another Hepburn, to whom I do not refer above, so as not to confuse the issue, Alexander Hepburn of Whitsum; he may be, and in the *Scots Peerage* is stated to be, the same as Hepburn of Riccarton, whose name appears often as a supporter of the Queen; he was also in Darnley's service, and at one time suspected of the murder; on this charge he was cleansed. He was a cousin of Whitcastle.

PLATE III

An "aeroplane" view of the scene of the tragedy from the S.S.W., after the explosion. It shows the postern gate in the Flodden wall, the three cottages in the south gardens, the "Thieves Row" between the wall of the latter and the Flodden wall, and the trees under one of which Darnley's body was found. It also shows the window in the wall.

Brymston and Brymstone; he was forfeited for the murder, but got his pardon through the mediation of the Earl of Moray in August 1566 (*Selections*, p. 164).

So far the record of both father and son is bad. Coming to the killing of Darnley, the list of names in the "Answer to Bothwell's cartel" includes as murderers with the hands, "Laird of Branston," also James Cullen and others, while the second or "not yet set up" placard includes the same names but describes the Laird as of "Beynston." Later, in July of 1567, we have the names of persons summoned for the King's murder, and at this time Sir James Balfour was manipulating the witnesses, and had already to all appearance succeeded in liberating James Cullen (Chap. II, p. 74). In this list neither Cullen nor Branston is mentioned, nor even Beynston, but Patrick Hepburn of Whitcastle is named. But so far as I can gather, Whitcastle was not seriously pursued.

That, then, is the problem. Was John Crichton or Patrick Hepburn the accomplice of Balfour in the matter of the key? I admit that a decisive answer cannot be given, but on three grounds I express the opinion that *Crichton* was Balfour's man. The first: against father and son were previous convictions of plotting to murder for personal gain; the Crichtons had it in them; Patrick Hepburn, on the other hand, has nothing recorded against him. The second: Patrick Hepburn was included in the Summons of Forfeiture, John Crichton was not. Sir James Balfour manipulated this list and excluded his friends, as, for example, Cullen, and Ker of Fawdonside, both of them certainly involved. Other Kers were included, as Hirsell and Dolphington, but they were Fernihirst Kers and at feud with the Cessfords, and presumably unfriends of Balfour. The third: Patrick Hepburn's proper designation was "of Whitcastle," and he is so styled in any official document, for example, the Summons and the Act of Parliament of August 1568. It is, on the whole, probable that the name included in the cartels to Bothwell, viz. Branston (according to Drury) or Beynston (according to Kirkaldy), referred to Crichton and not to Hepburn.

The point has a certain importance, in that if Hepburn should be held to have been Balfour's man as well as Bothwell's, it might argue a pre-murder alliance between them, and I think there was none, for each was acting independently.

THE ATTACK ON BORTHWICK CASTLE

It is merely a truism to say that Bothwell was aware of the combination of the Lords against him, many of them the very men who had consented to his marriage; he could not but know by now that all that business was a plot in his disfavour. Even so early as 25th May, Drury reported that all on whom Bothwell could rely had secret warning to be ready for action; of the confederated Lords he says, they had already contracted to punish the captors of the Queen and set her at liberty; not a word so far, openly at least, of accusing her of the crime. There were apparently two avenues of attack, the one from the south headed by the Lord Home, the other from Stirling, headed by Morton[1].

I think it is impossible to avoid attributing Bothwell's sudden move to Borthwick to the information that these opponents were in motion. I know that it is said he was about to raid Liddesdale, and that proclamation anent this had been issued; but, at such a juncture, it is unlikely that he would leave the capital, the possession of which, together with the person of the Queen, almost spelt sovereignty, unless he was obliged to do so. His natural refuge, if hard pressed, would be Edinburgh Castle, and it can scarcely be doubted that this was the occasion mentioned by Bishop Leslie: "The said Sir James had...driven from thence the very Earl himself...."

Leslie's story, true or not, can refer to no other period, for Bothwell was never again in Edinburgh after that day in June

---

[1] It is worth noting that Drury had for a month past egged Cecil on to send supports to Home; whether he did so or not is not said. The presence of Home against Bothwell connotes the support of the Cessford Kers, including Fawdonside, and Drury notes that young Cessford refused to take from Bothwell a pardon for his share in the murder of the Abbot of Kelso, because it had the condition of his adherence to Bothwell's faction attached to it (letter of 4th May). An additional reason to say that Fawdonside and Bothwell were not on the same side at the murder of Darnley.

when he retired to Borthwick. It was the first fatal step, which led in a few days to Carberry Hill.

Two recitals of the event are of importance; the one made by the Captain of Inchkeith, printed by Teulet[1], not very accurate in itself and composed from hearsay, in which he says, "It appears that the Castle (that is, Balfour) has intelligence with the Morton faction"; the other is a letter from John Beton[2], which gives some curious information. "The Lords," he says, "retired...that same night to Edinburgh, where they were received, notwithstanding any command sent by the Queen's Majesty in the contrary, to the town or castle." This was 11th June, and we are now clear that between 7th and 11th June, Balfour was in "intelligence" with the Morton faction, but it takes time for "intelligence," that is, negotiation, to express itself in action; I think we shall not be far wrong in believing that, when Balfour withstood the appointment of Hepburn of Beinston early in May, he had already made "gestures" to the Protestant party.

I do not want to take up more time on this subject except to draw attention to the somewhat inconclusive nature of the affair. Whether the confederates were really anxious to capture Bothwell is doubtful; certainly at that time they feared to lay hands on the Sovereign. Drury's letter of 20th June explains the situation by saying that "these Scottish lords" were awaiting the approval of Elizabeth. Most evidently what they did must be based on instructions from England. They intend, says Drury, to remain in Edinburgh and not to attempt any other enterprise: "till they hear how this that they have already done be liked by the Queen's Majesty, my sovereign, at whose devotion it seems they would, and desire to be, and to be directed wholly by Her Majesty." Drury is referring to the events of Carberry Hill, but the same thing applied to Borthwick. I repeat that, up to this time, *there is no hint in the official documents of any accusation of Mary herself.* On 23rd June Bedford writes: "The punishment

[1] *Relations*, II, pp. 300 ff.
[2] See Sloane, Coll. Brit. Mus. Add. MS. 3199; also printed in Laing, II, pp. 109 ff.

of the murder being had, they mean not to detain their Queen any longer in hold (as prisoner), but are to be ordered therein as our sovereign shall appoint." *Words* only, I admit, but showing, in this case as in the other cases already mentioned, that the *imprimatur* of the Sovereign of England was the pillar on which Scottish rebels rested. In the Borthwick case what they gained was control of the capital and, in effect, of the Castle.

THE EXERCISE OF HIS SECRET POWER

But Sir James Balfour was by no means done with when he ruined Bothwell by holding the Castle against him; he was far too astute to relinquish his position without value received. He sat daily in Council with the Lords at Holyrood, I suppose, and it is proof of the power he had over Morton and his colleagues that they did not seize him then. Not until the following August, after Moray had assumed the Regency, did Balfour give up his post, and then on terms which seem again to emphasize his influence. He received a large grant of money, an acquittance of all concern in the King's murder, the Priory of Pittenweem (a slice out of Moray's possessions) for himself and a pension for his eldest son[1].

The rest of the acts of Sir James Balfour belong to a period rather beyond our scope, yet to complete our estimate of the man it is necessary briefly to examine them.

Throughout the time of Mary's incarceration in Lochleven and the evolution of the indictment against her which was secretly advanced before Elizabeth's Commissioners[2], Balfour was in confidential relations with the Regent Moray, employed

[1] As recorded in the *Hist. of King James the Sext*, p. 18. Throckmorton, 13th August, merely says that he left "on good composition."

[2] *Secretly*, I wonder if the general reader realizes that all the information, which on the surface seems so complete, was absolutely unknown outside a very small and chosen group in Mary's time. Some of it was published after the case was closed, but even then only to a few selected persons, the bulk including the "evidence" of the persons condemned was never published at all. One is justified in suggesting that the story could not bear the light of criticism.

in the most secret affairs of the State[1]—employed, it cannot be doubted, with Archibald Douglas and Buchanan, in formulating and falsifying the "evidence" to be put forward. The perfidies of the months May to August 1568 would require a volume to detail[2].

Not long after Moray returned from England from his successful effort in persuading a jury, already suborned, that his Sovereign was a murderess, Balfour was discarded, either by reason that his usefulness was ended, or because some further negotiations in favour of Mary had been commenced by Elizabeth. These required the production of new "evidence," and Paris supplied it. His statement, as is well known, inculpated Balfour in a marked degree[3]. Balfour was accused and arrested (September 1569) but, and it is worth remembering, "freed, to return upon caution when he should be required, and that never befell, for some secret causes among them[4]." Taken with other facts it seems that the Regent Moray found him an inconvenient captive.

During the regency of the Earl of Lennox, he was again pursued and this time escaped by joining the party opposed to the Regent in favour of the Queen. Lennox dead, and, after an interval, Morton proclaimed Regent, Balfour deserted his temporary friends and used his power over Morton to obtain the reversal of his forfeiture[5]. On this occasion we are told he professed the true religion and received the King's pardon, date January 1573. The pardon was, however, merely a respite, for Morton found that it gave offence to many that "the said Balfour should enjoy the benefit of pacification[6]." Balfour retired to

[1] Drury, letter of 10th July, 1568.
[2] I have touched on a part only of this great fraud in my little book on the *Indictment of Mary*.
[3] There was something reminiscent of the habits of the shrike about these Scottish conspirators; the *bird* impales its victims on a thorn to be ready when wanted for its supplies, *they* appeared always to have a living victim ready as occasion required.
[4] *Hist. of King James the Sext*, p. 43.
[5] *Reg. of Privy Council*, II, p. 174.
[6] Spottiswood, p. 274.

France and, it is said, also to Spain to obtain monetary assistance from Philip for the then promising enterprise of Esme Stewart, Duke of Lennox, to reinstate the Roman Church in Scotland[1]. The conjunction of the names of Balfour and that of Esme Stewart has something peculiarly fitting. Both professed the "true evangile" and took occasion from time to time to express the fact, and both used it as a cloak to cover schemes for Counter-Reformation. There is a note of Walsingham's extant dated in February 1580[2], which mentions that Esme Stewart had conference, before leaving France, with the Bishops of Glasgow and Ross, Sir James Balfour *and* the Duke of Guise (Henry, third Duke). Let us remember that at that time the Holy League was in full operation for the extermination of heresy, warmly supported by Philip of Spain and the Pope. Nothing is more likely than that Sir James was in close touch with Spain, as suggested above, and the names mentioned above as in conference are very suggestive of connection with the extreme Roman party.

To this point I would ask special attention, because, from the time of Riccio onwards, there is, I think, no shadow of doubt but that Balfour, in all phases of his disguisement, was the channel of Catholic propaganda. In my view he had sought to spread this through Darnley, and not through Mary, who was averse from extremism of any kind; on this point there is more to be said later.

It was through the influence of the Duke of Lennox that Balfour was brought back to Scotland in 1581 to provide that evidence on which his former protector, Morton, was condemned. The evidence was almost certainly based on the famous "bond," which contained reference to "great persons now living."

With one more reference I will quit a character so full of evil. Mention has been made above of the pardon which Balfour obtained in January 1573, and regarding this there is extant a letter addressed by him to Killigrew dated 12th January, four

---

[1] *Simancas*, 15th January, 1581, quoted in Froude, XI, p. 20.
[2] Cotton, *Calig. C.* 6, f. 110.

days after the pardon. This letter has not been printed and is too long to be set out in full; but it commences:

> My very good Lord...after your departure[1] I was in hand with the Regent's Grace (Morton) and some of the Council...touching my appointment wherein I find not such satisfaction as I look for, albeit I cannot complain of any lack of goodwill in the Regent himself that things might be perfected. But vain pursuers, new lets (hindrances) and impediments daily cast in by some about him (the strict Protestants)....

Balfour then goes on to ask that any question of his further trial should be postponed for at least four years, and demands a letter from Elizabeth to the Regent confirming this. He ends thus:

> If these things be not granted, which I doubt not but your Lordship will think reasonable should be, I take God to witness that *if any further inconvenience arises* they (*sic*) will minister to the further unquietness of the harmony and quietness of this country, the fault is not in me, *for your Lordship knows my deliberation in all respects.* Nothing doubting but Her Majesty shall think it convenient that we (his brother and himself) have full surety, and that therein your Lordship will do your part, as many things *being in my power*, that may pleasure you, you shall always find me ready to be commanded.

I submit that this blackmailing letter shows as clearly as can be expected the arrogant assertion of a power to support a demand. I fear it is hardly possible to avoid the conclusion that, so far as Balfour knew, Elizabeth was cognizant of the matter which he held over her. He may have been wrong, as I have already said, but, if the "bond" was in question, and I think it was, it is clear that he believed her to be one of the great persons who authorized in the first instance the murder of Darnley[2]. It seems manifest that Balfour had taken steps to place the information where, in case of evil befalling him, it would still be available for publication. Even more, the concluding lines seem

---

[1] Killigrew had gone to Berwick to consult Drury about that matter, as disgraceful as any in history, the secret assassination of the Queen of Scots, if possible by the hands of her subjects.

[2] Lest I be misunderstood, let me repeat my opinion that the actual murder, even though authorized by England, was in fact brought about by circumstances unknown to and not planned by Cecil.

to hint that in the "matter of great moment" then on the *tapis*, that is, in the scheme of handing over the Queen, with the proviso that she would cease to be a trouble to either country, Balfour was offering his services. I suggest that he was a partner in that frightful piece of treachery.

One may hesitate to condemn too severely the treacheries of Cecil in England, of Moray, Morton and some others in Scotland; they lived and acted in a century when the mentality of mankind had scarcely acquired the rudiments of what is meant by "straight dealing," but at least they were, it *may* be said, imbued with the notion that they were acting for the ultimate benefit of their respective countries. Of Balfour, nothing of the kind can be thought; he acted always for self, cynically indifferent to results so long as he saved his skin and profited.

THE MISSION OF SIR HENRY KILLIGREW

Killigrew, Cecil and Sir Nicholas Bacon were "brothers" in the parlance of the day (they had married sisters), a trinity which boded ill for Mary Stuart. The first named had been employed on more than one mission which redounded little to Cecil's honour. Ostensibly he came to Scotland on this occasion to carry a letter from Elizabeth, partly of condolence, partly of exhortation to greater activity in pursuit of the culprits, partly with reference to Bedford's negotiations anent the Treaty of Edinburgh and the succession question. Actually, his duties were to spy out the land, and, as I believe, to sow a whirlwind for Mary's reaping.

Bishop Leslie[1], admittedly in this matter not completely trustworthy, says:

Meanwhile, Elizabeth sent a spy, or rather a traitor, as was usual with her, under the guise of an ambassador, whose business was to offer condolence to the Queen. This man's name was Killigrew, and he began at once to concert measures with the disaffected nobles for the purpose of creating revolution in Scotland and deposing the Queen. He made particular enquiries into the circumstances of the

---

[1] *Paralipomena*, Forbes-Leith translation, p. 120.

recent tragedy and the light in which the populace regarded it, wishing principally to gain time in which to arrange his plot against the Queen's place and honour.

So far as Leslie is concerned, I have some suspicion that he was not entirely clean handed, but his opinion of Killigrew is based on a good deal of knowledge which cannot be neglected, even if we discount it.

Elizabeth's letter was dated 24th February, but Killigrew could not have started northwards before the 27th, and he passed through Alnwick on 3rd March[1]. He probably arrived at Edinburgh on the 5th. Elizabeth's letter reads like a genuine expression of feeling, and adds to the impression which, to me, often arises, that she, left to herself and without the poison continually poured into her ears by her chief secretary, was capable of honourable sincerity. Yet one is puzzled whence Elizabeth derived the fears which she indites. The news from Edinburgh, reaching London before the 24th, had been scanty. M. de Clerneau had arrived on the 16th with Drury's letter of the 12th, but from neither could she have found reason to suppose that Mary would be backward in taking steps to institute enquiries. Three other letters of Drury would have reached London before she wrote, but none of these, on the surface, gave ground for her pointed remarks, unless the mention of the anonymous placard posted on the Tolbooth on the 17th, which, as alleged by Drury, probably wrongly, alluded to the Queen as a "doer," can be so considered. Moretta, whose words were chosen to give rise to suspicions, did not arrive in London until the 24th; he might have seen Elizabeth before she wrote, but it is not likely[2]—in any case he had left Edinburgh too soon after the event to know what would or would not be done.

To me it seems that the "atmosphere" in which Elizabeth wrote had been artificially created, and that the design to link Mary's name with that of Bothwell had an origin in London before ever it was thought of in Edinburgh. It was politically necessary for England to repel the early reports of the culpability of the Protestants by a counter-accusation against the Catholics;

---

[1] Forster's letter of that date.   [2] *Relations*, V, p. 10.

and to bring in Mary's name as responsible for her husband's death killed two birds with one stone. It shook the Queen's credit in her own country and also destroyed her influence with those English who retained the old religion. One might expect the reverse from the Catholic Ambassadors, yet "Every day," wrote the Spanish Ambassador to his master, "it becomes clearer that the Queen must take steps to prove that she had no hand in the death of her husband....The spirit of the Catholics is greatly weakened by this event, and more still by the news that your Majesty is not coming to Flanders, which I believe has also done great injury in that country (Scotland)...[1]." When de Silva wrote this he had as little to go on as Elizabeth, and I quote him to show the tendency to impute to Mary what so far was not imputed to her in Scotland.

If Mary had been the militant Catholic we are led to suppose it would be matter for astonishment that de Silva and Moretta should have done so much to foster indirectly the idea of her guilt. It cannot be thought that either of them would care in the least for the death of Darnley, or who was the cause of it, if it were not for its bearing on the Catholic revival. After all, Mary, and Mary only, had the birthright power to weld the two kingdoms into a Catholic whole, and in normal circumstances both de Silva and Moretta would not have hesitated to defend her innocence, even if they had positive proof of her guilt. But the circumstances were not normal, for Mary had shown herself resolute in refusing the policy of violence recommended to her, and her constancy to the Faith was under the deepest suspicion. The concern of the two Ambassadors shows that their present schemes centred round Darnley; the hopes of Spain and Rome were dashed rather by *his* death than by any loss of credit that might fall on her. What de Silva wrote to Philip in his open letters probably had no relation to what he wrote or sent by private message, and it is noteworthy that it was not until the 2nd June that Philip even acknowledged the receipt of the news of the King's death. Although he must have received it before the end of February, and it was certainly an event of the first

[1] *Simancas*, dated 1st March, 1567.

importance, he yet allowed three months to elapse before he mentioned it, and then in the most casual terms. It is impossible not to believe that the open correspondence was accompanied by secret and possibly verbal communication by courier.

The general impression one derives is that, at this time, both the Protestant and the Catholic elements were, for different reasons, combined to work for the downfall of the Scottish Queen. Knox expressed the view that the nation suffered for its "criminal lenity" in not taking the Sovereign's life; the Catholics were equally convinced that Mary suffered because of her leniency towards the Protestant nobles.

If Elizabeth's letter confided to the care of Killigrew indicates the tone he should adopt regarding the murder, "spoken of by most men[1] as done for her pleasure," there is a little more information to be derived from Cecil's letters of the 25th and 26th February which were also carried by Killigrew. Most unfortunately we have not the letters themselves, but we can gather something from the reply made to them by Maitland dated 13th March. It contains the following:

Although the matter be such as you have not good will to deal in or utter your mind freely to every man, your meaning ought to be taken in good part, and your wise considerations are to be allowed of (accepted by) any discreet person. And surely, as for my own part, I do like your intention, so I know the same does not offend such here as have most interest to wish the matter to be earnestly recommended to such as you be, for they mean to demand nothing but right, and that in due time and orderly[2].

[1] Yet on 24th February, Elizabeth had had communication with none outside her own capital.

[2] There is a curious similarity in the language here employed to that used by Cecil in a previous letter, which seems to indicate that Maitland was using a form of words, well understood by Cecil, to convey a hidden meaning. The letter referred to concerned Mary's marriage with the Earl of Leicester: "In desiring this (the acknowledgment of Mary's title in England) your (Maitland's) meaning is, I think, to have it in order and time, not against order nor before due time...." The meaning here is that before any assurance as to title would be given conditions as to religion should be agreed. In the present case the meaning may be to entrap the Queen into a Protestant marriage, and then get rid of the husband.

For the third mark which you do wish, in your letter, I should shoot at, to wit that her Majesty would allow of your estate in religion, it is one of the things in earth I most desire. I dare be bold enough to utter my fancy in it to her Majesty, trusting that she will not like me the worse for uttering my opinion and knowledge in that is profitable for her everyway, and I do not despair. But although she will not yield at the first, yet with progress of time that point shall be obtained. I pray God it may be shortly.

Cryptic though this may be, it indicates that Cecil had marked out a plan to take advantage of the present confusion. It had long been his aim to mould the Scottish Reformation to conform more nearly to that of England[1]. Almost one can read the bargain, "conform, and receive protection whatever your sins may be." As to the Queen, is it not suggestive that the present moment should be chosen to induce her openly to change her faith? Cecil knows that her moderation has lost her the favour of Rome; does he know, too, that the treachery of Darnley, supported by Catholic elements, would tend to alienate her from the old religion? Exactly what seeds were sown by Killigrew in his conversations with the Protestant Lords cannot be said; what he did and what he reported on his return were kept a close secret. There is one little sidelight; in a letter to Drury of the 10th March, Cecil announced his desire to resign. It was his way of coercing Elizabeth, for nothing was on the *tapis* at the moment except the treatment of the affairs of Scotland; I think we must conclude that one of his many dishonourable courses was being forced on his Sovereign, and it is not too much to say

---

[1] Cf. a letter from Randolph dated 25th August, 1560: "I have talked of late with them all, to search how a uniformity might be had in religion in both these realms. These (the leaders, I presume) seem willing that it so were....Howbeit I find them (the people in general) so severe in that that they profess, so loth to remit anything of that that they have received that I see little hope thereof." It is a tribute to Cecil's genius that he should have foreseen how little suited to the monarchical principle was the republican creed of Geneva. Except for immediate use, neither he nor Elizabeth had any sympathy with Knox. Had Cecil succeeded now, the animosity stirred up by Mary's son, in forcing the prelatic system on Scotland, need never have arisen, and Mary's grandson might have kept his head.

that it was *contra Mariam*. Mary was prostrate, banned by both parties, her intellect, for the time, clouded; now was the time for attack.

Did Killigrew have an audience with Mary on 8th March? He says he did, but I greatly doubt it. The reader knows my opinion that that monstrous libel of Buchanan is constructed on foundations of crooked truth. Referring to the audience, he says:

> For when Henry Killigrew was come from the Queen of England to comfort her...this gentleman stranger's hap was to spill the play, and unvisor the disguising; for when he was, by the Queen's commandment, come to the Court, though...he did nothing hastily, yet he came in so unseasonably before the stage was prepared and furnished, that he found the windows open and the candles not lighted, and all the provisions for the play out of order.

Buchanan is, of course, harping on his string that Mary should have been secluded from light and open air for forty days after her husband's death; this not being done was, to him, a sign of her indifference[1]. However, Buchanan did not foresee that Killigrew's own account of his audience would survive; he says:

> I had no audience before this day (8th March)....I found the Queen's Highness in a dark chamber, so as I could not see her face, but by her words she seemed very doleful, and did accept my sovereign's letters and message in very thankful manner, as I trust will appear by her answer, which I hope to receive within these two days.

I think that Buchanan's fragment of truth is not difficult to find. Mary was brought back from Seton to receive the Ambassador on, I believe, 5th March. For the next two days she was not in a state to carry out her duty, on the 8th the audience was appointed and the Ambassador would have been received in the ordinary way. At almost the last moment she probably broke down again and, as it was of importance to prevent the truth of her state leaking out, it is possible a dark chamber was hastily prepared, and the Ambassador received by an impersonator. Froude[2] has a fantastic account of the interview, but, in fact, few

---

[1] I do not think it can be shown that this was ever a Scottish custom, though it was so in France.

[2] Froude, VIII, p. 98.

words were said, and Killigrew was referred to the Council for his answer. My personal view is that he was not deceived by the impersonation, and I believe that Cecil was fully alive to the state of the woman he was persecuting.

An autograph letter from a Sovereign required a like reply, but there is no trace of what Mary said, if she wrote. Robert Melville, at a later date, 7th May, refers to a letter which may be the one in question:

> I have been in the country ever since Master Killigrew's departing....I understand that the Queen, your mistress, wrote to my sovereign a letter, wherein Her Majesty gave good advice and counsel, which letter was not so thankfully taken with as required, and over sharply answered. I doubt not but your Honor will excuse the same, and esteem rather it is the counsel of those about her than to come of herself. For you have experience that Her Majesty behaved herself more moderately when she had liberty to be at her own wise counsel.

Hardly anything could be better said to indicate the condition in which the Queen of Scots then was. We may assume that there were letters from the Council as well as, perhaps, an autograph from the Queen. The former would certainly not be couched in "sharp" terms, the latter would probably be Mary's own composition; however often her ordinary letters may have been written for her and her signature appended by others, I think, a letter to a Sovereign would not be so treated. Her letter was, one may imagine, not very coherent, and, likely enough, some of the many good reasons she had to complain of her "sister's" assumption of a virtuous superiority came to the surface.

En passant let me mention that I do not think any of the letters attributed to her, with the possible exception of the letter to Elizabeth just referred to, were from her hand. The correspondence with the Earl of Lennox is a case in point. Written in Scots as they were, she could not have composed them, then or at any time; it was alleged, one might say admitted, that her signature was often added by others. Drury definitely says that one letter to Lennox was issued by the Council; probably all were.

The day after Killigrew left Edinburgh, the Bishop of Ross went to Stirling to negotiate with the Earl of Mar as to the custody of the baby prince. Custody of the heir to the throne was almost an hereditary right of the Erskines. The present Earl's father, John, Lord Erskine, had had the custody not only of Mary herself in her infancy but of her father also. The Erskines were also hereditary governors of Stirling Castle, and this had been confirmed to them in the previous year[1], and Stirling was by usage the nursery of the royal children. I mention these facts because a great deal of cruel calumny has been cast on Mary in connection with the matter. It has been said that she only handed the child to Mar as a bargain, to secure the charge of Edinburgh Castle for evil purposes. In this there is, in my opinion, no truth.

It is true that Mary had to some extent departed from the general rule of keeping the child at Stirling, and, as Buchanan with much unnecessary emphasis tells us, had removed him to Holyrood, "in the deep of a sharp winter," that is, in January of 1567. But there was more in this than Buchanan chose to make known; even his rage is significant. At Stirling a plot had been brought to light, which shall be referred to again, having for its object the capture of the Prince and advancement of Darnley to the throne, and I am inclined to think that Mary was not well satisfied that the Earl of Mar, then at Stirling, had behaved in an entirely loyal manner. It was on these accounts that she had taken the step of carrying the Prince with her when she came to Edinburgh on 14th January, shortly after the baptism.

Now, two months later, we find the Prince again rendered to the care of Mar and, except for a brief moment in April, Mary never saw her son again. Was this act brought about by Mary? In her state of mental prostration, it is possible that she yielded to the persuasion of the Bishop of Ross and others, who could see that she was in no condition to protect the child. But had she been in the temper of callous defiance that her enemies describe, it is impossible to suppose her consent. The Countess

[1] Charter of January 1566.

of Mar, who would be most concerned in the care of the Prince, was sister to the same James Murray of Tullibardine, who, but a day before the Bishop went to Stirling, had been proscribed by the Council as the setter-up of the defamatory placards[1]. Not one of the Tullibardine Murrays was friendly to the Queen, and several letters of later date[2] add to the impression that the Countess was not the person whom she would willingly entrust with the care of her only son. It is true that, in a letter to the Earl written at the end of the following year from her prison at Bolton, she uses the expression, "Remember that when I gave you my son as my most precious treasure, you promised me to guard him, and not to deliver him to any without my consent..."; but this appears to refer to a personal conversation which could only have taken place when she visited Stirling in April 1567, a month later than the date of the Bishop of Ross' negotiation.

Arising out of this we have the confutation of some of the minor counts charged against the Queen. Mar made no difficulty in relinquishing his captaincy of Edinburgh Castle, indeed it was obviously inconvenient that, with so important a trust as that now given him, he should have a dual position. It is not true that Bothwell was given the vacant place; Sir James Cockburn, Laird of Skirling, was appointed[3]. I think we must deduce that, even if Bothwell's baneful influence over the Queen was at that time growing, he had not yet obtained complete mastery of her will-power nor the entire rule of her councillors—otherwise he would hardly have permitted the removal of the Prince to Stirling.

Remembering how closely the event followed on Killigrew's mission, it is difficult to avoid the conclusion that his influence had a good deal to do with it. He could see that Mary was in no condition to protect the child, and the mere fact that she

[1] p. 175.   [2] Bain, *Scottish State Papers*, III *passim*.
[3] See 'Diurnal' and Drury's letters. In the Douglas Peerage he is named William, but I think James, which accords with contemporary papers, is correct. Skirling and Lord Herries were "brothers," they had married sisters; and while Herries, with some relapses, was loyal, I cannot find that Skirling was ever a supporter of Bothwell or other than a true man to his Queen.

allowed the transfer without even going herself to see it carried out is eloquent of her state. But I wonder if this was the sole reason which moved Killigrew. Was there even then a plan to isolate the Queen and throw her into the hands of Bothwell? Was this the first act leading up to that almost inconceivable deed of perfidy known as the Ainslie Bond? On a subject so completely veiled one speaks with hesitation, but many things seem to point to the origin of all this mischief as coming from this period. If it were so, the removal of the child would be a first step. The baptism over, the father dead, the paternity, which his vile tongue might have set in question, laid at rest, the child in the power of the Protestant Lords—the mother mattered nothing. Bothwell's influence could not *then* have been great, else the first step could not have been taken, and yet from now onwards it seems to grow. Killigrew had been a plotter with the Protestant Lords the year before and concerned in the disgraceful affair of Rokesby; he would have changed his habits remarkably if he were not a plotter now.

One interesting little sidelight must be mentioned before we quit this subject. On the day Killigrew had audience of the Queen, 8th March, he dined with the Earls of Moray, Argyll, Huntly, Bothwell, and Secretary Maitland was also present. He tells this himself. What a dinner party! At the moment no discord, within a few weeks each trying to drag down the other. Was it the guest of the day who threw in the apple of discord? Bishop Leslie's opinion, quoted at the beginning of this section, furnishes, in part, the answer.

THE DEFAMATORY PLACARDS

I have said in the preceding section[1] that the connection of the Queen's name with Bothwell originated rather in England than in Edinburgh. The student will object that anonymous placards, or "bills" as they were called, were posted in public places in Edinburgh at a date earlier than could attach any influence from London. Unwillingly, I must turn aside to examine them.

[1] p. 165.

Defamation by anonymous placards was a method which was carried to a high degree of perfection in France, and both William Kirkaldy of Grange and James Murray of Tullibardine had been in France and learnt the art there. These two were the principals in the campaign. Kirkaldy has been invested with a halo as an heroic defender of the Queen's cause, and it may be that he expiated his sins and came to recognize his misjudgment of her when, some four years later, he defended the Castle of Edinburgh in her name. At the time we are now dealing with, he was without question a paid spy of England, and the sworn "brother" of Thomas Randolph; they had been students together in Paris years before. He had adopted the cause of the Reformation, and acquired a taste for English gold from the time of the Cardinal's murder. Elizabeth, who had seen some of his writings against his Sovereign, "utterly condemned" them and thought him the "worst in that realm[1]." Both he and Murray hated Bothwell with intense ferocity, and the Queen in scarcely less degree. Libels directed against either of them, coming from such sources, must be received with caution.

The first placard was set up on the night of the 16/17th February; it contained, according to Drury (letter to Cecil of 19th February), the words: "*I and* the Earl of Bothwell...were the doers of the same..." (the murder, that is). The same reading is to be found in a letter from the Spanish Ambassador in London, de Silva, to his master[2]. In other respects, however, the two readings differ, but we need not deal with this. There can be no doubt but that the personal pronoun indicates the Queen. We have, however, reason to believe that the two words italicized did not, in fact, appear in the placard; that Drury and de Silva should have used them merely shows their willingness to inculpate the Queen as much as possible.

There are two other records of the same placard. One appears in a letter from Cecil to Sir Henry Norris, then in Paris, dated 5th March. In it these words do not occur. Cecil has evidently neglected Drury's version, which he received on the 23rd Febru-

---

[1] Quoted in Stevenson's *Nau*, from a letter dated 10th May, 1567.
[2] *Simancas*, date 1st March.

ary, and adopted the true reading which he had had from some
other source. I call it the true reading because it agrees with
that published five years later in the 'Detection,' and this is
likely to omit nothing that may be against Mary. It runs: "...I
(that is, the poster of the placard), who have made inquisition
by them that were the doers thereof, affirm that the committers
of it were the Earl of Bothwell (and three others named), *the
Queen assenting thereto*, through the persuasion of the Earl of
Bothwell...." This is essentially different from naming the
Queen as a "doer," and, exaggerated and put in a wrong light,
there may be a shade of truth in the last quoted words (*supra*,
p. 98). It is not unlikely that the purport of the conversation
between the Queen and Bothwell on the fatal night may have
leaked out or been guessed at.

Neither this nor the next placard, which appeared two days
later and named three foreigners serving in the Queen's household, seem to have created much comment; they were apparently rather the product of private revenge than a serious effort
to elucidate the case. In them, excepting Bothwell and Balfour,
no name was mentioned on which suspicion afterwards concentrated.

The pictorial placard which first appeared on 26th February,
succeeded in a few days by the well-known representation of
Mary as a mermaid, stirred official circles to a greater extent,
and on 14th March a proclamation was issued, after a council
meeting, naming James Murray, brother of the Laird of Tullibardine as the author thereof, "tending to her Majesty's slander
and defamation." Drury's intimate acquaintance with these
placards, and the fact that he was able to send copies of them
to Cecil, shows that he was in close touch with the authors, for
copies of *pictures* were not easily procurable. It is an interesting
fact that a little later Kirkaldy was in a position to send to the
Earl of Bedford, who was the usual recipient of his reports, the
contents of a placard which had "not yet been set up[1]." On
another occasion the same person requested that copies of the

[1] *State Papers, Scotland, Elizabeth*, XIII, No. 43, dated 8th May,
1567.

libels should be printed for distribution on the Continent[1]. It is clear that Kirkaldy was closely connected with the libels, and probably it was he who kept Drury so well supplied, for, as Bedford was absent and Drury was his deputy, he would be the natural recipient of Kirkaldy's efforts to vilify his Queen.

In this connection it is worth noting that Drury mentions, in his letters of 21st and 30th March, two challenges set up by Murray offering to defend his accusation by personal combat, but there is no other mention of these. They seem to be in the order of "not set up" placards, and anticipating others of a like nature which are mentioned in April, after Bothwell's trial[2].

There is a little more to be said about this secret intelligence of Drury. The "not yet set up" placard mentioned by Kirkaldy on the 8th May included the names of six persons besides Bothwell, on whose bodies Murray and his friends offered to prove guilt according to the "laws of arms." These persons were: James Ormistoun, the Black Laird; the Laird of Beynstoun; John Hepburn of Bolton; John Hay of Tallo younger; James Cullen and James Edmonstoun. All these names are new; not one was mentioned in the first placards or in the letters written by Lennox, and, so far as that goes, one sees that, while the early accusations were wide of the mark and justified the little attention paid to them, the later conception comes much nearer the facts. But the point about Drury is this; in his letter of 19th April he says: "The copy of the answer to the Earl Bothwell's cartel of challenge I send you herewith, it is in general and *not with particular terms as I wrote you at the first* according to my first information." There were two answers to Bothwell's challenge set up by Murray and, I think, neither of them was "particular," that is, they did not mention names. There must be some part of Drury's letter of 15th March missing, but apparently in it he gave the list of names which is now in the Public

---

[1] *State Papers, Scotland, Elizabeth*, 20th April.

[2] It should be said that Bothwell's trial had been first fixed for the 28th March and postponed to the 12th April. Cf. *Hist. of King James the Sext*, confirmed by Drury of 30th March.

Record Office[1]; it agrees partly[2] with the "not set up" placard, but adds other names, it was not "set up" either. At least the matter shows how closely Drury and the placard makers were working together.

Remembering the animus of both Kirkaldy and Murray towards their Queen and the tendency of Elizabeth's officials in the north to egg them on, I think I am justified in saying that the campaign of vilification originated rather in England than in Scotland. As we have seen, up to the time of Killigrew's departure homewards, there is no sign of discord among the nobles, nor of calling the Queen's name in question.

Another matter arising from the placards must be referred to; it is to be found in Drury's letter of the 28th February. I will set it down in full, and, as far as I know, it has not hitherto been printed.

There have been other bills bestowed upon the church doors and upon a tree (that is, a post) called the Tron wherein they speak of a smith who should make (made) the key, and offers, as there might be assurance of the living (reward) that by proclamation was offered, he and others will with their bodies approve (prove) these to be the devisers, and upon the same venture their lives.

This is expanded by Tytler to read: "A smith was spoken of... who had furnished false keys *to the King's apartment, and who, on due security, promised to come forward and point out his employers.*" The words italicized do not arise in the original. The offer to come forward was not the smith's, but the posters of the "bill"; only one key is mentioned, and the addition about the King's apartment is imaginary.

But all the same it is a remarkable and puzzling piece of information. It indicates at this early stage a certain confirmation of Hepburn's deposition, in which he spoke of false keys made for the purpose of giving access to the King's lodging on the night of the murder—fourteen false keys *he* said. As the reader knows, I am sceptical about the necessity for false keys

[1] Bain, II, pp. 320–1.
[2] In this list the name mentioned above as "Laird of Beynstoun" is now spelt "Laird of Branston." This has been referred to above (p. 157).

when all the essential doors were, according to the story, at the command of the murderers. I am rather fortified in my opinion by the fact that, though both the 'Detection' and the 'Oration' mention keys, there is nothing to show that false keys were used.

However, so far as the story goes, the first news of false keys came to the ears of the Lords in the deposition of Hepburn, and that was not until the 8th December following. Are we to suppose them guessing through all the intervening nine months what the placard about the key could mean? It is quite extraordinary that in no other document is the matter referred to, for it was a remarkable clue.

Now, in that part of Hepburn's deposition which, for their own reasons, the Queen's adversaries suppressed, the words occur: "And towards the makers of the Keys (that is, regarding the makers, etc.) they were made between Benistoun and Sir James Balfour, and they two can tell" (p. 155). Just as it would have been perfectly easy to follow up the clue of the barrel already mentioned, so it would have been simple to root out the maker of the key or keys. Having before us the suppression of the name of Sir James Balfour regarding the keys, is it not some confirmation to the suggestion that his name was similarly suppressed regarding the barrel? The barrel was, I believe, a false trail; is it not likely that the key was the same?

THE HEALTH OF MARY STUART[1]

In my book *Mary, Queen of Scots*[2], I have referred several times to Mary's health during her sojourn in France. Her frequent fainting fits, her emaciation, her chalky pallor, the hopes

[1] This section was referred by the writer, shortly before his lamented death, to Dr J. S. Risien Russell for a professional opinion on the symptoms exhibited by the Queen. In a letter dated 21st February, 1929, Dr Risien Russell writes: "Having now made time to consider the matter carefully, I am in no doubt that the case was one of true epilepsy, and that General Mahon is fully justified in coming to this conclusion."

[2] *Mary, Queen of Scots, a study of the Lennox Narrative*, by Major-General R. H. Mahon, C.B., C.S.I., Cambridge University Press, 1924.

expressed by more than one observer that she could not long survive. Her pre-natal "history" was not good, her father died within a week of her birth in a state of mania, terrified by visions, and for a long time previously he had been a victim of depression and melancholy.

A few days before her arrival in Scotland, Randolph wrote of her as "A sick crased woman" undertaking a "stout adventure." Not many weeks after her coming, he wrote: "As she rode in the streets she fell sick and was borne from her horse. With such sudden passions she is often troubled after any great unkindness or grief of mind" (8th October, 1561). A year later the same person reported similar sudden seizures (10th August, 1562). Probably due to the terrifying experience of the murder, almost in her presence, of Riccio, she being pregnant, her labour was prolonged and excessively severe (June 1566); it is doubtful, indeed, if she ever fully recovered from it. During the next three months her peace of mind was disturbed by the extraordinary behaviour of her husband, and in October came her serious illness at Jedburgh, originated by physical fatigue and anxiety.

She became "dead," all her "members cold, eyes closed, mouth fast and feet and arms stiff[1]." From this state she was brought round by tight ligatures on her limbs, a common cure at the time for convulsive fits. At a much later date (May 1569), during her imprisonment in England, she fell into a somewhat similar condition, of which she wrote afterwards to the Bishop of Ross: "I fell several times into convulsions very similar to those you saw at Jedburgh."

From Jedburgh she travelled by stages to Craigmillar, from which place the French envoy du Croc wrote: "She is in the hands of the physicians, and I do assure you is not at all well." From this she went within a fortnight through the fatigues of the baptism, and of this the same writer said: "She behaved herself admirably.... This made her forget in a good measure her former ailments. But I am of mind that she will give us some trouble

[1] Bishop of Ross to Archbishop of Glasgow, 26th–27th October, 1566, in Keith, II, pp. 286 ff.

yet, nor can I think otherwise so long as she continues to be so pensive and melancholy.... She sent for me yesterday (20th December, 1566) and I found her laid on the bed weeping sore; she complained of a grievous pain in her side." There are numerous references to this complaint during her sojourn in Scotland.

Then came the fatigues and anxieties of the journey to Glasgow, the return to Kirk o' Field and the final shock of the death of Darnley. What effect do you think this would have on a woman whose condition is most briefly, and without exaggeration, given above?

There is silence regarding her state after the news of the tragedy was broken to her, yet we are not without glimpses of the truth. It can be understood that, at such a crisis, there would be hesitation in adding to the public dismay by an announcement that her life was in danger. Indeed, if I am not mistaken that she fell into violent hysteria accompanied by fits of a not less serious kind, it is likely enough that those around her had had experience of similar seizures and did not wish to talk about them. It may be noted that even so coarse an enemy as Buchanan partly confirms my supposition, though his intention was far otherwise, "She sweetly slept till the next day at noon" ('Detection'). Deep sleep is a frequent sequel of epileptic trouble. Those who, in the course of their affairs, had been in immediate touch with the events mentioned her distress, but it is evident that they knew no more than they were told. Robert Melville, who had started on his journey to London, the bearer of instructions to open the negotiations on which Mary had such high hopes, returned on hearing the news (p. 105). Probably he arrived in Edinburgh on the 13th or 14th, but he reported her as "too much distressed to see him." At a later date, 26th February, when in London, he says, "I have had no letter from my sovereign" (Bain, 11).

It is, in fact, more from her omissions to communicate with her usual correspondents than from the letters alleged to have come from her that one derives information. The Spanish Ambassador in London, de Silva, had informed her of the plot against her life[1], and in the ordinary course she would have acknowledged his courtesy, but, writing to Philip on 8th March, he expressed his surprise at not hearing from her[2]. Again, on 14th April, he mentioned that he had had nothing from her, and still later, 17th May, he repeated his surprise at not hearing[3]. It is strange that the letter sent to the Queen-Mother in France, announcing the murder, came from the Council and not from Mary herself; there is no hint that she wrote to her aunt of Savoy, her uncle of Lorraine, her grandmother of Guise, her aunts of Arschott or Nemours, in fact there is nothing of the old Mary, taking advantage of this courier or that to recommend herself to the recollection of her relatives in civilized Europe. "La petite reine sauvage" often felt her isolation, and longed to return to those whom she had learnt to trust, and now, more than ever, had she been in a normal state she might be expected to lean on the support of her friends; but there is nothing! It is unlikely that everything of this kind has been destroyed.

I do not forget that Bastian, the newly made husband of her faithful waiting-woman, Christina Hog, was sent to London and France. He passed through Berwick on 19th February[4] and was in London on or before the 26th[5] and arrived in Paris on 6th March[6], accompanied by M. Dolu, who was the Queen's treasurer for her French affairs. Bastian, it is said, carried a letter from Mary to Elizabeth. There is no trace of that letter, nor of any reply made thereto by the English Queen. Elizabeth's letter of 24th February was presumably sent before Bastian arrived; it was the often quoted letter, carried by Killigrew, telling Mary of her horror of the murder, and hinting that she (Mary) was not ignorant of the intention, and all that we hear of it is that Mary "accepted my sovereign's letters and message in very thankful manner." I have already expressed the view that Killigrew never saw Mary (p. 169), and it is hard to suppose that Mary in her senses would

[1] The same plot as reported by the Archbishop of Glasgow, news of which reached Edinburgh a few hours after Darnley's death.
[2] *Simancas.*   [3] *Ibid.*   [4] Drury of that date.
[5] *Simancas*, under date 1st March, 1567.
[6] Cockburn to Cecil, 19th March, 1567.

receive such a letter with gratitude; and even if she made a sharp reply, as perhaps she did (p. 170), it is significant that it is not preserved. On a somewhat similar occasion, when Elizabeth was known by her to have assisted her rebels, she wrote a letter of expostulation which should have made her sister ashamed; were it not, she said, that I know of the evil reports made to you by my rebels: "We could not think nor almost bear with the strange devisit letter which we lately have received of you..." (Bain, II, p. 267, dated 15th March, 1566).

Dolu, the treasurer, also carried a letter dated 18th February, the day on which he left Edinburgh or Seton, which he delivered to the Archbishop of Glasgow in Paris on 6th March; of this letter we have a copy[1]. It is mainly a business letter, replying to certain heads of a former letter from the Archbishop. Written in Scottish, it could not have been composed by the Queen, and it neglects matters in the letter under reply which I think Mary would have mentioned; and I judge that, like the letters written on the 10th of February, it is rather necessary business of State than a private letter from the Queen herself. Archbishop Beton replied to all three letters[2] on 9th or 11th March[3]; the bearer was Clerneau, returning to Scotland, who should have arrived in Edinburgh about 25th March, but there is little mention of his presence there, other than Drury's memoranda of 29th March in which he notes: "Clerneau's letters were much misliked and thrown into the fire. The Cardinal seems much to mislike with her for the death of the King." This information is not likely to be based on knowledge, for admittedly the Queen was closely guarded and none suffered to see her; nor does it agree with Clerneau's own account, for, writing to Beton on 14th May to apologize for his silence since his arrival, he says, "she has as yet neither listened to nor looked at anything that I brought from you or others."

---

[1] *Selections*, p. 170.

[2] That is, one of 20th January carried by du Croc, before the murder, that of 10th February carried by Clerneau and the one of 18th February carried by Dolu.

[3] *Selections*, p. 173.

The letter from the Archbishop is the celebrated one, of which so much is made by the Queen's enemies, which urges her, for her honour's sake, to make greater effort to pursue the conspirators, and tells her that she is "wrangouslie calumneit to be the motive principal of the haill of all." If Mary had yet any spirit left, can one suppose she would have taken this without reply[1]? But there is none! No more need be said; there is enough to make my point that the shock of the Sunday night, 9/10th February, had indeed affected the normal course of her understanding.

About a week after the death of Darnley, Mary went or was taken to Seton. Her enemies, of course, allege her reason to be a cynical indifference to the customary mourning, but Bishop Leslie gives another cause, namely, that she was "most earnestly dehorted by the vehement exhortations and persuasions of her Council, who were moved thereto by her physicians' information, declaring to them the great and imminent dangers of her health and life, if she did not in all speed break up and leave that kind of close and solitary life, and repair to some good and wholesome air" (*Defence*, in Anderson, 1). At Seton she remained[2] until the coming of Killigrew brought her to Edinburgh on or about 7th March. I suppose that she was then somewhat better, but again broke down at the critical moment (p. 169).

In Drury's memoranda of 29th March, intended, as I have said, for Cecil's eye only, he gives some further light on the situation:

She has been for the most part either melancholy or sickly ever since[3], in especial this week upon Tuesday and Wednesday (25th and

---

[1] I think this letter is liable to a very different interpretation to that generally put on it, but this belongs to the next chapter.

[2] I neglect a statement in the 'Diurnal' that she returned to Edinburgh on the 19th which is certainly untrue. The story of the junketing at Tranent is not more reliable. It is curious to note that this tale and some others find their way into the 'Book of Articles,' and are derived from Drury's collections of malicious spy-stories. It is not contained in the 'Detection,' and we are justified in concluding that Cecil's hand in the preparation of the 'Book' is apparent. See also Mahon, *Indictment of Mary, Queen of Scots*, p. 21.

[3] It is not quite clear whether by *ever since* he refers to the arrival of Clerneau with the letter of the Archbishop of Glasgow, or whether he means, in general, since the murder.

26th March) often swooned...the Queen breaketh very much, upon Sunday last (23rd March, the fortieth day after the murder) divers were witness, for there was Mass of requiem and dirige for the King's soul.

In his open letter of the day following, 30th March, the same writer merely says: "The Queen is troubled this last week with some sickness of which she is not yet all free of." I conclude that Elizabeth was not to know too much.

In his letter of 20th May, after her disastrous marriage with Bothwell, Drury speaks more plainly: "The opinion of divers is that she is the most changed woman of face that in so little time, without extremity of sickness, they have seen....It is thought the Queen *has long had a spice of the falling sickness and has of late been troubled therewith*[1]." At last the cards are on the table. Can it be doubted that all her life Mary was subject to a tendency to epileptic seizure, ordinarily mild, that it became more pronounced during her illness at Jedburgh, and that, having recovered from this, it recurred with violence and frequency after the shock of February?

Dementia, apathy, dreamy confusion, stupor are outward signs of the temporary post-epileptic insanity which may and often do follow severe cases; at that time little understood, they were attributed to witchcraft. The available evidence goes to confirm the hypothesis. Immense care was taken to prevent the outside world from having opportunity to ascertain her condition. While at Seton, we are told, the gates were closely guarded; when, later, she was taken to Parliament to declare her freedom, she was surrounded by soldiers, to the exclusion of the ordinary guard of the city burgesses; still later the Lords, in vindication of their action, declared that the Sovereign had been surrounded day and night by 200 harquebusiers, and few or none admitted to her speech[2].

At Lochleven we know that no independent outsider, French

---

[1] The last item is apparently one of several notes not part of the letter proper.

[2] Lords to Throckmorton, 11th July, 1567, printed in Keith, II, pp. 677 ff.

or English, was permitted to see her. Surely we are entitled to believe that there was something to conceal. Claude Nau, whose Lochleven information is reliable, tells us that there "she remained 15 days without eating or drinking, or conversing with any, many thought she would have died."

It need not be supposed that the Queen was in a state of madness equivalent to what, in those days, was described as "phrenzy"; her state, as I suppose, resembled that of Juana, mother of the Emperor Charles V, of whom it is told that she could on occasion be brought before public assemblies of the deputies, and could be discreet and sensible but was uncertain, and, in general, liable to extravagant actions[1]. One gathers this condition in Mary's case from many hints in the contemporary records.

In the vindication of the Lords referred to above occurs the words: "We thought...that within a short time her mind being a little settled, and the eyes of her understanding opened, she would better consider of herself...." A week later Throckmorton wrote: "I would to God that she were in case to be negotiated with." In the same month of July, the words put into her demission of the Crown included: "We are so vexed and wearied that our body, spirit *and senses* are altogether unable to travail in this room (position)." In August, the Secretary Maitland spoke of her thus: "Presently she is none other to be satisfied than a very sick person in an extreme disease is to be pleased in their inordinate appetites." Bedford reported in July: "The Queen is now somewhat calmed and better quieted than of late and takes both rest and meat." The rest and quiet at Lochleven might be expected to bring back her wandering mind, though I suggest that she never had more than a hazy recollection of the horrors of the fatal night in February.

There is a picture of this "shell" of the former graceful Mary, after the day of Carberry Hill, when her flint-hearted nobles carried her captive to the Provost's house in Edinburgh, which alone should prove the case: "She came to the said window

[1] Cf. Prescott, *Ferdinand and Isabella*, 1901; Merriman, *Rise of the Spanish Empire*, 1918; Villa, *Juana la Loca*, 1892.

sundry times in so miserable a state, her hairs hanging about her ears, and her breast, yea the most part of all her body, from the waist up, bare and discovered, that no man could look upon her but she moved him to pity and compassion[1]." It does not take a stretch of imagination to conjecture the effect of such a day as Mary had passed upon her enfeebled mentality—fatigued, excited, wanting food, "scarce to be holden upon horseback for grief and faintness[2]," thus she had come to her capital for the last time.

Once it is recognized that from that day of February the equilibrium of the Queen's mind was unsettled, some things otherwise inexplicable become clear—the day at Carberry Hill, for instance. Some wayward impulse induced her to free herself of Bothwell's influence and to throw herself on her people's mercy. Yet it has to be admitted that, in the later stages of her mania, the predominant note was infatuation for Bothwell; and this is a problem that cannot be set aside.

From the earliest records we have of her, obedience, submission to rule, gives the outstanding trait of her character. Her letters to her mother, her attitude during her married life in France, her sovereignty in Scotland, all point to an absence of assertion. Nowhere do we find that Mary *ruled*; on the contrary, at the outset we hear of the dominance of her brother the Lord James, then a certain timid assertion in her negotiations for a Spanish marriage; goaded by the subterfuges of Cecil into the Darnley match, she yields her will entirely to his; later, Leslie and Balfour control her, and finally Bothwell. I have said, and after close study of all the circumstances, I maintain, that Bothwell's influence did not become a *guiding* factor until after the death of Darnley. Before that she looked on him as a staunch supporter in time of need, but, as a councillor, or even as a capable leader, she had no reason to value him highly. The natural character of the woman, but most especially the weakened state of her mind after February, left her an easy prey to evil design.

[1] John Beton to his brother, 17th June, 1567, Sloane MS., printed in Laing, II, pp. 109 ff.
[2] Calderwood, II, p. 365.

"It must be added, as was believed at the time with every appearance of probability, that Bothwell threw the Queen's mind into a confused state by means of magical arts and so brought her to consent to the marriage." Thus wrote Bishop Leslie in his *Paralipomena ad Historiam*[1], and he was in close touch with all that went on. I do not pretend to knowledge of what is possible in imposing *will* on a suitable subject; I can only say that a more suitable subject than was the Queen of Scots at this time could not be found. Certainly there is a very widespread belief that such things are done, and Bothwell's skill in "necromancy" is confirmed, if that is a proper word to use, by at least half a dozen independent contemporary statements. While these pages were in the writing a remarkable article appeared in the *Morning Post*, by Mr Edgar Wallace; it was headed "The New Crime," and its object was to call attention to cases of criminals who "Can, by the exercise of his or her personality and mental gifts, dominate a weaker mentality and make a profit thereon." "The law does not recognize any such human power, but only the most stupid amongst us will deny that it exists." Whether this form of crime is *new* or not I must leave to the reader's judgment[2].

Lest it be argued that Mary's mental debility may have commenced after her illness at Jedburgh and that she gave way to homicidal mania at Kirk o' Field, I reply briefly that the facts of the crime set forth in the remainder of this volume in no wise harmonize with her complicity, and, secondly, that there is no sign that she was mentally afflicted before the fatal day. She was

[1] Translated by Forbes-Leith.

[2] Since this paragraph was written there is testimony even more closely touching our subject from such an authority as Dr James Drever, who in a letter to the same newspaper says: "Neurotic and hysterical subjects develop 'transference' with extreme facility, and are very easily hypnotized." By the word "transference" I understand that control of the power of will passes to the "master," and especially the emotion of affection, or rather, I should suggest, a kind of dog-like devotion not quite on the same plane as what we call "love." While on this point let me add that Mary's "submission" seems to have been intermittent and probably only complete when the dementia was acute.

seen of many, by Sir John Forster at Halydon Hill, by the Earl of Bedford, the Comte de Brienne, and a number of nobles neutral and unconcerned in the tragedy; there is no hint, no sign of such a case; there are, however, many *facts* to the contrary.

To follow further Mary's marriage with Bothwell is beyond the scope of this work. I have carried the question thus far because the *fact* of the marriage is held by her enemies as the strongest proof of her complicity in Darnley's death. A noted historian, Dr Robertson, I think, is alleged to have said on hearing of the publication of Whitaker's *Vindication*, "Tell me if he has proved that she did not marry Bothwell, if so, I will read it." He who made this remark had a narrow outlook; the circumstances I have set out above without heroics account for it[1]. Of Mary's horror and unhappiness at her situation there is record in plenty—and her enemies call it "remorse," forgetting that elsewhere they give her a character which could not include such a sentiment.

DARNLEY AS A PLOTTER AGAINST HIS QUEEN

The object of the last section of this chapter is to show that the plot at Kirk o' Field was not the only occasion on which Darnley had aimed at sovereignty.

Of Darnley himself not much need be said. He had not completed his nineteenth year when he arrived in Scotland; a tall, overgrown lad, one can imagine that he required rather to be kept back than thrust into the vortex of controversy. His father claimed the position of "second person" in the realm of Scotland, imputing bastardy to the head of the Hamiltons, both descended from King James II. His mother, born in England, claimed, as granddaughter of Henry VII, a right to the English succession,

---

[1] M. de Pimodan in his book, *La Mère des Guises*, has struck a truer note: "(She) seemed not to have had entire consciousness of her acts, her health was seriously affected, her reason was shaken under the weight of misfortunes unprecedented, and nothing could more excuse her than to see the catholic Queen, granddaughter of Antoinette, consent in her aberration to marry Bothwell according to protestant rites."

which, at all events during the reign of Mary Tudor, purported to be superior to that of Elizabeth. Strongly Catholic, she, and after her, her son, were regarded by many disaffected adherents of the old religion as the rightful occupants of the throne. Between the Earl of Lennox and the Scottish throne, neglecting the Hamiltons, stood Mary; between the Lady Lennox and the English throne stood Mary again, neglecting, that is, her alien birth. In the Catholic interest, Philip of Spain had shown favour to Lady Lennox and encouraged her, but had never, so far as I know, openly supported her in any active assertion of right. At the least, it can be said that, failing Mary, the Lord Darnley combined in his person a claim on both thrones, to which, given opportunity, the Catholic Powers would not hesitate to subscribe.

Whatever may be said about the Earl of Lennox, he was in his younger days a man of action; he was approaching the sixties when killed at Stirling, but there is no reason to suppose him other than sound of constitution; his wife had the reputation of exceptional strength of character, and she also lived to a good age (died 1578, aged 63); the son had apparently nothing against him hereditarily. Yet, nurtured on vanity and high aspirations, combined, as I have said, with his outgrown strength, his *naturel* was guided in channels which led to a vicious and violent disposition; it may be, I think probably was, the case that much that he did was put into his head by others, but even if that were so, they found a ready pupil, unrestrained by any code of honour or humanity.

From the beginning he aimed at the "Crown Matrimonial," a term which included succession if his wife died childless[1], and Mary would have granted it but for difficulties with the Hamiltons and the Estates. To Darnley, almost certainly, the Crown Matrimonial was but the stepping-stone to the Crown Absolute, and no compunction as to wife or child would weigh in the balance. Even his overweening vanity could hardly conjure up sufficient power to hold the position, without the promise of external support, and this I believe he had; but he was not wise enough to see all the difficulties.

[1] Cf. Robertson, I, p. 377.

I have already noticed the extent to which Mary submitted her will to his, and that the expulsion of the Earl of Moray from the kingdom was rather his act than hers, but we do not come in contact with his real aims until February 1566, some eight months after his marriage: "I know," wrote Randolph, "that there are practices in hand, contrived between father and son, to come to the crown against her will...many things more grievous and worse are brought to my ears, yea, things intended against the Queen's own person[1]." These words introduced, so to speak, the Riccio plot on to the stage, though it is true that Randolph when he wrote this letter was on the eve of expulsion from Scotland, and his spite, which I have not quoted, may be discounted; but, as an actor, he may be trusted to have known the details of the approaching murder of Riccio.

It is not my purpose to take up time with this affair, except as to two of its aspects. There is no need to strike a high note as to the abominable nature of the intention to "remove" Riccio; we are living in the sixteenth century, and the man was justly regarded as an important agent of the Catholic revival. The expulsion of the Protestant Lords was, as we shall see later, the first plank of the revival, and Darnley, urged by Riccio, had already done something towards its realization. The expelled Earl of Moray was at Newcastle, the Earl of Bedford was at Berwick where he was soon joined by Randolph, the Earl of Morton was at Edinburgh. These, the principals, were in communication with each other, and with Cecil in London. To destroy Riccio and restore the Earl of Moray was, according to the sixteenth-century standard, a *clean* plot.

Unfortunately it could not remain so—Darnley was a necessary adjunct. He hated Moray and would gladly have seen his forfeiture passed by the Parliament now called for that purpose. He was, and I would ask that this may be noted, imbued with the same desire to get rid by any means of the Protestant leaders which runs through all the writings of the Catholic party—a desire, again please note, to which Mary had refused to subscribe. Yet, without Darnley, who alone, in his position of

[1] Letter to Leicester, 13th February, 1566.

titular King, could prorogue the Parliament in the temporary absence of the Queen, the plot would fail. Moreover, the shield afforded by the connivance of the King was of importance in this act of highest treason, the warding of the person of the Queen.

It is well known that Darnley was lured into the net by the promise, under signed bond, of the Crown, failing the Queen's issue. But, and this is my second point, it is not so fully recognized that the murder of Riccio in the presence of the Queen was Darnley's own addition to the plan of the conspirators. There is not a shadow of a doubt that he intended the death of his wife as well as that of the unborn child. Necessarily this must be so, for, the Queen living and the child born, his treasonable acquirement of the Crown Matrimonial would be not merely useless but detrimental. The story that he planned the murder of Riccio in defence of his honour would have weighed nothing in the eyes of the Catholic powers against the fact that he reinstated the Protestant Lords and swore to establish their religion[1].

The opinion on the Continent is succinctly given by the Venetian Ambassador, Barbaro, writing after Mary's illness at Jedburgh, some seven months after the murder of Riccio. He attributes her illness, as usual, to the effects of poison, and adds: "By whom and with what design this great wickedness has been

---

[1] A word about the so-called Ruthven Narrative, which purports to give the whole details of the event by an eyewitness. Whether the dying Lord Ruthven had indeed the leading part in dictating this long document of some 6000 words is doubtful, it is far more likely that Randolph put the whole in a form that would best suit the requirements of Cecil. It is at least certain that the writing was sent to Cecil for correction on 2nd April (Bain, II, of that date), and the result of his emendation, returned to Berwick, was issued dated 30th April (cf. Keith, III, pp. 260 ff.). It harps almost altogether on the King as the originator of the murder; on the other hand, another document similarly purporting to be from the hands of Ruthven and Morton, and sent to the Earl of Bedford for the information of Elizabeth, stresses that the execution "tended to no other fyne (end) but to the establishing of the religion," conservation of the amity, and relief of the Earl of Moray and his friends, "whose actions and ours are coupled and convened all in one" (*Selections*, p. 169).

perpetrated, your Serenity, who remembers past affairs, may form your own judgment." The truth of the Riccio affair was a long time in reaching Paris, and all the first reports, apparently emanating from London[1], were to the effect that the King of Scotland had murdered his wife, admitted the heretics and seized the kingdom. It must be concluded that this, the anticipated ending of the revolution, had been spread by Cecil or had leaked out through his messengers. De Silva, writing to Philip, definitely says that Cecil told Lady Margaret (Lennox) of the murder the night *before* it occurred[2].

One word more, it is not possible to suppose that Darnley and his father, or even Darnley without the father's advice[3], acted thus with any sincere intention to promote the Protestant cause. Neither could have been so foolish as to rely on the permanency of the undertaking to place him (Darnley) on the throne. Their only strength lay in Philip and the Catholics, and neither would have exchanged this asset for the doubtful support of Elizabeth. What was the attitude of King Philip in the matter? I wish I knew the answer; Catherine de Médici drops a little hint, but it rather whets one's curiosity than satisfies it: "I am unable to believe that the news (of the Riccio murder) has not already reached Spain by other means than ours, which I beg you will ascertain and inform me, *as also how the King Catholic received it...*[4]." At least Catherine suspects the special interest of Philip, and, if her innuendo that he had provided a means of early information is correct, it seems to infer that Philip was not unaware that a catastrophe was approaching. Fourquevaux's answer *to Catherine* is not forthcoming, but—and this is another little point which adds to our curiosity—there is his answer addressed to Charles IX which, though it is not at all the same thing, yet, even in the smooth phrases of the diplomatist, yields a good deal.

---

[1] Cf. Pollen, p. 472.   [2] *Simancas*, 6th April, 1566.
[3] De Silva gives a significant little hint in referring to "the unwillingness of the King to be controlled by his father in all things" (*Simancas*, 11th February, 1566).
[4] *Letters*, C. de M. to Fourquevaux, 8th April, 1566.

Fourquevaux's reply to the Paris letters of the 8th April is dated 30th April[1]. The Queen of Spain, he says, had not received the news before he told her, that was on the 25th April. He then had audience of Philip and expatiated on the fact of the murder and the ingratitude of Darnley, couching his language so as to excite the monarch's wrath. Philip replied that he knew about it since last month (March), his news coming by way of Flanders; he expressed his dislike of the outrage:

Then (says Fourquevaux) I carried the conversation a little further, to see if I could induce him to say or offer that he would aid in supporting the just quarrel of the said Lady, *but no such word escaped him now* (mais ce mot ne lui est point échappé maintenant), though I am told that at the time of the late rebellion (Moray's rising of July/ October, 1565) he said he would employ his whole power to assist the said Lady to bring her rebel subjects to obedience.

It may be that I see molehills where there are but worm casts, yet, in this broad hint—in the one word *maintenant* which contains a volume—and in Catherine's pointed enquiry, am I unduly suspicious in believing that Philip's attitude towards Mary had changed during the eight months or so succeeding her marriage; was there already something in Philip's secretive mind pointing to Mary as having committed the great sin—interference with his regality of the Netherlands—and the lesser sin, infidelity to Holy Religion? It is a minor point but strange, that Mary's companion from infancy, the Queen of Spain, was kept in the dark as to these occurrences.

Let us note, *en passant*, that in these early months of the year 1566 the turmoil in the Low Countries was definitely shaping to a struggle between the Spaniard and the nobles. Philip, the spider of Segovia, was already luring the flies who had dared to disturb his web; Egmont had been invited to Spain[2] but had

---

[1] It is another straw, if a small one, that there is a letter from Fourquevaux to Catherine of the same date, but it treats of indifferent subjects, without reference to her questionnaire. This seems to add to the probability that the carrier had verbal instructions. (*Bibl. Nat. Fonds Français* 10,751.)

[2] Gachard, I, p. cxxxii.

gained another eighteen months of liberty and life by refusing; Montigny had gone in his stead and never returned; and Carlos was under observation. Mary—she had sinned, too[1]. Secrecy of movement was carried by Philip to the level of a fine art, and we can expect to find little evidence; yet I think he was not guiltless of inciting Lennox and his son to take the place of Mary—unworthy though they were to fill it—and thus to further the cause of Holy Religion and private revenge at the same time. A bold statement; I am conscious of my difficulties—they belong to the next chapter.

The baptism of the infant prince, and the events immediately preceding it, are factors in the fate of Mary to which insufficient weight has been given. Darnley's ambition Crownwards, crushed for a time after his failure in the Riccio affair, was by no means dead. The birth of a legitimate heir, whether the mother lived or died, threw his pretensions out of gear; the best he could hope for was a Regency and the care of the infant's slender life. The ceremony of baptism, the father being present, would, it might be hoped, give the quietus to that calumny known to everyone who mattered, that Riccio had been slain as a matter of the King's honour. The presence of representatives of England, France and Savoy[2] would set the seal of official recognition.

"Darnley," wrote Catherine de Médici on hearing of the birth of the prince, "is so bad that I do not know if he feels as he should[3]." This is the keynote, and, as it appears to me, he set himself to make what profit he could out of his

[1] Cf. Mahon, *Mary Queen of Scots*, pp. 45 ff.

[2] It is remarkable that Spain was not represented. De Silva (*Simancas*, under date 25th June, 1566) hints that there were reasons why Mary refrained from an invitation, but she asked Savoy as "she considered him a person attached to your Majesty." Perhaps it was the old question of precedence, but on such an occasion this might have been surmounted. Less than a year previously, de Silva had represented Philip at the Parma marriage in Brussels. Had there been desire for his presence it could have been arranged. The tardy coming of the envoy from Savoy is also difficult to explain. Spain and Savoy certainly acted in common.

[3] Letters to Duchess de Nemours, 30th June, 1566.

position. At this stage, however, it will be better to pass over the methods by which Darnley sought his ends. All that went on during the months that passed between the birth and the baptism is so bound up with external influences that the Second part of this book is more suited to the subject. Indirectly the plotting against the Queen continued, but here let us confine ourselves to direct action—local action, we might term it.

Chiefly by means of the second and third narratives of Lennox and by the 'Book of Articles,' we get an indistinct notion of what has been described as the "quarrel" at Stirling. We learn from these documents, which are, of course, written with intent to inculpate the Queen to the maximum possible extent, that the Earl of Lennox did, in fact, appoint certain gentlemen of Lennox "and others the King's friends" to resort to Stirling. The exact time of this assembly is not given, but we must conclude that it preceded the baptism, and must have been between the 11th December, when Mary arrived there, and the 14th, when the Ambassadors gathered for the ceremony. It is clear that suspicions were aroused by the number of these partisans of Lennox, and precautions were taken against surprise. Mary complained personally to Darnley, according to the story, and in reply he was truculent, declaring that he would take his adherents whithersoever he wished. These seem to be the broad facts without the "colour" added by the narrators. We can imagine that neither Mary nor her councillors wished to make any fuss at the moment.

But a little more light is thrown on the matter by the affair of William Walker, and of this we are on more certain ground in referring to a letter sent by the Queen to the Archbishop of Glasgow, dated 20th January, 1567, in which she says:

Lately a servant of yours named William Walker came to our presence, being for the time at Stirling (she left Stirling on 12th January), and ... declared to us how it was not only openly rumoured, but also he had heard by reports of persons whom he esteemed lovers of us, that the King, by the assistance of some of the nobility, should

13-2

take the Prince, our son, and crown him; and, being crowned, as his father, should take upon him the government[1].

Walker was examined before the Council, and various witnesses cited by him were sent for at different times, so that quite a number of days must have been spent on the enquiry, bringing the date of Walker's first information at least to early January, and therefore removed from the "quarrel" at Stirling by not many days.

It is easy to understand that Mary did not desire to prosecute the matter to the end, for her whole thoughts were directed towards the *rapprochement* opened by Elizabeth[2], and peace with her husband was essential. For our present object it is only necessary to point out that at a date during the later half of December, when Kirk o' Field and everything connected with it was still six weeks and more in the future, there were rumours, and to some extent definite action, indicating on Darnley's part an intention to seize the Prince, to crown him, and assume the government. This involves two things, the destruction of the mother and the support of some foreign power, for Lennox and Darnley had not of themselves sufficient following.

What foreign power? The reference made by Mary to the assistance given by "some of the nobility" is puzzling. One may feel almost assured that none of the principal nobles was at this time on Darnley's side—very much the contrary, for, while Lennox could count on a number of the lesser barons or lairds, and probably on the Tullibardine Murrays and some of the Borderers as the Cessford Kers, all these together would not count for much. This was no Protestant plot, as was the case when Riccio was murdered. All Darnley's recent efforts had been Romewards or Spainwards; Philip, said rumour, was certainly coming to the Netherlands, Alva had already been appointed and would shortly be in motion. I will say no more at present. One thing emerges, when Mary left Stirling she carried her

---

[1] The letter is in Labanoff, 1, pp. 395 ff.

[2] Who had at last agreed to a revision of the objectionable clauses of the Treaty of Edinburgh, and a consideration of the question of the succession.

child with her, in "the depth of a sharp winter," as Buchanan puts it; the reason is clear, she did not trust the Tullibardine Lady of Mar, nor what might happen in her absence.

Darnley escaped from Stirling on the 25th December, 1566, most likely at night. I use the word escaped, for he certainly went without notice given, and had his going been known he would probably have been stopped. Whether Mary followed him to try and persuade him to remain with her is a moot point on which I can add nothing to a note in a previous volume[1]. Presumably he joined his father in Glasgow on the 26th, and there within a very short time fell ill.

I confess to having some doubts if Darnley was as sick as he made out, though there is not, it is true, much on which to found suspicion. The Queen sent her physician to visit him, so says Bedford on the 9th January, at a time when truth was not at such a discount as it afterwards became; but Buchanan in his 'Detection' says precisely the reverse: "The Queen would not suffer so much as a physician to come to him." As Buchanan's frequent method was to use facts and turn them inside out, one rather gathers that the physician was sent but refused admission to the patient[2]. It is likely that the condition of the sick man did not bear too much expert inspection. In any case it is clear from the "long" Glasgow Letter that an extended correspondence had taken place between the Queen and her husband, at the time when his malady should have been acute: "I asked him," says Mary, "about his letters, wherein he complained of the cruelty of some," and the answer was, that *she* would not accept his offers and repentance, and then he vowed never to sin any more if but this once he might be forgiven.

And Mary forgave him, though I think it was rather policy than spirit that moved her, for the *pourparlers* with Elizabeth were just commencing, reconciliation was imperative. But, though

---

[1] Mahon, *Indictment of Mary Queen of Scots*, p. 51, n. 14.

[2] It is worth noting that Buchanan in the 'Indictment' omits his former statement altogether. Moreover, he tones down all the original story of poison which embroidered the Latin work. See Mahon, *Indictment of Mary Queen of Scots*, pp. 38–9.

she forgave, she did not trust him. We can hardly doubt that the Lennox family dwelling at "Stable Green" in Glasgow, where Darnley lay, could have accommodated her, and he "was very fane that I should lodge in his lodging"; but she refused to quit her confined quarters at Provand's Lordship. There she was guarded by the Hamiltons and Lord Livingston.

That Darnley's repentance was sincere is not to be believed for a moment; the black-hearted scoundrel of the Riccio murder *could* not be sincere. He knew well enough how important it was to the policy that he should remain with Mary, and my reading of the garbled tales is that he cajoled her into the visit to Glasgow by his letters of contrition coupled with a promise to return with her. Whether he hoped for an opportunity to carry out his nefarious design at Glasgow I cannot say, but I think it very probable. It was at Glasgow that he received the "report" of Sir James Balfour that Kirk o' Field was a suitable place for his purpose.

Mary's visit to Glasgow must have been a State necessity of the most important kind[1]. Darnley's health alone certainly did not require it. Her mind must have been fully occupied with the advances made by Elizabeth towards the settlement of those outstanding questions which had been causes of anxiety during all her active reign in Scotland; a ten days' absence from Edinburgh was the last thing she would choose. Bedford's mission included the long-deferred acknowledgement that the Treaty of Edinburgh did in fact contain words "prejudicial to her title as next heir," and offered "a new treaty between us." Mary had replied that she would send some of her Council to "treat, confer and accord with you and your Council...." Sir Robert Melville was despatched on 8th February to London to open the new negotiations, and it is remarkable that his 'Instructions' have not been preserved. It is probable, I might say certain, that they

---

[1] In case you have not thought of it, just picture to yourself the effect on the forthcoming negotiations if the father of the heir-expectant was in the Netherlands, attached to the Court of the Duchess of Parma, and placing all the influence of his inherited position at the disposal of Philip.

contained much in confirmation of Cecil's own report to Sir Henry Norris: "My Lord of Bedford...arrived here but of late and has brought us good report from the Scottish Queen, of her good disposition to keep peace and amity with the Queen's Majesty[1]."

I can understand that it would not be politic to preserve a document, drafted on the eve of the Kirk o' Field tragedy, which would show how much the mind of the Queen of Scotland was occupied with the matter which for years had been so near her heart, and how little she was thinking of all the horrible things laid to her charge; but I do not understand why no historian mentions the fact of Melville's dispatch[2]. To me it seems a matter of importance, and, if there were not one other scrap of evidence to show Mary's innocence, I think that Bedford's mission and the subsequent action thereon, occurring at the very time when Mary was alleged to be taking steps which must inevitably destroy her dearest hopes, would be strong presumptive testimony in her favour.

THE CRISIS

I had another object in referring to Melville's dispatch, and it brings us to the conclusion of this chapter. Writers who circumscribe their story by a narrow circle drawn round an alleged passion of Mary for Bothwell must employ a wider lens to get at the truth. To carry the reader with me in my estimate of the political situation at the close of the year 1566 and the first few weeks of the new year is my great desire, and I feel uncertain of my ability to do so with the necessary brevity. I will not use expressions of probability or doubt, I will simply state what I believe.

It was obvious that a crisis was at hand. Elizabeth, in agreement that Darnley must go—as witness the secret bond with Moray and Morton,—was inclining to a policy of agreement with Mary on all outstanding questions, including the succession, with conditions, and, it may be, confined to Mary's son. She

---

[1] Cabala, 10th February, 1567.
[2] Except Froude, who misrepresents it (VIII, p. 82).

was feeling the pinch of the *Drang nach Osterreich*—the Austrian marriage—into which she was being drawn. She had just emerged from a serious conflict with her Lords and Commons on the question, and marriage was abhorrent to her who knew well that she was physically unfit. She had stormed about her right to marry as she chose, but in fact the choice was being forced on her. Mary and her son were her means of escape. Bedford's mission was genuine; the question of religion was not insurmountable; Mary was at least as open-minded as the Archduke Charles, and both were known to have middle views, that is, a Lutheran tendency.

It is a remarkable fact that the Archduke as a suitor was accepted by both Cecil on behalf of Elizabeth and by the Cardinal of Lorraine on behalf of Mary. I do not want to repeat what has been said elsewhere, but the inference is clear that, from different poles, the two had the same end in view. In a recently published work, *Queen Elizabeth and some Foreigners*[1], we have laid open before us all the complexities which were confronting the political parties at the time.

Cecil, with his inborn hatred of Lorraine, yet favoured the Austrian, perhaps only because he knew nothing could come of it, but, unquestionably, the alternative found from him no support. There was a violent dispute with his mistress; he threatened to leave her; ultimately he dragged her with him to Mary's destruction.

But in the months October–December 1566 the crisis was culminating. To the Ultramontanes the final loss of all hope of Counter-Reformation if Elizabeth should agree with Mary; to Cecil and the English Puritans the dread of another Mary controlling England.

Of Cecil's action to destroy the hope (Darnley) of the English Catholics we know; of the ultramontane effort to destroy the Queen and to capture her son, something has been said, but now we must go farther. From the day that Elizabeth undertook to be "gossip" to Mary's child, and the gold font was made, the forces of the churches militant were in motion.

[1] Von Klarwill, tr. by Professor T. H. Nash, London, 1928.

PART II

Chapter IV

CAUSE

COUNTER-REFORMATION

PROFESSOR SIR JOHN SEELY[1] has painted with a large brush the inception of the idea of Counter-Reformation. He launches it fully equipped in the year 1564, "when the Council of Trent closed its sittings. This event was in a manner the settlement of the religious question of the age. It was a settlement which had the effect of giving to Catholicism a superiority in Europe...." In the painting some outlines are blurred which had been better preserved. The results of the Council can hardly be regarded as satisfactory or as a settlement. The decrees were never accepted in France, and with demur even in Spain[2]. It was necessary to pack the jury and bring the Council to a hasty close in order to preserve the Papacy itself from subordination to the Council.

Whether it be true, as claimed by a great authority[3], that Pius IV pressed from the moment of his election for the assembly of a Council, or whether, as alleged by others, his intention was rather to talk than to act, it is at least certain that he had no real design to bring the leaders of the heretical sects into equal debate with the Fathers of the Church of Rome. Safe conducts might pass the solemn assent of the Council, but freedom was not possible in a body ruled by Legates instructed from Rome. It is hard to believe other than that the fear of national action in France to settle the matter by conference at home was the goad that brought the Council into being; it might be added that,

---

[1] *The Growth of British Policy*, p. 27, Cambridge, 1895.
[2] Cf. Pastor, *Gesch*. Pius IV, p. 550.
[3] Pastor, tr. xv, Intro. p. xxxiv.

however Philip might rail against Gallicism, he had very similar ideas as regards Spain, and this was an additional spur in Rome.

The main achievement was reform within the Church, and in this Charles of Lorraine was the protagonist; it was not in the scheme of things planned at Rome that reform should come by instruction from without. The deliberations exhibited the divisions within the fold quite as clearly as did the progress of external heresy.

But it may be agreed that the very failure of the Council to face the crisis with unanimity brought home to the Papacy the paramount necessity of urgent action. As to this, however, the French historian M. Henri Martin expresses a view which should be considered: "Pius IV would ask nothing better than peace, but it depended no longer on Rome to check the movement begun in Europe; the true centre of the Catholic action was in Spain." Pius was old, his health broken, his time occupied by a mass of business consequent on the Council; no strong measures issued from Rome during the two years of life that remained to him.

Philip, it can be admitted, was the material stay of the Papacy, but his personal bigotry did not prevent him from exploiting his power to his own ends: "Ye in Spain would be Pope and carry all to your King's advantage," is a remark attributed to Pius; religion and political advantage went hand in hand with the Spanish king[1].

But, besides Philip, there was another and even more powerful weapon for the defence of the Church. In the Council of Trent the man whose incisive and determined language went far to maintain the authority of the Papal Chair was the Spaniard, James Lainez, successor of Loyola as Father-General of the Society of Jesus. One of the founders, he was imbued with the straitest conception of the rules of the Order; it is said indeed that he was their author.

In him was none of the vacillation which marked the speech of the majority in the Council. Ruled by Lainez, the Society

[1] Pastor, *Gesch*. Pius IV, p. 555.

was little likely to lose the impetus given by Loyola, and no one knew better than he the difficulties confronting the Counter-Reformation in Scotland. He had attended the conference at Poissy and had become aware of the atmosphere which surrounded Mary Stuart when she left France; and he had been the recipient of the reports sent by Father de Gouda of his mission in 1562 to Scotland. He knew of her refusal to enter on a course of violence, and it cannot be doubted that he shared de Gouda's opinion that, without marriage with a strong Catholic prince, there was no hope that the Queen would or could make headway against the forces opposed to the reinstatement of the old religion. Father Lainez died a year after the closing of the Council. It may be assumed that he had expressed his views as to the course to be followed; but, to put them into execution, required a more determined attitude than could then be expected from the Pontiff.

The election of Michael Ghislieri to the Holy Chair in January 1566 as Pope Pius V was the real commencement of counter-action, to quell the rising force of the Reformation. In him the Church found a champion ignorant of the dilatory methods of diplomacy; austere and rigorous in his own life, he insisted on the same from those around him. Cardinal and Grand Inquisitor of the Roman Church, he had acquired the reputation of unshrinking disregard for mere human suffering, if thereby souls could be brought back from heresy. He declared in solemn assembly after his election that heresy, false doctrine, and schism should be banished, and the safety of the Church assured[1]. It was natural that he should employ the militant organization of the Society of Jesus to penetrate the ramparts which had been reared to divide Christian unity.

The Society had stood high in the favour of Pius IV, who had confirmed and extended their privileges. The Council of Trent had acknowledged the Constitution. Lainez and his successor, Francis Borgia, were esteemed at Rome, but their scope was limited to peaceful penetration by education[2]. They were, during the lifetime of this Pope, to use a term employed by Father Pollen, "the handy men of the Catholic Church." To the new

[1] Pastor, *Gesch.* Pius V, p. 211.   [2] *Ibid.* Pius IV, pp. 352 ff.

Pope the combat resolved itself into a duel to the death with Calvinism, and the Jesuit Fathers became the *Sturmtruppen*, selected for courage and endurance, to lead the attack.

SCOTLAND IN THE PONTIFICATE OF PIUS IV

SOME ENVOYS OF CATHOLICISM, 1564–65

"The year 1563 closed and the year 1564 opened with singularly little done by the Holy See on behalf of Scotland. Indeed another twelve months was to pass before any affair of importance was taken in hand." This is the dictum of Father Pollen, and is doubtless correct. The mission of the Jesuit, de Gouda, has already been referred to. The missioner had been ill chosen, and the general ignorance in the outer world of the condition of Scotland was shared by him. We have only to remember the advice given to him to fit himself out with imposing array, and to carry himself so that all should know of the grandeur of his work, and compare this with the weeks of hiding, the hairbreadth escapes from the vengeance of Knox and his disciples, to recognize how small a chance a man who was already worn out, and spoke no modern language but his own, had in contending with such odds.

At this stage of our enquiry the emergence of Edmund Hay as the companion and guide of de Gouda is the interesting point. He was third son of Peter Hay of Megginch or Melginch, of ancient lineage; his two brothers Peter and James were distinguished, and their descendants were respectively Earls of Kinnoull and Carlisle. There was a fourth brother, Walter, also a member of the Society. Their mother was Margaret Crichton, of the Ruthven branch of that family.

In 1562, when Edmund Hay accompanied Nicholas de Gouda to Scotland, he was aged 28, a priest, bachelor of theology, studying at Louvain, and postulant for admission to the Society of Jesus, in which he subsequently became a distinguished member. His rapid promotion indicates his ability, and he became Rector of the Jesuit College in Paris in November 1564, and Provincial of the French Jesuits in 1574. He is described as eloquent, prudent, of noble bearing and great spirit.

With him was associated his cousin, William Crichton, also a member of the Society and distinguished for his zeal, his politico-religious activity, and his advance to high position. Megginch, where Father de Gouda lay hidden for months, was a stronghold of the most pronounced Catholic views, and in the two cousins were to be found the extremity of ardour for the Faith and the most rigid adherence to the rules of the Order.

If de Gouda's mission was a failure, so far at least as its original intention was concerned, the views carried back by Edmund Hay were clear cut and typical of the neophyte fervidly in earnest; addressing the Father-General, he said:

> What I particularly want to impress on your paternity is, that all plans hitherto suggested (to bring about counter-reformation in Scotland), however prudent and pious their authors, will be premature, not to say absolutely useless, as long as the Queen's illegitimate brother (Moray) is alive, or at any rate as long as he continues to govern the Kingdom[1].

In the hands of Lainez this warning perhaps lay unattended, for he was closely occupied with the affairs of the Council.

The year 1564, also, indicates little cordiality by way of correspondence or sending of envoys between Rome and Scotland. Stephen Wilson, a Scot, mentioned during the time of de Gouda's mission as a servant of the Queen, was present in Rome; but there is nothing to show that he was sent there by her, nor indeed is it at all clear that he was in Mary's service. To him the Pope entrusted a letter, dated 15th June, 1564, together with a printed copy of the decrees of the Council of Trent. Mary's reply[2] is dated 20th October of the same year, but the reason for the long delay is not known. Her letter is in French, which was unusual in addressing the Pontiff. It seems distinctly lukewarm so far as the decrees are concerned and, for the rest, it contains the common formulæ of devotion and her hope for union in the

---

[1] Forbes-Leith, p. 80, dated 2nd January, 1563.
[2] Printed in Labanoff, VII, p. 6.

Church, if by the grace of God the heresies can be overcome under the efforts "which Your Holiness *will be* able to employ." Intentional or not, the phrasing seems to imply that so far Rome has done little, and seems an echo of sentiments expressed in France concerning decrees and other things.

Possibly Mary's answer was brought back by Wilson, but again no haste was made in carrying the letter. He was in Paris about January 1565, and was viewed with a little suspicion by the Jesuit fathers: "We shall see how he behaves in Paris, here (Rome) he was *poco quieto*[1]. We wish he could make some spiritual exercises there[2]." Not until April 1565 did Mary's letter of the previous October reach Rome, and the response thereto was purely formal[3]. To encourage her to accept the decrees she is told that the other Catholic kings have accepted the Council very cheerfully, a statement that she must have heard with surprise.

However, the point is that "papistical" Mary was at the moment not very much *en accord* with the Papacy. Indeed her thoughts appear to have moved in courses very unlikely to find favour either with Pius or Philip. We are within the span of Mary's great intrigue, or rather, of the intrigue in which she was a timid partner. Enough has already been said of the secret negotiations carried on between her and the Netherlands nobles, through the Duchess of Arschott (in which Egmont was a principal, and Cardinal Granvelle a participant, ready to sell the pass if danger threatened)[4], and of the strange fatality which brought about the simultaneous ruin of all those concerned—of Egmont, Horne, Ann of Arschott, Carlos of Spain, Mary herself, and of Cardinal Granvelle who suffered least, but remained for years in semi-exile, fearful to put himself in the power of his master Philip. Besides these the fate of Montigny, Berges, and many minor victims seems to point unerringly to a cause not fully explained either by coincidence or by religious strife.

But for the present purpose it is necessary to consider a few

---

[1] Which with the context means, perhaps, "not very fervent."
[2] Pollen, p. 486.   [3] *Ibid.* p. 189.
[4] Major-General R. H. Mahon, *Mary Queen of Scots*, p. 45.

details regarding William Chisholm, at the time Bishop Coadjutor of Dunblane, whose name is often connected with Mary
to indicate her subservience to Rome.

In February of this year of 1564, Chisholm was sent to Ann
of Arschott with some of Mary's secret correspondence on the
great matter[1]. Whether he returned to Scotland during the year
seems doubtful. In April Mary writes to Ann that she is anxiously
awaiting him[2], and there is a reference in a letter from Ann to
Cardinal Granvelle, which might indicate that he had come back
to Scotland some time in May[3]; it seems more likely, however,
that he sent his letters by Mary's French secretary Raulet, who
came to Scotland in the early days of May. At all events
Chisholm spent August and perhaps the preceding months at
Louvain, where it seems he developed a desire to join the Society;
his assiduity in Mary's service was, apparently, somewhat lax.

Chisholm's intention to join the Jesuits was gently thrust
aside by the Father-General[4], and, at the same time, a reproof
was administered for his desertion of his flock at home, and a
hint that, "in the retirement you now enjoy," preparation for
more activity may be made. It was not until the following March
(1565) that he returned to Scotland, arriving a month later than
Darnley. But, in the meantime, the views of the Jesuit head-
quarters in Rome regarding Chisholm seem to have hardened:
"The Scots Carmelite may be helped...but do not mention
entrance into the Society. We should not take him even with
the Pope's dispensation." Something was wanting in this man;
at a hazard one may guess a tendency to lip-service rather than
real service.

Early in July of 1565 Chisholm went abroad again. A curious
document is extant dated at "St Johnstoun" (Perth), 28th June,
1565, asking for safe conduct for "The gentleman, bearer hereof,
Master William Chisholm" to pass through England. Mary was
not at Perth on this date, and the irregular description of the
"bearer" makes it doubtful if the Bishop had any commission

---

[1] *Pap. d'État*, Mary to Duchess of Arschott, 20th February, 1564.
[2] Pollen, p. 450.   [3] *Pap. d'État*, 6th June, 1564.
[4] Pollen, pp. 482 ff.

from Mary at all; nor does he appear to have carried any credentials by way of letter from the Queen[1].

It is said that his mission was to obtain a dispensation for the marriage with Darnley, but this is very unlikely, for, nearly a month before he reached Rome, on the 19th August, a request for the dispensation had already been received there, through the Cardinal of Lorraine. We know of this by a letter addressed to the Papal Nuncio in France from Rome, dated 25th July, 1565, asking his opinion as to whether it should be granted[2].

Within a few days after his arrival "Master William," who had resumed his style as Lord Bishop of Dunblane, made an impassioned harangue before the Pope. The tenor of it leads one still more to suspect that it did not originate with the Queen, although he claimed to speak in her name; among other questionable phrases is this: "Her plan is that she may destroy all the enemies of the sacred faith and make away with those who disturb religious peace. To restore the Church, and the obedience and calm of former times...which she hopes she could, by the Grace of God, easily accomplish, if human council and aid do not fail her[3]."

Father Pollen observes that there seems to be an omission of some words, for which the lacuna has been left above; but he does not say if there is any indication of such omission in the original manuscript. That lacuna could be rationally filled by attributing to Mary the intentions which crop up at intervals from the time of de Gouda's visit and onwards, viz. the arrest and execution of the leaders of the Protestant party.

Probably such an idea, however obvious as a preliminary to secure the desired end, was as abhorrent to Pope Pius IV as it was to Mary, and this may account for its suppression in the records; but to suggest it as authorized by the Queen, who had

---

[1] See the passport printed in Pollen, p. 202.

[2] Pollen, p. 201. The Nuncio took time to reply but apparently did so on 27th August, received in Rome shortly before 25th September (*ibid.* p. 216), and near about that date the dispensation was sealed, though it seems to have been antedated.

[3] Pollen, p. 205. I have not exactly followed the translation on p. 208, for it seems to me that a full-stop is required at "perturbent."

already refused it once, and did so again later, proves how little she had to do with the discourse of Chisholm. It must be added here that this measure of drastic action was invariably voiced by the Jesuit Order, or by those closely affiliated with them. They alone on their side had the unflinching vision to perceive the only cure for the disease; "to chop at the very roots" was an expression used also by the Protestant party to indicate those whose removal was sought. The same sixteenth-century code in both camps!

Another point must be noticed: Chisholm mentioned that a force of ten to twelve thousand men would accomplish the purpose, and Cardinal Pachecho, writing at the same time to King Philip, mentions the same force—in a word, Spain should provide the material and Rome the gold. However, whatever the reasons were—and they may have been doubts in the Papal mind as to how far support of Mary would further the cause—the answer received by Chisholm was but cold: "Our help will never be wanting, but will be given at an opportune and suitable time....We do not think that that moment has yet arrived[1]."

Notwithstanding the urgent needs of his flock, which the Bishop had impressed on the Pope, he did not return to Scotland on leaving Rome but remained in Paris throughout the winter of 1565, residing at the Jesuit College until the spring of 1566, when, after the election of the new Pope, Pius V, he was called to fresh activities.

THE FOREIGN NEGOTIATIONS OF SCOTLAND, 1565

The correspondence which took place during the year 1565 is to be found scattered in volumes by various writers who have utilized this part or that to colour their views. Nowhere is it brought together, and only by a review of the whole can judgment be given.

The reader will recall the general circumstances of the year. The treacherous sending of Darnley to Scotland, the secret satisfaction that Mary had fallen to the bait, the feigned dis-

[1] Pius IV to Cardinal of Lorraine, 25th September, 1565, in Pollen, p. 225.

pleasure in the result, the attempt to capture the Queen and her intended husband at what came to be called the "Raid of Beith," the rebellion of the Earls of Moray and Argyll, fostered and financed from across the border; finally, the military preparations of England to force submission. The letters drafted by Cecil and signed by Elizabeth—masterpieces of hypocrisy. The galling assumption of superiority. All this and more is well known; can anyone blame the Queen of Scotland if she sought foreign assistance?

But Mary, so far as her personal part was concerned, acted openly towards her sister of England. On or about 24th July, 1565, she wrote a private letter in her own hand to Elizabeth; the letter itself is not extant, but we know something about it. That it was clearly of a most conciliatory kind is shown by the reply dated 30th July[1], "We (Elizabeth) cannot deny (that) there are many good and friendly offers therein," and again, "We were much moved in our old affection (by the letter)[2]." Of Mary's offers, conveyed by her envoy, there is a full statement in a paper preserved by Bishop Keith, though he has not correlated it to this occasion[3]; among others were the following:

Neither directly nor indirectly should any intelligence be had with England, to the detriment of Elizabeth and her lawful issue. No alliance should be made with any foreign prince to the hurt of England, but there should be a league with England for the perpetual amity and welfare of both sides. No innovation or change in religion, laws or liberties of England, should be attempted, even if, in the future, the Scottish Queen should be called to rule there.

Here at least was enough on which to build, and the wit of diplomacy should have been able to devise safeguards to obviate double dealing, if any there were. But, it must be said, peace was not desired; and if, at first, there was some show of acceptance and talk of a Commission to settle details, it was clear from the first that the English Queen, impelled by her evil genius, Cecil, had not the power to agree.

[1] Bain, II, p. 185.   [2] Bain, II, p. 187.
[3] Keith, III, pp. 232 ff., confirmed by Camden, *Annals*, p. 79.

Mary's private letter also contained this sentence, the only one preserved: "I cannot believe this comes from you[1], and without other retaliation I shall have recourse to all princes my allies to unite with me in demonstrating what my kinship is with you. You know well enough what you have done about *that*[2]." This is open and above board, hardly to be condemned by anyone of unbiased mind.

This letter was carried by John Beton, and on the same date, 24th July, she wrote to King Philip probably sending it by the same bearer. This letter[3] cannot be regarded as entirely free from equivocation; yet strongly extenuating circumstances must be admitted. It was obviously impossible for her to tell Philip she had issued a proclamation confirming freedom of conscience to all, provided she was allowed to have the same freedom. She had every reason to believe that England was about to attack her, and she was threatened at the same time with civil war; her Crown, even her liberty, were in danger; and Knox was doing his utmost to stir up rebellion, not for freedom of conscience but for exclusive privilege of his own.

What she actually said was perhaps a quibble:

I have always resisted as much as possible those of a faith contrary to my own....I am resolved to marry the son of the Earl of Lennox in order to strengthen my position...and to check this new sect[4]. They have attempted to force me to abandon my faith....I am assured that you will grant me aid and succour to maintain the faith ...nothing is more pernicious to the obedience due to princes than the tenets of these new evangelists[5]....I beg for your good will and to be in bond with you, and that your ambassador be instructed to tell the Queen of England that you will not permit anything to be done there to my prejudice....

If this letter was sent to London by Beton, it seems that it was to be forwarded only if no favourable reply to the offers of

---

[1] We have not got the context, but, expanded, this perhaps means, "I cannot believe that all the treachery of the past few months comes from you."

[2] Bain, II, p. 189.   [3] Printed in Labanoff, VII, p. 340.

[4] Of the Scottish Genevans, not more disliked by Mary than Elizabeth.   [5] Evidently the Calvinists.

conciliation with Elizabeth eventuated. Certainly its despatch, or at least its receipt, was delayed, for Philip does not acknowledge it before the 13th October, nearly three months later; and by that time new conditions had arisen.

Mary, impelled by the pressure of the Earl of Lennox, Darnley, and the Catholic extremists, was, with perfect right and justice, successfully pursuing her rebel lords. There is a letter from Paul de Foix to Catherine de Médici dated 18th September, 1565[1], which describes the situation:

She (Elizabeth) asseverated solemnly that she greatly desired to pacify the affairs of Scotland....I said to her that I had heard that money had been sent from here, which she positively denied. As to the four thousand men (she said) it was false, but I am certain...that there were raised in this country certain troops, which, as I hear today it is decided to send into Scotland to join with the said lords....I told her clearly that, if the Queen of Scotland found herself in difficulty, you could not but afford her succour for the security of her person and estate....The Queen of Scotland says that they of her contrary party plotted the capture of the King...or if they failed, to attempt the lives of both her husband and her....

No comment on the falsehoods of the English Queen is necessary; no doubt her conscience was sufficiently salved by the fact that what was being done was in other names than hers[2].

Yet, though Mary was in the field, there are several stray remarks by Randolph which go to show that she was not vindictively opposed to compromise: "I believe for all the words written in her letter she is better willing to accord than would seem"[3]; "To have a reconciliation, I see her not unwilling"[4]; "Robert Melville has been a suitor for Moray, he finds yet no favour, which proceeds more of her husband than herself[5]." It was at this time that the Queen was said to be dominated

[1] *Relations*, II, p. 226.
[2] Elizabeth's instructions to the Earl of Bedford, directing him, "as of yourself," to employ £3000 sent him, in aiding Moray and procuring men for his defence, are extant. They are dated 12th September, that is, a week earlier than her mendacious statement to de Foix (printed in Robertson, III, App. xiii).
[3] Randolph, 9th September, in Bain, II, p. 206.
[4] *Ibid.* 31st October.   [5] *Ibid.* 25th December.

by her husband, and that the names of Sir James Balfour, Riccio, and the Earl of Lennox are often found coupled together. Mary was already finding the interference of Lennox with his son and the affairs of State irksome, and she "wished he had not set foot in Scotland[1]." Here there is better evidence than that of letters written in the stress of circumstances that the real Mary is genuinely in favour of conciliation, and of freedom of conscience.

It was about this time that Francis Yaxley arrived from Flanders. As already stated above, he was a servitor of the Lennox, an ardent plotter in the cause of Rome, and had been appointed secretary, so it is said, to Darnley, who met him with rejoicing. He came secretly at the end of August 1565 and was despatched again almost immediately on a mission to Philip, to whom he carried letters dated 10th September, from both Mary[2] and her husband. Darnley's letter is not recorded, but in her letter Mary says:

> Your desire to maintain religion, caused me lately[3] to seek your favour and aid, foreseeing that which has now happened in our kingdom, tending to the ruin of the Catholics and the establishment of these unhappy errors. My husband and I, in attempting to resist, shall be in danger of losing our Crown, and at the same time the rights we have elsewhere, if we do not obtain aid from one who is a great prince of Christendom.... We have chosen to appeal to you before all others for your counsel, and we count upon your support; for the which purpose we send this English gentleman (Yaxley), Catholic, and faithful servitor of the King and me, with ample credit to explain our situation... Send him back soon for the matter is urgent....

Looked at dispassionately this letter might have been so much more vehement that it might almost be called restrained. There is in it no repudiation of her own moderation, the note is of the attempt to overwhelm both freedom and the State. Her action in calling for aid on Philip was perhaps not one to applaud. Still, it was political, and it was controlled by circumstances brought about by others whose level of morality was below her own— even if hers was not of the standard we *claim* to-day. To describe Yaxley as her "faithful servitor" shows clearly enough that she

---

[1] Randolph, p. 243. [2] Printed in Labanoff, I, p. 281.
[3] Refers presumably to her letter of 24th July already mentioned.

alone was not behind the pen, for she had never seen him until some ten days previously.

It is apposite to quote here from a document[1] of later date:

Sundry servants of ours (of Elizabeth) have repaired hither (Scotland) upon several pretences of great offers....And though our sister (Mary) owns that there hath been such offers and tenders, yet she gave no consent or allowance thereto that might in anywise impair the amity....

The "servants" referred to included Yaxley and Anthony Standen. It rests on Mary's word that they were not drawn to Scotland by her wish, and that may not be sufficient for some readers, yet to most it will be some additional certificate that Yaxley was not acting for Mary. Anthony Standen the elder was a gentleman of Darnley's household and a noted intriguer on the Catholic side up to and even after the Gunpowder Plot of 1605[2]. It appears that he came to Scotland either with or shortly after Yaxley.

Of the reception by Philip of Yaxley's budget a good deal is learnt from the *Simancas Records*[3]. A reply to Mary's letter of the 24th July, which announced her approaching marriage, had just been drawn up when Yaxley arrived (about 13th October) with the letters of the 10th September. The messenger started to return on the 23rd October, carrying Philip's answer to both communications. To the first there were separate formal letters to Mary and Darnley conveying his felicitations and hoping for good furtherance of religion therefrom. To the second it would appear that Darnley only was addressed—one might suppose that Philip had small confidence in the "Regiment of Women."

[1] Instructions to the Earl of Bedford, proceeding to represent Elizabeth at the baptism in December 1566, Keith, II, p. 479.

[2] It is worth mentioning that Anthony Standen, elder, is found in Spain in the year 1589, in company with one Sir William Stanley, an English Roman Catholic, and later a noted intriguer in the Gunpowder Plot of 1605. It is not beyond probability that Standen's knowledge of the Kirk o' Field Plot, which I have no doubt was complete, *may* have given the idea to Stanley. Guy Fawkes was later in Stanley's company. (*Cal. of Dom. State Papers*, CCXLII.)

[3] Quoted by M. Mignet, *Mary*, II, pp. 433 ff.

The letter is formal, but was accompanied by a detailed reply to the matters put before him by Yaxley, verbally it appears (*Lo que Francisco Yaxles le ha dicho*). In this Philip mentions that he is sending 20,000 crowns as an earnest of his goodwill, a matter to be kept secret lest it bring Elizabeth to greater contrary effort; if she makes open war there will be opportunity to do more. He begs the Scottish Sovereigns to do nothing rash in regard to England, to keep their party there alive until he be "where he can with greater facility assist them." The time to address Elizabeth on the subject of her treatment of Lady Lennox is not yet come, nor is it now desirable to make any treaty of closer friendship. To call in assistance from France is a matter on which he advised caution, for the remedy might be as bad as the disease. For the rest, they should keep his ambassadors in London or Paris well acquainted with their movements.

Yaxley was shipwrecked and drowned on his return journey in January (1566), the Spanish money was seized by the Earl of Northumberland, and whatever papers he had with him were either lost or kept by England. But it appears that the above-quoted reply from Philip was not with Yaxley but had been sent by a different channel to de Silva in London. For some reason it was not forwarded to Scotland, ostensibly because no safe messenger was available, and as late as June 1566 de Silva still held it[1]. The reason for delay given by de Silva was probably not the true one as John Beton had passed through London, and by him confidential letters to the Queen could have been sent; moreover, about mid-June, Stephen Wilson, conveying the results of the Bishop of Dunblane's mission to Rome, had passed. De Silva says that he imparted some of his matter to him but evidently not all, although, on the face of it, one might suppose Wilson to be an ideal messenger. At the same time that Wilson arrived in Scotland, there came also, by way of Flanders, the late Yaxley's servant, Henry Gwynn, who entered Darnley's household; he must have been able to impart to Darnley much if not all that his master had been charged with by the King of Spain. It is true that, at the moment, Mary was in her confine-

---

[1] *Simancas*, under date 4th June, 1566.

ment; but that would not account for de Silva's long delay, which suggests that some part of what was to be said was for Darnley's ears only, but that his recent temporary junction with the Protestant lords had decided de Silva to proceed with caution.

The words quoted above in Philip's message are important[1], and obviously mean that when Philip comes to the Netherlands, a project then much discussed, his help might be looked for. This journey to the Netherlands was an expressed intention that caused extraordinary perturbation in the Courts of England and France, and, as we shall see, had a marked effect on the fate of Mary.

The position of the actors engaged in promoting counter-reformation in Scotland at the end of the year 1565 may be summed up thus: in Scotland there was a Council, comprising the Earl of Lennox with Darnley, partly under his influence and partly following his own unbalanced promptings, Balfour, Riccio, Yaxley, Standen elder[2] and junior, Welche or Walsh (of whom it is known that he had no favour with Mary), and others whose names are little known, all of them ardently for Rome or Spain. On the Continent there were James Beton the Archbishop, loyal to Mary so far only as she was loyal to the Church; Chisholm, Bishop of Dunblane, and Jesuit by intent; Edmund Hay, Jesuit, wholehearted in the "Cause"; William Crichton, Jesuit, Hay's cousin; Francois de Alava, Ambassador in Paris and link with Philip; Solaro di Moretta, envoy of Savoy; and others more shadowy—some honestly for faith, some for self; and Mary a shuttlecock between them.

---

[1] It is worth noting that this expression of opinion is derived from a letter written to Philip by the Duke of Alva: "Your Majesty being in Flanders, could more easily encompass that which would further her interests" (*Relations*, v, p. 13, Alva to Philip, 29th June, 1565). It is very frequently the case that the Spanish King seemed more guided by the advice of Alva than any other.

[2] The two last, rather as travelling agents than as residents.

SCOTLAND IN THE PONTIFICATE
OF PIUS V

MARY BETWEEN THE HAMMER AND THE ANVIL

The wide interest taken in the history of Mary Stuart by some serious foreign historians, and particularly German historians, may be traced rather to the search for connected details of the part played by Scotland during the religious strife of the mid-sixteenth century than to particular interest in the tragedy at Kirk o' Field. It is not to be expected that, in a matter so essentially local as the tragedy itself, any valuable work is likely to result; but, in the larger question of the underlying Cause, it is from foreign writers and foreign archives that most can be expected. Our home authors, following the well-worn rut of Casket Letters, Detections, and "evidence" from one side, have been content to follow the beaten road, to the almost entire neglect of external sources of information. Of late years research has moved abroad, and a most notable contribution has been made by Father Joseph Pollen; but there are still treasures to be found by those who have the leisure and the learning to ransack the collections on the Continent.

Yet even at the very start there was an Englishman, Sir Henry Norris, English Ambassador in Paris, who gave a lead which was not followed. In a letter dated 5th April, 1567, nearly two months after the death of Darnley, which to me seems of special importance, he said: "As at first I thought, therein I remain not to be removed, which was *that the original of that fact* (the death of Darnley) *came from hence* (Paris)[1]." This, though an anticipation, is quoted because Norris was unusually level-headed, and he certainly had reason to believe that the Gunpowder Plot of

---

[1] It is true that the context indicates the idea that *from hence* means rather from French machinations, than from Paris, as a centre of plotting apart from *French* impulse; but, though Sir Henry was an acute observer, he might easily overlook that Paris as centre did not necessarily connote France as promoter. Norris to Throckmorton, 5th April, 1567, in *State Papers, Scotland, Elizabeth*, LXXXIX.

1567 did not find its cause in a vulgar love affair between Mary and Bothwell.

It had taken over four months to decide the election of Pope Pius IV; it took barely three weeks of closed conclave to decide on his successor, Pope Pius V. Cardinal Borromeo, favoured nephew of the late Pope, saintly of character, but by no means seeing eye to eye with Ghislieri, was the chief actor in the election of the latter, though Philip was behind the scenes. Scarcely anything could better indicate the urgent need of a directing mind. The new Pope, "on fire with consuming zeal," would inspire his forces with his own spirit—torture and the stake for deserters, death even for those suspected of lukewarmness to the Cause, the policy of "frightfulness" to replace the policy of persuasion. The end justified the means, he believed himself "responsible before God for the souls of the whole world[1]." The late Pope had found it necessary to curb his excessive violence when in his office of Inquisitor[2].

In Western Europe, England was the grand enemy, lost and won and lost again, English gold fostering the foes of the Church, in France, in the Netherlands, in Scotland; leagued with the princes of Germany; hardly vulnerable except through Scotland. And Scotland, governed, if it could be so said, by a young woman aged 24, of whom it had been reported three years previously,

The leading men in the government acknowledge the queen's title, but do not let her use her rights. They have many ways of acting in opposition to her, and they set themselves to draw her over to their way of thinking....What, I would ask, should a young lady do in such circumstances....She is alone, and has not a single protector or good counsellor[3].

Following with too great slavishness the written word, our authors tell of Mary's humble submission to the Pope, her reiteration of her constancy to her Faith, and in the letters sent to her are the expressions of confidence in her pious intentions to overwhelm all opposition to the Church. But it is not safe to build too largely on such expressions, much of which are

[1] Pastor, tr. xv, p. xlvi.   [2] De Thou, v, p. 130.
[3] De Gouda's report, in Pollen, p. 136.

mere formulæ, and one could point to similar letters addressed to the Pope of the day by persons of acknowledged leaning to reform; but Mary's case had this excuse in addition, that, repelled in her endeavours to agree with Elizabeth, she was obliged to go further with the allies left to her than would otherwise have been her wish. It is, however, with the expressions of confidence in her that it is necessary to deal. It cannot be supposed that Pius V felt that Scotland was in strong hands, he cannot have been ignorant of the past history of Mary, who had been, for four years and more, not only announcing freedom of conscience but acting up to her word.

In the wide survey undertaken by von Pastor over the field chosen by him in his history of the Popes one may expect to find occasional vagueness in particular cases; he tells us, for instance, that "To make end of such conditions and to set the ancient religion on its former footing, *or at least on equal terms with the Protestants*, was the decision of Mary after her victory over her rebels[1]." These words, true though they are, harmonize ill with his general argument; but the point is, it cannot be imagined that Mary could really have the confidence of a man of views so stern as Pius V. Would it not be justifiable to say that he, who feared not to threaten ruling princes for even the suspicion of leniency towards heretics, would only await the occasion to replace one who not only offered heretics equal terms but retained them as her chief advisers, and later on pardoned them when they rebelled, and finally refused all advice to destroy them? It must be obvious that Mary Stuart, from her early associations onwards, cannot have acquired a high place in the eyes of Rome. As a leader prepared to wade through blood and accomplish stern deeds towards a Catholic triumph, she had no qualification of sex, of temperament or of conviction.

In such views the Pope could count on the agreement of Philip. As already stated, the Netherlands were to the Spanish monarch as much almost as Religion itself. Even if Mary was innocent of having listened to offers of regality there, it is still clear that a hostile England greatly endangered his dominion;

[1] Pastor, *Gesch.* Pius V, p. 394.

and, therefore, a Scotland wedded to Spain and ruled in his interests was an object to scheme for. Could he be satisfied with a Mary whose constant aim had been union with England, and who, for recognition there, was willing to engage herself to recognize and promote a union of religion? It is not enough to say that Philip believed all these undertakings to be merely feigned; he knew as well as most people that policy, safeguarded by parliamentary enactments and public declarations, could not be abandoned. He knew quite well the Lutheran middle point, very slightly removed from the English form, towards which Charles of Lorraine had moved, and towards which Mary had moved or could move with little difficulty, and at the same time never believe that she had deserted her Faith.

Obviously, neither Pius nor Philip could rest secure so long as Mary remained. In her marriage it is possible that they hoped to see better prospects, yet they can hardly have been ignorant of the character of Darnley. It was less on the youth himself than on his family that they founded hope. Margaret Lennox was a power, and Elizabeth's wisdom in locking her safely in the Tower can hardly be questioned; Lennox himself, if not a strong pillar, was at least of average value. It is almost certain that ostensible confidence addressed to Mary, and the support given or promised to her, were in fact intended for the Lennox party. The parents with claims to both Crowns, concentrated in the son, were assets which more than balanced any interest accruing to France through the Hamiltons.

Philip had once expressed himself hopeful that the young Queen might die, "it would save us from serious complications." It is true that Mary was then in France; but, whatever she might write to Philip in the stress of temporary circumstances, she was French still, and Philip's sentiment no doubt held good. Her claims, even if distant and shadowy, to overlordship in the Netherlands could not be overlooked by Philip, the more so that the idea had been mooted. In all respects—if Mary were out of the way—the Lennox interest had possibilities worth pursuing. Philip worked slowly but relentlessly—the *removal* of obstacles, no one can deny it, being a factor in his methods.

THE FOREIGN NEGOTIATIONS OF 1566

Mary's last year of sovereignty opened with news of the death of Pope Pius IV. The name of his successor would be still unknown for several weeks, but by the end of January 1566 she prepared to send representatives to the customary ceremony of the Obedience, which she desired should be clothed with the magnificence given to it by other princes. Bishop Chisholm, who was still on the Continent, was chosen as her Ambassador, and her letter and commission to him is dated 31st January, but was not despatched until after 7th February by the hand of Stephen Wilson. By that date the news of the election and its result had reached Scotland[1]. Possibly the Papal Brief of 10th January, 1566, had been also received. In this letter the Pope sounded a note of optimism as to affairs in Scotland, not well warranted by facts:

We congratulate your Highness on having by this notable fact[2] commenced to dispel the darkness that has for so many years brooded over that kingdom....But the Lord has promised rewards for good and holy works not when begun but when ended. Therefore complete what you have commenced....

It may well be doubted if His Holiness realized how incomplete the work was; a section of the Protestant party had been driven out for rebellion in arms, not for religion—driven, too, into England, there to receive comfort and to form a fresh centre of trouble. Worse still, two-thirds of the party, fostered by England, remained in Scotland. Short-sighted optimists of the Lennox and Catholic group might shout victory, but Mary, more clear-sighted, saw the blighting of her hopes of closer relations with Elizabeth.

Unfortunately for her reputation in the eyes of the man whose praise belonged only to those who went relentlessly forward, Mary began at an early date to show that, in victory as in peace, she preferred the middle course. Before the end of April 1566

[1] *Selections*, p. 153.
[2] The expulsion of the rebels under Moray and Argyll is meant.

she had pardoned Moray and Argyll, two principal pillars of heresy, and later all the others on whose extinction Rome had too confidently counted.

Reference has been made above to a letter of 24th July, 1565, from Mary to Elizabeth making offers of reconciliation which even the English Queen acknowledged as satisfying. At the time these proposals had been condemned, for Elizabeth never expected that Mary, with her slender resources, would retain her authority against the nominees of England on whom she herself relied and whom for years past she had bribed and incited. But towards the end of the year matters assumed a different complexion; not only was Mary in a stronger position, but Elizabeth could not but be aware that armed interference in Scotland, as recommended by her Council, would bring Spain, urged thereto by the Pope, into the lists. In these circumstances the parley was reopened. Elizabeth may perhaps be given credit for a disinterested attempt to over-ride the prejudices of her ministers by a personal negotiation with her "sister"; but it must be recorded that, at the moment this new offer was being made, rumours were current that the recent meeting at Bayonne foreshadowed united activity on the part of the Catholic powers. Though in fact it was not true, it is easy to believe that a rumour which has been woven as a fact into history by many modern writers caused real anxiety at the time. To confirm the rumour, or at least to add to the anxiety, the first whispers of an approaching journey to the Netherlands by the Spanish King began to be breathed. The letters of Fourquevaux to his master in France contain several references to the collection of ships and troops in Spain. "Quand l'Espagne remue, l'Europe tremble," and Philip, with what was perhaps a malicious pleasure, kept Europe trembling for the next two years or so. The news of his coming waxed and waned, and traced, so to speak, a "graph" of pressure, the peaks in which corresponded with storms in Scotland.

Reconciliation with Scotland was a necessary precaution, and perhaps Elizabeth desired a legitimate method; if so, her desire was quenched by Cecil, who preferred a more violent way to reinstate the Protestant exiles.

Of this remarkable incident, which in the long run could
hardly fail to thrust Mary towards Rome and Spain, something
must be said. In its first phase one finds some indication of
honesty in the English Queen. She had been led into a course
of action, treacherous in itself, which had brought her Scottish
friends to ruin. She would now come back to her own promptings and do something to come to an understanding with her
"sister," while at the same time giving a helping hand to her
dupes—the Earl of Moray and his friends. Mary had opened
the way and had sent messages by Castelnau that, notwithstanding the discourteous silence regarding her previous offers, she
was as anxious as ever for reasonable accommodation. A reply
was drafted for Elizabeth's signature, presumably by her orders,
offering to send a Commission of persons of estimation, "to
conclude a firm and perfect league between us." The persons
chosen were Lord Lumley and Sir Walter Mildmay, the former
leaning to the old faith, the latter the reverse, but both with the
reputation of honesty.

At the same time, in the form of a long document of twenty-
five pages[1], instructions were drawn up on 24th October, 1565,
by Cecil to govern their conduct of the Embassy. In every
sentence falsity peeps out. The first eight or nine pages are devoted to an enumeration of Mary's alleged offences; the Treaty
of Edinburgh, the treatment of Tamworth, the hardness used
towards the Earl of Moray and others, "who meant to use no
force against her," and of whom, "you (the Ambassadors) shall
plainly answer and affirm with truth that we (Elizabeth) never
did or meant anything to comfort them or any of her subjects in
any rebellion or offence against her." Of this last statement even
Froude is constrained to say, "She stooped to a deliberate lie."

There follow many pages of what Mary should give to obtain
forgiveness, for the most part things that she had already offered.
The treaty should be amended as to the clause excluding Mary

---

[1] A copy, with marginalia in Cecil's hand, is in the Cotton MS.
Calig. B. 10. f. 364, and another copy, which I believe is similar though
I have not collated them, is in the Record Office. The former is dated
November 1565, the latter 24th October, which is the correct date.

from the succession, but any *right* she might have was too great a question to be discussed. There was nothing tangible, in fact, so far as Scotland was concerned, but much of importance for England.

This document was never sent; Elizabeth must have been conscious that her recent comic reproof of the Earl of Moray—who, "sitting on his knees" before her in the presence of the two French ambassadors, had, by pre-arranged agreement, solemnly denied receiving incitement from her—would excite the risibility of Europe. To issue this fresh document would stamp her as a clown; within four days of its cancellation, however, Randolph had instructions to put the case before Mary; but evidently most of the original matter was omitted.

Mary welcomed the proposals for a *modus vivendi* on the basis of a new treaty. Presumably the names of the Commissioners were not mentioned, but Mary undertook to send representatives to meet whomsoever Elizabeth should send. Nothing remained now but fulfilment of the pledges; but that was wanting. It is clear enough from Randolph's letters that Cecil disliked the idea from the first. Unable to check Elizabeth's impulse, he devised other means to render the negotiations abortive. The first rift appeared when "on good consideration" it was decided that Commissioners would not be sent to but would be *received* from Scotland; and Randolph was commanded to explain that he had mistaken the message. A lie so obvious deceived nobody; the Scottish Council plainly indicated what they thought of an ambassador so discredited, and refused to have any more to do with him. But Mary still desired to continue the endeavour, and persuaded the Council to accept the new situation; answer was accordingly given that "The Queen our Sovereign is content to send Commissioners to the Borders...and to do anything else to maintain amity[1]."

It rested with Elizabeth only to name her representatives, and, on 24th January, 1566, Randolph, with fresh instructions, did so. He explained that, as this was to be a Border meeting, the persons concerned should be Border officers, Bedford and Forster.

[1] Randolph to Cecil, 23rd December, 1565, in Bain, II, pp. 245–6.

Mary named Home and Cessford, and, on objection being taken
to Home's rank, she substituted Bothwell[1]. Regarding this,
Froude permitted this remark to appear in his *History*[2]: "The
Queen of Scots, as if in deliberate insult, named Bothwell as a
fit person." The historian cannot have been ignorant, but of all
his many misrepresentations this seems one of the worst; it is
intentionally misleading[3].

To cut down the original proposals of sending two reputable
Commissioners to treat for a league of friendship to a mere
Border committee, and to appoint the man who was the head and
front, on the English side, of the late rebellion, the man who even
at that moment, though Mary did not know it, was plotting
another and not less serious *coup*, was indeed an insult, which
Froude omits to mention; but why the appointment of Bothwell,
similar in rank and office to Bedford, should be so the historian
does not explain. In any case Cecil had gained his point, and
the notion of any treaty of peace and reconciliation was again
indefinitely shelved. This incident is hardly mentioned elsewhere. A fortnight later Mary's Chief Secretary, Maitland,
recently forgiven and restored to office after his part in the late
rebellion, wrote to Cecil that the only way to restore the Protestant lords was "to chop at the very root—you (Cecil) know
where it lieth"[4]: and thus the murder of Riccio was initiated,
with Bedford as chief agent for Cecil. Randolph was dismissed
from Scotland on clear proof that he had conveyed Elizabeth's
money to the late rebels.

Mary was inclined to peace, and was moved thereto both by
Castelnau and by Throckmorton[5], neither of whom was dis-
interested. Throckmorton's letter of advice is contained in
Melville's *Memoir*, at pp. 119 ff. It cannot be supposed that

[1] *Selections*, Randolph to Cecil, 24th January, 1566.
[2] Froude, VII, p. 367.
[3] It is no excuse to allege that, on the faith of a dismissed servant,
Bothwell had been accused of using opprobrious terms regarding both
Mary and Elizabeth. The story was a year old, was never tested, and
was very improbable.
[4] Maitland to Cecil, 9th February, 1566.
[5] Pollen, p. 466; *Relations*, II, p. 250.

Melville had no authority for his text, yet taken *à la lettre* the whole is so treasonable that it cannot be imagined to come from a cautious Protestant, closely in the councils of Elizabeth, without her cognizance. It would be the kind of skilful pleading likely to achieve the object of inducing Mary to pardon her rebels—and the advice is probably not out of discord with that which Elizabeth in her heart wished for.

Castelnau's advice corresponded in some points with that of Throckmorton—friendship with England, and avoidance of unprofitable civil war. The rebels, he said, asked nothing but to live in peace and liberty of conscience. In these words must be dissimulation, for none knew better than the Ambassador what the truth was. Mary's reply was frank and reasonable; she could not with honour seek to compound with those who sought to dethrone her—she had not molested their conscience. Her desire was for French support; that denied, she must put herself in the protection of another prince. Amity with England was her wish, but it must be on mutual terms.

It is noteworthy that during part of this conversation Sir James Balfour was called in, obviously to emphasize the case against the rebels.

The basis of all this is clear. Elizabeth and Catherine were nibbling at the notion of a united front versus Spain; to neither, for different reasons, was the idea of Spanish influence in Scotland palatable[1].

Elizabeth, stronger in character and power than Mary, was herself as wax in Cecil's hands; it is not surprising if Mary in these circumstances listened to those who pointed her to the only sources of succour—Philip and the Pope. She listened and took the steps of common prudence, but she never set aside her desire for moderation.

In February 1566 two persons arrived in Scotland—James Thornton from the Archbishop of Glasgow, and Clerneau de Villemont from the Cardinal of Lorraine. The principal duty of the latter was to convey to Mary the Pope's Brief of 10th January referred to above[2]. What Thornton's specific message

---

[1] Pollen, p. 466; *Relations*, II, p. 250.   [2] p. 221.

was, or whether both envoys had an identical note, is not known. Randolph's statement that their purpose was to urge Mary to proceed to her utmost against the rebel lords, although suspect, may be true. For months past he had been stirring the flame and pouring into Elizabeth's ears every kind of untruth regarding the movements of the Queen of Scots. The Cardinal, the Archbishop of Glasgow and William Chisholm, Bishop of Dunblane, were all, apparently, in Paris at the time of the sending of the envoys, and it may be that, as a matter of policy, they would deem it the better part to advise the Queen to use her advantage for the securing of some tangible acknowledgment from Elizabeth, and to that end to proceed in the approaching Parliament against the rebels.

It is likely enough that this was the advice tendered to Mary by the two envoys, but it is certain that after their arrival she sent Robert Melville to London; he, who was known to be a friend of the Earl of Moray, must have been selected to act in his interests. From much that will appear, it was not Mary who desired to proceed against the exiled Protestants, but her husband and the Lennox party generally. Whatever advice was tendered to Mary we may be sure that still more was poured into Darnley's willing ears, added to by Riccio and Sir James Balfour. Up to that time it was certainly Darnley who desired the permanent proscription of Moray. Yet, within a short time thereafter, he and his father were forming a combination to acquire the " Crown Matrimonial " by the " temporary "—which in fact could only mean the final—effacement of the Queen. The murder of Riccio was but a peg on which to hang other things of more moment.

Both Thornton and Clerneau de Villemont were present in or near Edinburgh during the tragedy of March 1566. There is tantalizingly little information of what they reported to their respective masters. Thornton was sent back to France on 3rd April, bearing Mary's account of the Riccio plot, to be communicated to the French King, the Cardinal of Lorraine, and the foreign Ambassadors. This was probably the first accurate news received, though de Silva from London had sent an account to Philip on 23rd March. Fourquevaux, writing from Spain on 30th April, 1566, mentions the grief of the Court there at the news, but, apparently, it was rather the grief of the Queen of Spain at Mary's troubles than astonishment of Philip that Darnley, whose marriage he had but recently rejoiced in as a means of furthering the cause of Religion, should be now siding with the Protestants in an attempt on the Queen's life.

One cannot deny that Philip had cause for chagrin; his money intended for Mary had gone into Elizabeth's coffers; the secret of his aid which he wished to be so carefully guarded had been exposed by the accident to Yaxley; his advice to hasten slowly had been neglected. If he was mollified later, and he appears to have been, some strong explanations by Lennox on behalf of Darnley must have been made to show that what was done was with good intentions. It is not surprising that Lennox after the murder was "sore troubled in mind[1]."

THE EMBASSY OF THE BISHOP OF DUNBLANE

As stated above, Stephen Wilson was sent to France about 7th February, 1566, the bearer of a Commission to Bishop Chisholm to represent the Queen and King of Scotland at the ceremony of Obedience to the Pontiff; the expenses of the embassy were to be found by the Cardinal of Lorraine from Mary's funds in France. In addition to his formal Commission the Bishop was to carry a letter from Mary to Pius V. This letter[2], which is signed by Mary only, makes no mention of her husband at all. At the time of writing the name of the addressee was not known in Scotland, but this would have been added after the arrival of Clerneau and before the despatch of Wilson on or about 7th February. The writing of this letter was practically synchronous with the evidence that England was playing false in the matter of the Anglo-Scottish Commission, and it contains what might be expected, an urgent demand for help in view of the probability of a desperate final attempt on the part of the

---

[1] Randolph, 4th April, 1566, in Bain, II.   [2] Labanoff, VII, p. 8.

rebels to overcome her. The effort did in fact materialize on 9th March, 1566, with disastrous results—the murder of Riccio.

Wilson, travelling with ordinary fortune, would reach Paris within the last week of February, and there he found the Bishop of Dunblane who, in accordance with his instructions, went to Varennes to see the Cardinal of Lorraine. He was to obtain from the Cardinal a plan of the best procedure to be followed in addressing the Pope. The Bishop, as was usual with him, delayed his journey, for he was still with the Cardinal when the first inaccurate news of the insurrection in Scotland arrived. The result was that the Cardinal decided to curtail that part of the programme which entailed large expense and, it must be supposed, added considerably to the matter which was to be spoken before the Pontiff. The circumstances were now obviously of an even more serious nature than at first supposed.

The Bishop arrived at Lyons on 29th March[1] *en route* to Rome, which he reached about 26th April. By that time he must have been in possession of a correct outline of the events in Scotland. At least he knew enough to suppress the Commission signed by Mary and her husband, for the latter, so far as the news went, was not a fitting person to address His Holiness. It may very well be the case that Mary's letter to the Pope may have been altered or rewritten to leave out Darnley's name, for it is difficult to believe, as both had signed the Commission, that the letter of the same date should be from one only.

At all events the Ambassador omitted the formal ceremony of Obedience, and proceeded at once with an Oration before the Pope. Of this Father Stevenson prints two copies; the first, evidently written before the news from Scotland had been received, makes several mentions of King Henry, but the second, although it is apparently the one actually delivered and mentions the part played by the King in the affair of Riccio, also seems to convey the idea that his defection was but a temporary aberration. It contains such expressions as "Neither our queen nor our king have the slightest inclinations to swerve from the path trodden by their ancestors," and in general "they" ask for aid.

[1] Pollen, pp. 493–4.

As the orator cannot have had any certain knowledge of the extent of Darnley's lapse, it must be supposed that he was anxious to put it in the best possible light, in order that the hoped-for subsidy should not be withheld. It is noteworthy, however, that writing to Philip immediately after receiving the news, the Pope omits all mention of the King, and confines himself to an appeal for help for Mary[1]. There is nothing in the address of the Bishop about asking for a Nuncio to be sent to Mary; it seems more likely that, when the Pope decided to send monetary help, the Nuncio was at the same time named, to see that the help was properly utilized.

The Pope's letter to Philip was received by him on 7th June, but although no reply is forthcoming, Castagna[2] says he promised to do his best; there is no record, however, that he did anything. Pius also wrote a letter to Mary on 12th May[3] in which he does not mention Darnley, exhorts her to be firm and announces the sending of a Nuncio and a subsidy. This letter was carried by Stephen Wilson, who arrived in London on 16th June[4] and in Edinburgh about 22nd June. The moment of arrival was not a very convenient one as Mary was unable to attend to business, but her reply made on 17th July expresses gratitude and eagerness for the arrival of the Nuncio and the money. Probably the latter was the main question at the time, for she had already indicated to Laureo (the Nuncio) that she could not yet receive him.

Bishop Chisholm remained rather over a month in Rome, but arrived again in Paris about the 24th June, and there remained awaiting the arrival of the Nuncio. If his mission had in the first place no other object than to offer the customary duty to the new Pontiff, it developed into much greater importance. At a very critical time the Curia became informed of the actual situation in Scotland, with all its weakness. It cannot be doubted that, whether he would or no, the Bishop had to explain the small extent of Mary's effort to further the Cause, and we see

---

[1] Nau, p. 199.   [2] *Cor. Dip.* I, p. 261.
[3] Printed by Pollen, p. 236.
[4] *Simancas*, under date 23rd June.

the reflection of the Pope's misgivings in the limitations drawn round the disbursement of the money, which he had collected with difficulty. But, though the evidence is slight, it appears that Chisholm was from the first no warm believer in Mary as an instrument to put into action measures which required ruthlessness. This will be referred to again at the end of the final tragedy. A very important decision was arrived at, to attach Father Edmund Hay to the Nuncio, for the purpose of sending him in advance to Scotland to report on the real situation as to the reception of a Papal Ambassador. It does not appear that any intention of sending the Bishop of Dunblane to Scotland was at first entertained, but rather the Archbishop of Glasgow[1]; and the reason probably was that the former was held to be too hotheaded for a task requiring prudence.

Pius V was thoroughly alarmed and conscious that a crisis was in view and that the loss of Scotland would be of enormous importance; in choosing Laureo to save the situation we may be sure that the most careful consideration was given.

THE NUNCIATURE OF VINCENZO LAUREO, BISHOP OF MONDOVI

THE MAN HIMSELF

Vincenzo Laureo, appointed by the new Pope to succeed him in the Bishopric of Mondovi and, even before taking up this position, selected to the immensely important task of making a supreme effort to stem the tide of heresy in Scotland, must be supposed to have had the same qualities of character as had Pius himself. Father Pollen says of him that he was an advocate of strong measures, without being a strong man[2]. As to the latter estimate, the Bishop probably knew from the beginning that the appointment of a foreigner to enter Scotland officially, as a representative of Rome, was impossible. It seems out of the

---

[1] Pollen, p. 499, Manare to Borgia, 26th June, 1566.
[2] Pollen, Pref. p. cvii.

question to attribute such a proposal to the Cardinal of Lorraine[1], who knew what had happened when the Jesuit, de Gouda, was sent in somewhat similar circumstances. If the idea arose through Bishop Chisholm, it is likely enough that he had marked himself out for the post; but, whatever the reason, he did not inspire full confidence in Rome.

That the Bishop of Mondovi was deeply tinged with the self-sacrificing ardour of the Society of Jesus admits of no doubt. De Thou[2] describes him as closely in the counsels of Lainez and Polanco, a protégé of Cardinal Tournon, and an advocate of such strong measures as bringing Spanish troops, and even Philip himself, into France to quell the reform in 1561. Fouqueray describes him[3] as a familiar of Tournon, and we know that the Cardinal was an advocate of pontifical absolutism. It was Mondovi's influence which obtained the foundation of a Jesuit college in Tournon's native town. Father Polanco, writing to Hay to announce the Nunciature, describes the Bishop as "an old, true and devoted friend of the Society[4]." In this probably lies the reason for the choice; Pius V was not more devoted to the Society than his nominee[5]. It was not lack of devotion that kept the Nuncio out of Scotland but the knowledge that his presence would hinder the Cause. Yet we shall find that absence from the scene of action, and it may be also an inelastic view of the remedy to be applied, did, in the long run, tend to subtract from his value as Nuncio and to leave in the hands of others the task of facing the realities on the spot, and devising the steps to be taken for the "greater glory of God," as they saw it.

"The humanitarianism of our day will not fail to be shocked at the test which we shall hear him (Bishop of Mondovi) propose to Mary to prove her sincerity," says Father Pollen; but it is unnecessary to compare the sentiments of to-day with those of nearly four centuries ago. If we made a practice of being shocked at what was said and done then, the pages of history would destroy our peace of mind. Yet, taking the phrase as it stands,

---

[1] As suggested by the Nuncio himself; see Pollen, p. 299.
[2] De Thou, IV, p. 126.   [3] *Hist. Soc. Jesus*, I, p. 291.
[4] Pollen, p. 497.   [5] Cf. Fouqueray, p. 446.

should not our humanitarianism extend sympathy to a young woman, already verging on collapse under the load of treachery and desertion of those she had a right to deem her friends, who stoutly refused the test, and thereby damned herself in the eyes of those who alone held out a helping hand? Does our humanity hesitate to pile up calumny on her name for deeds following on this refusal?[1] What that test was will be shown presently[2].

THE BISHOP OF MONDOVI ARRIVES IN PARIS AND MAKES HIS FIRST REPORT

We have already considered the circumstances which originated the mission of the Bishop of Mondovi, and have noted the exaggerated language in which the merits, not only of the Queen of Scots but also of her husband, were extolled before the Pontiff. It is true that Darnley was included rather tentatively in the later orations of the Bishop of Dunblane; but, although the Papal Briefs echoed the high hopes of restoration of the Faith by their, or by her, means, it may be doubted if the Pope or his advisers were in fact without knowledge that Mary was little to be relied on for serious effort, whether arising from want of inclination or from want of power to act, had she wished to. Yet it is more than probable that there was a certain failure to grasp the full extent of her weakness; the Curia, accustomed to deal with Sovereigns who, even in the midst of rebellion, retained large reserves of strength, could hardly realize one whose authority extended no further than her subjects willed. We may trace in this knowledge, the necessity for exhortation

---

[1] Cf. Pollen, Pref. p. cvii. It would appear that before Father Pollen had fully digested the fruits of his own magnificent research, he was inclined to be horrified at the drastic boldness of Laureo and willing to shield him. Writing in *The Month* (January–June 1898) before the publication of the *Papal Negotiations* he says: "The Bishop of Mondovi speaks of the *execution*, not of persons, but of a plan, and a plan suggested not from Rome but from Paris." It is unlikely that he would have maintained this thesis at a later date; the plan to attain an end by violence was common to the times, whether on the Catholic or the Protestant side, and in this case was fully known and approved in Rome.   [2] pp. 241, 242.

to greater endeavour, and in this ignorance, the means taken to assist her.

To appoint a Nuncio publicly was a step far removed from sound policy. It could not but be known that, for any effective result to ensue, the power of Spain must be called in, and it need not be said what effect this would have on the Cabinets of London and Paris. It was neither asked for nor desired by Mary, and this much the Nuncio was obliged to admit in the first letter written by him after arrival in Paris[1]; he learnt, he said, that the request for a Nuncio was at the suggestion of the Cardinal of Lorraine, who thought it would incite the Pope to be more inclined to liberality in a subsidy. One may doubt if this is literally true, but it is useful as showing that between the Cardinal and the Bishop there was no great co-operation. The Cardinal's name would not have been used thus freely had the writer been his friend, or believed him to be *persona grata* in Rome. Indeed, from days dating four years back, when Tournon and Lorraine were opposed in essential principles, it can be understood that the protégé of the former was not at one with the other.

Although there is no document giving in form the instructions which guided the Nuncio in his mission, and it is not unlikely that these were verbal, he carried a Brief addressed to Mary, dated at the time of his departure from Rome (6th June), which exhibits in a high degree the enthusiasm, even the religious exaltation, of the Pope towards the task of his representative. The Brief, *Ex quo tumultus a perduellibus tuis*[2], hints that, but for his age and heavy responsibilities, he would himself go to Scotland, a statement which could not fail to spur the Nuncio to the maximum endeavour. There is also the reference, seldom absent, to support to be expected from the King of Spain. The reader should note again to how great an extent Philip's projected visit to the Netherlands affected the hopes of Rome.

The Bishop journeyed from Rome by way of his new See of Mondovi, from which place he paid two visits to the Duke of

---

[1] Pastor, *Gesch.* Pius V, p. 398, offers the opinion that "Whether a papal ambassador was wished for, can well be doubted."

[2] G. Conn, *Life of Mary*, II.

Savoy. Though the purport of these visits was to discuss a move against the Swiss reformers at Geneva, it is none the less likely that Scottish affairs were also talked of; and it is not improbable that he there met Bertino Solaro, sometimes known under the name of Moretta. As this person was a member of the Duke's Court and had had considerable experience of Scotland and knowledge of Mary, it is likely that he would be called in to any consultation on these subjects. Such a meeting, if it took place, would be of importance. At the date of the second visit (25th July, 1566) the news of the birth of the Prince must have reached the Duke, and, considering Mary's close affection for the Duchess, he had probably been already asked to be a sponsor at the baptism[1]. Whether Moretta had then been nominated is doubtful, but it is very remarkable that he did not reach Edinburgh until the 25th January, 1566/7, a month too late for the ceremony.

Moretta was present in Edinburgh at the time of Darnley's death, and it is not unjust to say that his movements, then and afterwards, give rise to suspicion. Whatever opinions are formed of the Nuncio's intentions, it will hardly be gainsaid that Moretta too had a mission; his presence in Scotland would be otherwise unintelligible. Whether his instructions coincided precisely with those of Laureo is for consideration.

In his letter of 21st August to Rome, written after arrival in

---

[1] It is not overlooked that the Duke's acceptance of the office is provisionally placed as dated in November (see Pollen, pp. 454–5), and this is confirmed by the letter from the Duke to Elizabeth dated 10th November stating that he was sending Moretta to represent him; see *Cal. For. Eliz.* under that date. But, on the other hand, there is evidence that he had been expected long before that; thus, de Silva, writing on 11th November, says: "There is no news yet of the Savoyan representative; perhaps he went by sea" (see *Simancas* under that date and still earlier, 9th September). Laureo mentions that the Duke had been invited. Again the Venetian, Correr, reported, dated 23rd January, 1567, that the Queen of Scots had postponed the baptism by two months awaiting news of Moretta's coming. See *Venetian Cal.* VII. Certainly the baptism took place later than at first intended, for the Earl of Bedford left London early in November and was awaiting the arrival of Moretta; see Bain, II, under dates 13th, 17th, 25th November.

Paris, the Nuncio gives us some account of his itinerary from Lyons. "As I was bound by his Holiness' commission to talk with the Cardinal of Lorraine before my interview with the King of France," he resolved to meet the Cardinal, and did so near Châlons. The conversation appears to have been confined to the subsidy intended for Mary from Papal resources, on hearing of which the Cardinal was greatly pleased, and blessed so saintly a giver; a Brief from the Pope was also handed to him, but what it contained is not known. Finally, the Bishop arrived in Paris on the eve of the feast of St Lawrence, that is, 10th August, 1566.

An interesting little sidelight is thrown here by him, which may be noticed. He carried Briefs for the King and the Queen-Mother of France, but the wording of these only indicated a request that all Catholics should be caused to observe the decrees of the Council of Trent; this was a half-measure which did not please the resident Nuncio in France (Bishop of Ceneda), who had already issued instructions of a more drastic nature. These indicated that all persons, whether Catholic or not, should be forced to acknowledge the decrees. To this measure, Ceneda had been only able to obtain verbal consent on the part of the King and his mother; he had failed to obtain an Edict. At this moment Catherine was, in the opinion of His Holiness, three parts Huguenot[1]; yet the surface language of mutual admiration did not alter, a condition which was very similar to the case of Mary Stuart, whose heresy was rather of the less dangerous Lutheran type. Eventually Laureo agreed to send the Briefs back to Rome for alteration, and to avoid any difficulty at Court, "I will excuse myself by saying that I left Rome believing that the Pope would send me the Briefs afterwards, and that I expected them daily with the Bull of my Faculties." From this we see that the Bishop did not hesitate to confess to the Cardinal-Secretary his lapse from strict verity. His Holiness, who it is said hated a lie, approved of this one; perhaps it was too diplomatic to be venal.

Arrived at Paris the Nuncio found letters from Mary express-

[1] Cf. Pastor, *Gesch.* Pius V, pp. 358–9.

ing polite assurance of the value of his assistance, but begging him to defer his departure for Scotland, since the seditious would prevent her from receiving him properly. His reply was the usual exhortation—to use all endeavour to restore the Faith to its original state. Whether in this letter he offered the bald proposal to accomplish this object by executing the leaders of the Protestant reform, and especially Secretary Maitland, cannot be said. The letter itself is not available, but only a general summary of what was said and done at the time[1]; it was sent on 9th September, and was carried, together with the first instalment of the subsidy, by John Beton, who arrived at Stirling on the 22nd September, 1566.

Attached to the Nuncio's letter to Rome of 21st August was a private and very secret communication, intended perhaps for the eye of the Cardinal-Secretary only, but shown to the Pope, who was "delighted" with it—not so much with the general news, as with the steps suggested to put matters right. Darnley is therein described as an ambitious and inconstant youth, desirous of rule. He continues to go to Mass, but consorts with heretics[2]; the Queen is forced to pardon the Protestant leaders, in whom she now shows confidence. The concluding paragraph, which interests us most, ran as follows:

These difficulties might be obviated if the King of Spain should come, as one hopes, with a strong force to Flanders, or else, as certain persons of weight believe, that one might execute justice against six rebels who were the leaders and originators of the late treason against the Queen, and whose deaths would effectually restore peace and obedience in that kingdom. These are, the Earls of Moray and Argyll, the Earl of Morton; the Laird of Lethington; Bellenden, the Justice Clerk; and James M'Gill, Clerk Register....The King himself (so these signory say) could execute it without any disturbance arising.... The danger is that the Cardinal of Lorraine and the Queen, in their excessive clemency, would not consent to such an act[3].

This remarkable paragraph shows once more the importance attached to the expected coming of Philip to the Netherlands;

[1] Pollen, pp. 408–9.
[2] This last was not quite true at the time the letter was written.
[3] Pollen, pp. 272 ff.

it indicates the grounds for the fears, expressed in England and France, that the extensive preparations, greater as was said than were warranted by mere intention to overcome the politico-religious uprising in the States, were designed to attack one or other or both these nations; it voices the reason for the temporary friendship of Catherine of France and Elizabeth. To Laureo the notion of calling on Spain accorded not only with the policy of the Curia but also with his own previous record; and Francois de Alava, Spanish Ambassador in Paris, and reputed friend of Darnley[1], was we may be sure one of the persons of weight invited to assist him in his council of advice. It should be noted that the Queen is thrust aside, her clemency and her femininity rendering her unfit for work such as this, and it is the King on whom they rely. Inconstant though he be, his desire for rule, aided by the presence of Spain, make him a factor to count on; and probably Alava and some of the others could tell the Nuncio of Philip's previous support of his "faithful servitors" the Lady Margaret and Matthew, Earl of Lennox, her husband, heirs reasonably near to both the Thrones. The "King himself" could do these things; aided by Protestant promptings he had done something similar barely five months before, and endeavoured to get rid of his wife at the same time; now, aided by Catholic suggestions and with the same lure, but backed by a greater power, could he not be expected to do at least as much? But neither Margaret, nor Lennox, nor their degenerate son could attain the goal while Mary lived. And the reference to the clemency of Mary and her uncle of Lorraine must also be noted; here we find a perfectly neutral witness, obviously without intention of favouring either—rather the reverse—deponing to what has been brought out in the preceding pages.

There was nothing new in the proposal in itself; it is indeed likely enough that de Gouda made the same suggestion four years before. Buchanan in his *History* hints as much. It was not only to Scotland that the "cure" was to be applied; here and there through the records of these four years the shadow of similar plans appears. We hear of the Queen of Navarre and

[1] *Simancas*, de Silva to Philip, 29th June, 1566.

some of her advisers being haled before the Inquisition, of the settling of apostacy in France by removal of a few heads; and in both cases the shadow is cast from Spain. The only real difference between the system of the two parties was that the Catholics, in possession of the machinery of the law, would execute, or talk of executing, by "Justice"; the Protestants acted more effectively by assassination without any empty words at all.

In this particular case the Ancient Church was staking almost everything on this last attempt to recover lost prestige. The work was to be entrusted to the titular King of Scotland, a weak instrument, but, with aid from local sources, and above all fortified by the coming of Philip to the Netherlands, perhaps strong enough. But, as on the previous occasion when acting for the Protestants, his reward must be real not titular kingship.

THE WOOING OF THE CARDINAL OF LORRAINE

It is not necessary to follow the whole course of the correspondence between the Bishop of Mondovi and the Cardinal-Secretary; for the most part these are translated by Father Pollen, and can also be read in transcripts of the originals in the collection in the Public Record Office. From the beginning the importance of the coming of the King of Spain is frequently stressed, and, in the first letter received from Rome by the Nuncio after his arrival in Paris, dated 16th September, 1566, he is warned to be chary in disbursing the subsidy unless he has some guarantee that the money will be properly spent in furtherance of the Holy Cause. In this proviso the doubts lingering in Rome of Mary's orthodoxy, or at least of her zeal, are more in evidence than in the flowing periods of the official letters. It is clear that the hopes of Rome are placed rather on Philip and the Lennox Stuarts.

By the 30th September, 1566, the Pope was beginning to have doubts whether the Nunciature had been wise, "Your going into Scotland, it seems, depends upon the coming of his Catholic Majesty into Flanders...as in his own letters he has lately said that he meant to do": should this be delayed, the Nuncio should return to his Bishopric. The Bishop's next letter of 21st October is important; much of it is taken up by the relation, exaggerated as usual, of the pious aspirations of the Royal family in France, their willingness to spend their lives for the Cause and so on, words not corresponding well with deeds, but very similar to those official utterances from and to Scotland which have already been mentioned. Towards the end he reports that he has paid two visits to the Cardinal of Lorraine, the first about the 12th to 15th October, the second on 21st October.

The importance attached to attempting to induce the Cardinal to exercise his authority to persuade or coerce Mary to take a course against her will is apparent. The instructions to visit him on first arrival, these two visits, and what resulted from them, are the proof. Notwithstanding the lavish eulogy of the open letters it is evident that Mary was expected to be *difficile*, and I think this adds some confirmation to Buchanan's statement that the proposition now in question had been put to her before and refused. Evidently, too, the Pope was weakening in the matter, and what was to be done should be done quickly. Von Pastor puts it thus: "In Rome the inner circle had come to the conclusion that Mary's religious eagerness had been over-estimated[1]."

The Nuncio's first report on his negotiations is written in "clear," and is more restrained than a later report dated 12th November written in cipher. They should be taken together, though neither can be relied on as exactly true, for the Nuncio, urged by zeal to accomplish his mission, would be moved to heighten his colours to improve his picture. His first point, unnecessary if the Cardinal had been wholehearted in the affair, was to impress on him that the Papal subsidy was intended to promote one purpose only, to wit the service of Religion. His private news led him to suspect that Mary was anxious enough to get the money, but by no means inclined to have conditions attached. His opinion of this attitude is made clear from his commentary: "I am inclined to believe that it was for this that God suddenly visited her with that very grave and dangerous

[1] Pastor, *Gesch.* Pius V, p. 400.

illness[1]. Let us hope He may have touched her heart thereby, and inspired her with some good and holy resolution."

He then goes on to say that "I had great difficulty in persuading him (Cardinal of Lorraine) that there ought not to be further delay in doing something signal for the service of God in Scotland." Not only was the Pope ready to help to any extent, but his influence with Philip was well known. The service in question was undoubtedly the "removal" of the Protestant leaders, and the Cardinal evidently tried to escape from having a hand in it; the Pope's health, he said, was not good, he could not undertake so important an enterprise if there were danger of its being abandoned. Ultimately the Cardinal agreed to send one of his gentlemen,

in whom he confided much, to advise and persuade the Queen to decide on restoring Holy Religion in her kingdom; and, as there seemed to be no more expeditious remedy, in the opinion of the Cardinal himself, and the Archbishop of Glasgow and the Bishop of Dunblane, and also Father Edmund the Scot, than the punishment of a few seditious wretches, the Queen should execute with a brave heart this most just punishment for God's glory....The said gentleman should arrive in Scotland before M. Stephen, the Scotsman, leaves that Court, so that if the Queen, moved perchance by the persuasion of the heretics, were calling me to Scotland for some other purpose than zeal for religion, we might hope that, on the arrival of this gentleman, and especially after such a dangerous illness, she would decide on carrying out the pious and prudent advice of the Lord Cardinal. But to avoid, as far as possible, every suspicion of deception, and to discover the will of that Queen, and what hope there is for religion in that kingdom, the Bishop of Dunblane, and the Scottish Father Edmund, of the Society of Jesus, started at the news of her convalescence, and, both being full of zeal for Holy Religion, they will give courage to the Queen to prosecute the Holy Cause....

The Bishop's second visit to the Cardinal was to tell him of the Pope's command that he (Laureo) should return to Mondovi; and the Cardinal, evidently seeing the whole Papal subsidy vanishing and Mary overwhelmed, begged the Nuncio to await an answer to his letter sent by the "gentleman," or at least until

---

[1] The illness at Jedburgh is referred to.

after the baptism which would take place within a month[1]. The Nuncio agreed, "in order to show that on the part of his Holiness' Nuncio no effort or diligence has been spared to carry out the pious and holy intention of our lord the Pope."

Here, then, in the plainest language, we have the "test" to be proposed to Mary. Whether it is true that the Cardinal of Lorraine fell in with the plan to the extent suggested is perhaps open to doubt; it was so evidently a strong plank in the Nuncio's schemes that Mary's uncle should join in the advice, and he required so much persuasion to do so, that it is likely the agreement to send a gentleman would be given more prominence than in fact was due. At a later date, the Nuncio is himself inclined to think that the Cardinal was rather "driving time" than seriously pushing the proposal: "I begin to fear, either that the said lord cardinal did not use all the urgency needed to convince the Queen in such a matter, or that her Majesty has another end in view"[2]; and, in another place: "The truth is that the principals who managed this business, really did not from the beginning proceed with becoming sincerity[3]."

It is now necessary to consider what was going on in Scotland while the Papal Nuncio was evolving his plans to fulfil his mission, and how Mary received his proposals. The period to be covered is from, say, July to end of November 1566.

THE SITUATION IN SCOTLAND, JULY TO NOVEMBER 1566

CROSS CURRENTS

Mary's annalists are silent, or supply but meagre details as to the sub-surface movements which were shaping her destiny during the five or six months following the birth of the Prince. In truth they are difficult to define. One learns of them as much from what has not been said as from what is recorded, from little tremors rather than great vibrations.

[1] That would be say by 20th November, an additional proof that the waiting for Moretta did in fact cause delay.

[2] Pollen, p. 323.   [3] Pollen, p. 381.

Broadly speaking, since the murder of Riccio on 9th March, 1566, the Queen and Darnley shaped different courses. He, impelled by Lennox, Gwynn, the Standens and Sir James Balfour, reached definitely towards the power of Spain; he had lost ground to make up, but no doubt had his explanations. She, impelled by sheer necessity to preserve her Crown and her son's rights, inclined towards Rome and accepted the steersmanship of her pilots—the Cardinal, the Archbishop of Glasgow, and the Bishops of Dunblane and Ross. Spain was within her course too, but it was Spanish influence with Elizabeth rather than force that she required; and, if pecuniary aid were forthcoming, it should be sent through Rome and not direct. Wittingly or not, in this the wishes of Philip were respected; he did not desire to figure personally. Nor, since the Lennox missioner, Yaxley, had obtained his money, did Philip show any disposition to supply more. "I tried to induce him to support the said Lady but no such word escaped him *now*," said the French Ambassador; and, in fact, whatever the cause, Philip's sympathy at this time does not extend towards Mary. "The ready will of the Pope...was clearly to be seen, and the great influence he had with King Philip, though, in the opinion of the Ambassador of Scotland and the Bishop of Dunblane, the help of the Pope alone was sufficient[1]." It was the Pope who found the subsidy, Philip gave words only.

In the thoughts of Mary and of Darnley, two impending events claimed in different degrees the first place. To Darnley, the coming of Philip to the Netherlands gave rise to renewed aspirations, which were probably based on some assurances from the source. To Mary, the accomplishment of the baptism of her firstborn outweighed all considerations, and Elizabeth's cordiality gave rise to renewed hopes of settlement of a permanent kind.

To Mary this ceremony was something which perhaps can only be dimly comprehended. West was nearer East than it is to-day, and some who have knowledge of the ecstasy of an Eastern mother at the advent of a firstborn son can perhaps enter into

[1] Pollen, p. 314, Mondovi to Alessandria, 12th November, 1566.

16-2

her mind. In the East a firstborn son is the crown and glory of the mother. She is now placed among the honoured women, she has secured favour before the gods. To Mary, if something less than this, it was more in other ways; she was mother to a prince of undoubted right to succeed to both Crowns; the ceremony, of infinite importance in her eyes as a Christian, was to set the seal on her natural ambitions; in her son would come the solution of the agelong struggle between the two nations. She would be able to look to a time when she could lay aside this heavy Crown in his favour[1]. She shared, too, the dreams of her uncle of Lorraine of uniting the Churches on the middle line. But, not less than all this, the great ceremony was to set at rest the calumny put about by the man who should have guarded her honour. If Mary's dreams pictured her son as progenitor of a long line of Royalty, it was given to her to taste the bitterness of learning that he inherited his father's nature. Can anyone doubt what manner of man Darnley was when they know what James became?[2]

To complete this ceremony with circumstance far beyond her means, to outbid the bribery of Cecil, so as to obtain from her treacherous nobles permission to hold the office according to her Faith[3], she would go to almost any length. Unquestionably she diverted the first instalment of the Papal subsidy to this purpose —as much as she could get of it; equally certain it is that she exaggerated the willingness of her Calvinist masters to receive the Nuncio, hoping to secure the rest of it. She mortgaged her

[1] If we can trust Brantôme it was only a sense of duty that induced her to quit France to take up her sovereignty; and, from the time of Riccio's murder, there are several statements, from widely different sources, of her desire to retire from a task for which she felt herself physically unfit.

[2] If any reader doubts what James became, a recently published book, *King James' Secret* by Professor Rait and Miss Cameron, will settle that question.

[3] It is worth noting that the Archbishop of Glasgow thought that Elizabeth's envoys at the baptism, "though they are Lutherans, should not refuse to take part in the holy ceremony, as the mode of baptism in the Lutheran sect does not differ much from that used in the Holy Catholic Roman Church" (Pollen, p. 291).

dowry in France for two years[1] and pawned her credit to the Edinburgh merchants; she humbled herself to beg where she should have commanded. All this in order that the pomp should lack nothing that could help, in the presence of England and France, to bury the last whisper of Darnley's unmanly lie.

And that scoundrel, knowing her position, blackmailed her by threatening to leave the country before she had accomplished her "triumph." Can one wonder if, when on 5th November she received one of his letters,

which when she had read in presence of the Regent, the Earl of Huntly and the Secretary, she cast a piteous look, and miserably tormenting herself, as if she would have fallen down again into her former sickness, she plainly and expressly protested, that, unless she might by some means or other be despatched of the king she should never have a good day. And if by no other way she could attain it, rather than she would abide to live in such sorrow, she would slay herself.

This extract from the 'Detection' of George Buchanan may contain truth; but, knowing the source, one may expect insinuations. It is natural that Mary, barely a week recovered from a serious illness, should lose control of herself and, if she used the words imputed to her, it indicates her overwrought feelings regarding the baptism; and, though the letter from Darnley probably contained other things, one cannot doubt that it aimed at a further hindrance to her hoped-for success[2].

No pen has yet been able—no pen will ever be able—to convey *all* the tragedy that lies behind this hunger of the mother to ensure that her son should not suffer by the calumnies heaped on herself. "You know," wrote du Croc, "very well that the

---

[1] By some jugglery the money seems to have been withheld, see Pollen, p. 475.

[2] Admirers of J. A. Froude may wonder why he, deliberately, having the 'Detection' and the 'Book of Articles' before him, falsified the extract to turn it more to Mary's disfavour; see his *History*, VII, p. 491. It may also be asked why the "Noble Moray" of Froude's imagination did not explain all the circumstances when he read this story in the 'Book of Articles'; most likely it was he who supplied Buchanan with the tale and indicated its usefulness.

injury[1] she has received is exceeding great"; much of what these words include is hidden from us, but it is at least certain that he refers to the outrageous conduct of her husband.

To Darnley the great event was the rumoured coming of Philip to the Netherlands. So far back as June of the preceding year (1565), during the conference at Bayonne, there had been conversations between the Cardinal of Guise[2], the Archbishop of Glasgow and the Duke of Alva; the last had expressed his Sovereign's satisfaction at the decision taken by Mary to marry her cousin, and a great deal was said by the other two as to the reliance placed by Mary on the support of Philip, which may or may not have been justified by their instructions[3]. Cardinal Louis was more inclined to seek violent issues than his brother. Of the Archbishop it can be said that he was always extreme, but not always "Spanish," as on this occasion. At the moment our point is that the Duke assured his visitors that Philip, "being in Flanders, would be able with more convenience to attend to that which would be suitable to her (Mary)[4]." Whether this statement came to Scotland or not is not known, but a similar promise appears in Philip's letter of 23rd October in the same year, addressed to Darnley personally, to which reference has been made.

Thus it may be said that the notion that Philip's coming to the States was synonymous with some action towards Scotland was already planted in Darnley's mind; and now, in this year of 1566, with ever-increasing definition came the report that the intention was about to materialize. To what extent Darnley had lost value in Philip's eyes, as a prospective instrument, by the Riccio affair, is a difficult question to answer. With Pope Pius V one might be safe in saying that to league with heretics to accom-

---

[1] This is Bishop Keith's translation; the original is not available, but we may be sure that the French word was *injure* which would be better rendered "slander" or "insult."

[2] Louis de Lorraine, *not* Charles.

[3] Mary made the announcement of the birth herself a month later, and it seems a little unlikely that she had authorized what may be called an *ad interim* report.

[4] *Relations*, v, pp. 12 ff., Alva to Philip, 29th June, 1565.

plish any end could not be justified; with the King of Spain it was probably different, and the failure to attain the end in view only counted, to which may be added the premature action which he particularly disliked. Still the Lennox Stuarts, mother, father and son, had inherent value which could not be thrown away because the son was a fool. One thing is certain that what de Silva from London, or de Alava from Paris, wrote about it is not worth much, for these astute counterparts of Philip himself were adepts at concealing any secret matter, and of communicating by means other than open letters.

The first whispers of Philip's coming, other than the hints referred to above, appear to have come in the letters of the French Ambassador in Madrid; during the last months of 1565 and the beginning of 1566 he reports the collection of men and money and ships, the purpose of which was doubtful. Catherine frequently writes for more information, and is evidently suspicious of the end in view. In May (1566) comes the first definite statement that a journey to Flanders is contemplated and, from that time onwards, it is frequently referred to. The Netherlands were ablaze and Philip, by acts of almost abnormal tergiversation, seemed to fan the fire[1]. The Pope was urgent in exhorting him by his presence to quench the flame which seemed to threaten the continued existence of Holy Religion, and in August Philip replied: "If success were wished for, so must the King appear with an army, not only for personal protection, but also to overawe the rebellious Netherlands, and their friends in France, Germany *and England.*" For this, he said, money was wanted, and hinted that a papal subsidy was appropriate[2]. When all was ready he would start, undisturbed by any personal danger. In the same month of August, Fourquevaux reported that his coming was certain.

All this was the common talk of the Courts, but besides rumour, Darnley and the Lennox family had special information. Lady Margaret, though in the Tower, had means of communicating with Scotland, not, we may be sure, with Mary who

---

[1] Cf. Motley, chap. VIII.
[2] Pastor, *Gesch.* Pius V, pp. 344–5.

was in opposition to the whole Lennox faction, but *via* Flanders[1]. The Spanish Ambassador, de Silva, was able to keep her informed of doings outside her prison. Opportunely, too, we have the scrap of information in one of de Silva's letters[2] that surprise was expressed by the English Ambassador in Paris at Darnley's friendship with de Alava. The explanation given for this, that they had been intimate in Paris, can hardly be true, for de Alava was not resident there until February 1564; it is true that he had paid flying visits there previous to this[3], but it is unlikely that Darnley had been in Paris unless in his boyhood. Hence we may take it that the friendship now spoken of was deduced from intercourse by letter and messenger; and, coming at this particular time, it is significant.

At all events it is clear that, whether by suggestion from the Spanish Ambassadors in London or Paris or on other incitement, Darnley was engaged in plotting in England, and the manner of his proceeding gives the impression that it was intended to co-operate with a Spanish plan of campaign. To seize Scarborough Castle and capture the Scilly Isles may seem a foolish enterprise; but, in fact, the one would be an important asset to an invading force from the Low Countries, and the other a useful base for a descent on the West of England. So much so, in fact, that it is probable the idea originated in a more military brain than that of Darnley or his father. Of Darnley's dreams at that time this interpretation may be offered; to fly to Flanders—the record tells us several times that this was his intention—to denounce his child as a bastard, to join the Spanish forces, to await the coming of Philip, and then a "merry war," escorted by Philip's carefully selected ten thousand, in an England prepared as to one-half to receive the invaders—so he erroneously thought—with open arms; finally a coronation at Westminster, by favour of his mother, and the united rule of Great Britain in the Holy Catholic faith, supported by all the might of Spain and the Papal power. This was a foolish dream, even without its gravest omission—that Mary still lived. After the coming of Laureo's

---

[1] Bain, II, p. 310. [2] *Simancas*, 29th June, 1566, to Philip.
[3] See Mahon, *Mary Queen of Scots*, p. 135.

missioners to Scotland, the dream changed, as will be shown later.

Confirmation of these aspirations in high quarters cannot be expected, but there is a remarkable warrant from a source which, while it certainly lacks in weight, has none the less an air of truth that carries conviction. The evidence is that of one William Rogers, a fugitive from justice in England, who was evidently seeking to ingratiate himself with Cecil by assuming the self-imposed duties of spy. He was, it appears, in Scotland during the latter half of June 1566; the Queen was at this time "lying-in" at the Castle of Edinburgh and, though what he says does not suggest any participation by Mary, it is as well to note that in all probability she never heard of him. Rogers passed into England towards the end of June and had reached Oxford, whence he wrote to Cecil[1].

By confessing himself an offender against the laws of England, not a recommendation that adds to the reputation of those who received him, he wormed himself into the confidence of the two Standens, henchmen of Darnley, and also into that of the King himself. He rode with the King at hunting and hawking, and was taken to be his man. The matter learnt by Rogers through this intercourse was—that Henry Gwynn had brought letters from Lady Margaret for Darnley and also other letters from nephews of the Cardinal, Arthur and Edward Pole, the former of whom had been in the Tower since an abortive attempt to raise insurrection four years previously, the latter apparently at large. Arthur Pole transmitted an offer to resign his claim to England as direct heir of the Plantagenet line, in favour of Mary and Darnley—no new thing as regards the former, for he had done so in 1562 and no notice had been taken of it; he claimed also to have interest sufficient to raise the West of England in support of any plot against Elizabeth. If he could get out of the Tower he would be shortly in Scotland, there to serve the King at his own charges. There was also one Martin Dare, a companion of Edward Pole, who was or had been a captain at Scilly, and must have been acquainted with the strategic position there.

[1] Bain, II, p. 293.

Gwynn had also brought from a merchant 2000 crowns to Darnley, with offer of more if necessary for his purpose. Others in the North, such as Sir Richard Cholmeley and his son, were prepared to deliver Scarborough Castle; and one Moon—who appears later as a servant of Lennox—came every month from the west country with communications from the gentlemen there.

Had the political atmosphere abroad been clear, Cecil would no doubt have treated the matter more lightly, but, with the coming of the Spanish King looming on the horizon, with Darnley's family claim on the allegiance of the English Catholics, and with the knowledge that communication by all the parties with Flanders, which meant with Spain, was in progress, the affair became serious. It may be taken as certain that the outcome was the urgent demand for the return to Scotland of the Earl of Morton, and the drawing up of the Cecil-Moray-Morton bond for the "removal" of Darnley, to which reference has already been made. It is not likely that any of the conspirators knew of the information given by Rogers—Cecil would more probably carry on bogus correspondence through him until all the names concerned were in his toils. It must be emphasized that, in all this plotting in England, Mary's name is absent. A little later perhaps she heard of it, and the fact added to her dismay at her husband's conduct; for, in this respect, it is obvious that he was directly across her path of carrying her great ceremony to a successful conclusion, with the friendly co-operation of Elizabeth, and all that that connoted.

During the weeks following the birth of the Prince on 19th June, Mary did nothing to confirm any confidence that Laureo might still retain in her. Moray was received to full favour and shortly after, about mid-September, Lethington was restored to his office of Secretary and reconciled to Bothwell, and Argyll was called again to Council—all in precise contrast to the plans which the Nuncio was formulating in Paris.

After the hunting in Meggotland wherein Mary, Darnley, Moray, Mar, Bothwell and others had joined, all apparently on good terms, the party, or at least the Queen and Darnley, had returned to Stirling at the end of August. About 12th Septem-

ber, Mary returned to Edinburgh to hold what is described as
the usual audits of accounts. Whether Darnley had refused to
accompany her on this occasion, as is said, is not certain. It was
at this time that she reconciled Maitland with Bothwell, received
the former to his old office as Secretary, and restored Argyll to
favour. On 21st September she returned to Stirling, and it was
then apparently that Darnley began again to show his cloven
hoof. That he saw in this reconciliation between the Queen and
his former associates in the Riccio affair danger to his own life
is unlikely; rather, he probably saw an opportunity to do something noteworthy to restore himself in the estimation of Rome
and Spain. It has been seen already that he was plotting on
behalf of the latter; he had probably not yet had any news of
the proceedings of Laureo—unless Stephen Wilson, who was
still in Scotland, had given him more information than he had
imparted to Mary; but he was well aware that Mary's present
course was altogether opposed to Counter-Reformation.

The arrival of John Beton from Laureo on 22nd September
with the instalment of the Papal subsidy no doubt caused Mary
to return to Edinburgh on the following day. There was no
secret about the matter, as she discussed it with her Privy
Council. On this occasion Darnley certainly did refuse to accompany her, and sent for his father, who came to Stirling from
Glasgow and remained two or three days in conference with his
son. We are told that Lennox undertook this visit in order to
remonstrate with Darnley on his proposal to go abroad to Flanders; but probably this was not the only matter discussed; and
it is much more likely the chief subject was how best to take
advantage of the present situation.

Several letters, written in October by Du Croc, the Lords of
Council, and Robert Melville, give insight into the nature of the
discussion[1]; all agree that, after the conversation with Darnley,

[1] Du Croc to Archbishop Beton, 13th October, 1566, in Keith, II,
p. 448; the same to Queen-Mother, 17th October, in Labanoff, I,
p. 374; Lords of Council to same, 8th October, in Keith, II, p. 453;
Robert Melville to Beton, dated London, 22nd October, in Keith, II,
p. 460.

Lennox notified the Queen of his son's intention to leave Scotland. On the day that this notification came to Mary's hand, 29th September, and apparently by pre-arrangement, Darnley arrived in Edinburgh, and, on the following day, was questioned by the Council as to his reasons for such a step. One gathers that the idea uppermost in the minds of those present, including Mary herself, was that his departure might compromise the Queen's honour, and possibly interfere with the baptism. Mary "prayed him not to dissemble the occasion of his displeasure"; she said she had a "clear conscience, that in all her life she had done no action which could anywise prejudge either his or her honour." It is easy enough to comprehend what she meant, "you are going away to slander me, to deny your own son, unless...." Unless what?

Two of the letters above referrred to give a partial answer; that of Melville specifically mentions the Secretary Maitland, Bellenden the Justice Clerk, and McGill the Clerk Register, as persons whose dismissal was demanded by the King. Du Croc's letter, in more general terms, refers to his jealousy of certain nobles, meaning Moray, Argyll and the absent Morton. All these six persons were on the "black list" of the Catholic party. The only conclusion possible is that the interests of the Papal Nuncio were the interests of Lennox and his son, and the conversation between father and son resulted in agreement that this demand should be made, with a threat of the consequences of refusal.

It was now, or about, this time that Darnley wrote or sent to the King of Spain and the Pope describing Mary's remissness in religion, and no doubt reporting to them her pardon of the Protestant lords, her favour extended to Maitland, the most feared of them all, the probability that Morton would soon be recalled, the reasons why she desired the presence of the Nuncio, namely to obtain the rest of the subsidy, and her misapplication of the part already sent. To this, Froude adds that he wrote, "the Queen of Scots having ceased to care for religion, they must *look to him only* for the restoration of Catholicism[1]." This,

[1] Froude, VII, p. 440.

as a statement of fact, is imaginary on Froude's part, but it is very much what one would expect Darnley to say.

Some writers question if such letters were in fact sent, and point to Philip's denial[1], though that in itself would hardly suffice. Quite possibly there were no letters but a messenger only, and, though Anthony Standen, elder, had it appears[2] already left Scotland about six weeks previously, it is likely enough that he, with his full knowledge of the plotting in England, may have received instructions to proceed to Madrid and Rome[3]. There seems connection between this Darnley's propaganda and the "secret information" received by Laureo, that "the Queen formed the determination of sending for me with great difficulty...in order to avail herself of the remainder of these moneys[4]."

The Council which Mary held at Edinburgh on the 23rd or 24th September was presumably that at which the question so much in Mary's mind was opened, *i.e.* the consent of her heretic advisers to hold the baptismal ceremony according to the rites of the Catholic Church, and the question, less urgent to her, what was to be done about the Nuncio. One gathers that much discussion went on, and that Mary did not gain her point at once, at least as regards the Nuncio. Bishop Leslie in the *Paralipomena* states that consent to the advent of Laureo was refused, particularly by Moray[5]; it is difficult therefore to account for the instructions given to Stephen Wilson. These contain a paragraph in effect as follows: "You shall declare to the Nuncio that the cause of delay in answering his letter was the necessity to await the consent of the nobility to his coming. Which consent, for that and the Baptism was obtained in the beginning of October." Wilson's despatches were dated 9th October, but he

---

[1] *Simancas*, under date 17th February, 1567.

[2] *Cal. For. Eliz.* 1566/8, under date 17th August, 1566.

[3] This person remained on the continent until the time of the Gunpowder Plot of 1605, always plotting in the Catholic interest. See also Nau, pp. c ff. for some, not very reliable, account of himself by the person in question.

[4] Dated 12th November 1566, in Pollen, p. 313.

[5] Forbes-Leith, p. 114.

had not started when Mary's illness at Jedburgh delayed him again. Finally, he did not reach Paris until about 20th November. He carried a letter to the Pope which announced that the Nuncio would be conducted to Scotland with all honour[1], and also a covering letter to Laureo telling him that he could only be received under some other colour than that of Religion![2] The Nuncio, very naturally, said he did not understand what that meant.

To the zealots sitting in council in Paris there appeared to be no difficulty in the "removal" of those persons who were responsible for Mary's dilemma; one can imagine the opinion formed of a Queen, believed to have that power, whose every act indicated heresy and whose words attempted deception. It is not surprising that they—or one of them—dubbed her *peccatrix*. Her enemies have fastened on that epithet to deduce therefrom that she was guilty of her husband's death; even Father Pollen, not an enemy, expresses that view[3], though all the information collected by himself with such admirable research proves definitely that Hay used the term to express her want of fervency in a cause in which he himself would willingly submit to any torture to make even a small step forward.

Thus the course so far taken by the Queen set her in further antagonism with the elements that the Lennox Stuarts had cultivated since the time of Mary Tudor. Her orthodoxy had often been questioned before, but now that the Counter-Reformation was in new and vigorous hands, a woman, and especially a woman brought up in contact with all that was moderate in France, was a positive hindrance to progress. On the other hand, Darnley, worthless and incompetent in himself, was a useful tool—a figurehead—for the attack.

THE RECEPTION OF THE TEST, NOVEMBER 1566

We have seen that with "great difficulty" the Cardinal of Lorraine had been persuaded by Laureo, Bishop of Mondovi, the Papal Nuncio, to send a "gentleman" to advise and persuade the

---

[1] Labanoff, I, pp. 370–1.   [2] Pollen, p. 323.
[3] *Catholic Encyclopedia*, Art. "Hay, Edmund."

Queen "to decide on restoring Holy Religion in her kingdom," and we have noted some doubts expressed by the Bishop as to whether the Cardinal "used all the urgency" that the case required[1]. The zealous Bishop goes on to tell that the Cardinal was anxious that "this last counsel of his" should be kept secret, lest the Huguenots in the French King's guard should assassinate him[2]. This latter statement is probably not strictly true, but at least it is likely that the envoy chosen would travel with a minimum of publicity. There is no trace of the arrival in Scotland of any special messenger from the Cardinal; and in such matters we greatly miss the letters of Randolph, who would assuredly have discovered something to go on. Judging by the date of the Cardinal's consent to send a man, his departure may be placed as about 17th October, and at or about that date the Comte de Brienne commenced his journey to Edinburgh to attend the baptism as representative of Charles IX, arriving there on 3rd November[3]. In his train was the younger du Croc, son of the French Ambassador or agent[4]. This person had already a position in Mary's household, probably honorary, as "Pannetier[5]," and, as such, would have easy access without remark. According to the best accounts he was a dependent of the house of Guise. He may have been the bearer of the momentous "test." At the time of his reaching Edinburgh the Queen was barely convalescent from her serious illness at Jedburgh; she left that place on 5th November and came to Kelso on her slow return journey to Edinburgh. The younger du Croc, if haste was made, could have come to her there; but that is the earliest possible date.

That Mary did in fact receive some intimation[6] from her uncle

---

[1] p. 241.　　　　　　　　　　[2] Pollen, p. 314.
[3] *Cal. For. Eliz.* Forster to Cecil, 2nd November, 1566.
[4] Keith, II, p. 452.　　　　　　[5] *Relations*, II, p. 270.
[6] There is but one contemporary reference to the reception by Mary of the advice sent to her by the Cardinal of Lorraine. It is contained in Buchanan's *History*, p. 320: "She was incited to this (the murder of Darnley) by letters from the Pope and the Cardinal of Lorraine. For the summer before having, by her uncle, desired a sum of money from the Pope for levying an army to disturb the state of religion in Britain, the Pope more cunningly, but the Cardinal plainly, advised her to

at about this date is borne out by a letter by Laureo dated 3rd December. The Nuncio had then recently received a letter from the Cardinal announcing that Mary would not consent to the project. This report from his "gentleman" must have been carried to the Cardinal by Stephen Wilson, who left Edinburgh on or about 8th November, passed through London on the 13th[1], and reached Paris about the 20th, so that, allowing for halts and delays, the Cardinal probably had the news of Mary's decision by this post. The point is that Mary came to her momentous decision on or about the 5th November.

Now it was on that day that Mary is said to have received that letter from her husband which reduced her to such a state of misery, as already mentioned[2]. One would suppose that Darnley had already reached the depth of insult in his previous conduct and his letter of Michaelmas day in which he threatened to leave the country and all that that connoted. What can this new letter have contained that to Mary in her weak state of health seemed so insupportable? The answer can perhaps be gleaned from de Silva's letter to Philip of 13th November. He says: "He (Wilson) has been instructed to tell me that the Queen had heard that her husband had written to your Majesty, the Pope, the King of France and Cardinal Lorraine that she was dubious in the faith...."

A light is here thrown on Mary's character which, to the most prejudiced reader, can scarcely fail to give a favourable impression. She is ill, friendless, surrounded by men whose treachery

destroy those who were the greatest hinderers to the restitution of popery, and they took care to specify the two earls (Moray and Argyll) by name. If *they* were once taken off, they promised whole heaps of money. The Queen thought some distant tidings of this was brought to the ears of the nobility, and therefore to clear herself of suspicion, or the least inclination to such a thing, she showed them the letters." Neglecting the constant tendency of Buchanan to intermix truth and falsehood and substituting the name of Laureo for the Pope, we have a perverted representation of the facts.

[1] *Simancas*, of that date.

[2] p. 245. The receipt of the letter is mentioned in the 'Book of Articles,' the 'Detection' and other places.

has but recently been demonstrated, even if for the moment they appear to be in harmony with her, her every thought, in circumstances already mentioned, is concentrated on the accomplishment of the baptism and *entente* with England, and now she is confronted with the question which, in those days of intense religious feeling, would most surely cause mental agony. Womanlike, she had attempted to skirt round the problem, to woo both Rome and England, to obtain the material support of the one in order to give her a stronger position before the other. To a degree she was succeeding until her graceless husband, with no lofty motive of exposing duplicity, wrote or sent to Laureo and to Philip to reveal her thoughts and to accuse her of laxity in her faith.

To accept the test and confute this statement, to refuse it and complete the circle of enemies by antagonizing Rome and Spain, to weaken herself, possibly to put a bar to her high hope of killing the great slander by a magnificent ceremony—that was the question. Whether she hesitated or not we do not know, but the answer returned was that she would not stain her hands with the blood of her subjects.

Mary was *dévote*, but, like other exalted persons of her day, there was to her nothing illogical in believing herself the humble daughter of the Church, while holding views too broad to be orthodox[1]. Her character was not strong enough to permit her to utter her mind, and perhaps not even to define it to herself; to be rudely accused of want of faith was all the greater shock if in her conscience she knew it to be partly true. At the least, spiritually and materially, she knew her decision would be to her disadvantage.

---

[1] Cf. Rodocanachi, *Renée de France*, pp. 164 f.

FATA TEXUNT

The conditions at this time are of the greatest importance. Archibald Douglas was already carrying notes between Morton and Moray, Morton was in communication with Cecil, the name of the Queen's Majesty of England was being pledged, perhaps without her consent. The bond intended to seal the fate of Darnley was in the making, the attempt to draw Mary into the plot was formed, based speciously on the events just referred to, and Mary will reply: "I will that you do nothing whereto any spot may be layed to my honour or conscience...rather let the matter be in the estate as it is, abiding till God of His goodness put remedy thereto."

Darnley and his father were pursuing their schemes "to come by the Crown," plotting in England, hinting of Mary's unfitness to govern in the Catholic interest, and, by inference if not directly, indicating what could be done if Henry Stuart were king, plotting at home to capture the Prince and destroy the mother.

De Silva wrote on 4th November to Philip his master one of those open letters, so indicative of his attitude to Mary throughout, in which so much is hidden between the lines: "The Queen had made her will, leaving the prince in charge of her brother the Earl of Moray, to whom she entrusted the principal part of the Government jointly with the Council; and she enjoined them all to make no changes in religion but to let people live freely in accordance with their consciences as she had ordered." A letter sufficient to damn the subject of it in the eyes of the religious fanatic of Spain, even if he had no other ground for condemnation; a letter which indicates that the servant, aware of his master's feelings, is at no pains to soften the case against Mary. Philip had just held a Council[1] and ordered the Duke of Alava to prepare to carry fire and sword into the Netherlands and elsewhere, if opportunity should offer. The doom of Egmont, not unconnected with Mary, had been decreed.

---

[1] 29th October, 1566. See Gachard, I, p. cl.

The Papal Nuncio charged with the restoration of Holy Religion by Pope Pius V, to whom success alone counted as merit, having failed in his first attack, was now sending out his *Sturmtruppen*, the Jesuit Father Edmund Hay, and the Jesuit at heart, William Chisholm, Bishop of Dunblane. His Holiness was forming that opinion of the Queen of Scotland which he soon afterwards uttered: "It is not his intention to have any further communication with her, unless indeed, in times to come, he shall see some better sign of her life and religion than he has witnessed in the past[1]." These words arose chiefly from the matters in progress at the time, and in no sense indicated any complicity of Mary in the tragedy of February. At the moment he was withdrawing his offered support, and it must be assumed he was informing Philip of the fact—in other words, he was about to abandon Mary.

De Alava, *liaison* between Philip and the Counter-Reformation, was in close touch with affairs in Scotland, and Catherine, as always happened in a crisis, was beginning to show an interest in his mails[2]. Moretta, the inscrutable envoy of Philibert Emanuel, had, apparently, left Savoy *en route* for Scotland, and wandered—perhaps to Spain—before coming to Paris to consult with de Alava and Laureo, then to appear in Edinburgh as the hour struck.

Mary, meanwhile, was physically broken, weak in her great humanity, mastered by fate, and it seems almost a mockery that, while at the beginning of her "hundred days," the French envoy had written, "I never saw her Majesty so much beloved, esteemed and honoured[3]," at the end of it she might exclaim as Faust did:

> Die Uhr mag stehen, der Zeiger fallen,
> Es sei die Zeit für mich vorbei.

The suspicions of the Nuncio regarding the sincerity of the Cardinal of Lorraine in urging Mary to violence were undoubtedly well grounded, and, writing on 12th November, he says:

To avoid, as far as possible, every suspicion of deception and to discover the will of the Queen, and what hope there is for religion...

---

[1] 2nd July, 1567, in Pollen, p. 397.
[2] See p. 272.   [3] October, in Keith, II, p. 431.

the Bishop of Dunblane and the Scottish Father Edmund (Hay) started (for Scotland)...being both full of zeal for holy religion; they will give courage to the Queen to prosecute the holy Cause...[1].

It is clear from the letters that neither of the two missioners was under delusion as to the dangerous nature of their work[2]; from the first they appear to have recognized that something more than mere encouragement of the Queen would be expected from them, but it is clear too that from the first, Hay was regarded as the man in whom the greater trust could be placed.

They sailed from Dieppe on 3rd December, after delay there by contrary winds, which gave them the opportunity of meeting Stephen Wilson, fully acquainted with all that had happened in Scotland up to 8th November. The hopelessness of their task, so far as the Queen was concerned, must have been apparent to them. They arrived in Edinburgh on 13th December, Mary being then in Stirling; it is probable that they had been several days in the country before that, for the voyage with a favourable wind would not have taken so long as ten days. Father Edmund may have been in disguise or at least keeping out of sight. Certainly when he left Scotland after the death of Darnley he did so in an assumed position.

According to his own account, as expressed by Laureo[3], "after having done reverence to the Queen and presented my (Laureo's) letter to her was unable to converse with her about anything, her Majesty being entirely taken up with the celebration of the baptism." He hoped to have an opportunity after the ceremony, but it is pretty certain that no such opportunity occurred before Mary's return to Edinburgh from Stirling on 13th January. The similarity of Mary's treatment of this Papal envoy, as we may call him, and that accorded to de Gouda some four years previously must be noted. It is obvious that on neither occasion was she eager to hear what the messenger had to say, and the fact is worth more than the flowers of speech put into

[1] Letter of the Bishop of Mondovi, dated 12th November, 1566, in Pollen, p. 314.
[2] Pollen, pp. 317, 499, 501.
[3] *ib.* p. 342.

letters by herself or others, as to her desire to be guided by the advice sent to her from Rome. As to Father Edmund there is no evidence, whether from himself or any other, that she saw him at all, or that the Bishop of Dunblane accompanied him to Stirling.

If Mary did give audience to the Bishop of Dunblane, it was in Edinburgh during the week preceding her journey to Glasgow with the alleged murderous intentions regarding her husband. The only account of the conversation is contained in a document of doubtful authorship[1]. It is not very reliable, but it says that he told her how easy it would be to purge the kingdom of heretics, that foreign troops were ready, that money was available in Antwerp, that, if she should neglect this offer, no other would ever occur during her life. The answer has been already quoted, she would not stain her hands with blood, her "sister" of England now regarded her as her lawful heir and had sent her tokens of love and goodwill. It is unnecessary to enlarge on the impossibility of harmonizing these sentiments with the alleged intentions of Mary; this has been dealt with sufficiently.

Of the part taken by Father Edmund Hay there is a remarkable silence. There is, it is true, a general letter written at a later date stating that he went about the country freely and openly, disputed with a Calvinist doctor, made sundry conversions, and that, when in London on his way home, he animated and consoled many[2]. The writer must be held to have over-coloured his narrative. It is impossible to suppose that a Jesuit priest could at that time have shown himself openly in the country. It must be remembered that, when de Gouda visited Scotland, the hue and cry after the same Father Edmund was such that he was obliged to hide and leave the less well-known Father Crichton to conduct the Papal envoy[3]. In contemporary secular history there is no mention of him at all, nor does John Knox refer to him[4]. When he left Scotland, after Darnley's death, it is evident

---

[1] See Pollen, pp. 404–5; also Nau, p. 123.
[2] Pollen, p. 507.   [3] Pollen, p. 147.
[4] Knox was in fact absent in England from the end of December 1566, and the fifth book of his *History* which contains the relation of this

that he travelled in the train of Moretta, though Drury, who mentions that Moretta passed Berwick homeward bound, on 14th February, says nothing about Hay. Nor is there any mention of his doings in London during Moretta's stay there of some nine days between 24th February and 6th March. Not until 15th March did Moretta, with Hay in his company, arrive at Paris[1], and shortly thereafter a correspondent of Cecil wrote to him, "The principal of the college of Jesuits in France, that was in Scotland with M. Moret, returned with him to France." It would seem that this was the first that Cecil knew of the fact[2].

It is enough that, from the date of Moretta's arrival in Edinburgh on or about 25th January, 1566/67, Father Hay attached himself to him, and, whatever the part taken by the Savoyard may have been, we must admit community of thought between the two, and further that what Hay had to do was done secretly and under assumed position. Before Moretta came, Hay was presumably in the company of his fellow-envoy the Bishop of Dunblane, who appears to have come openly, under pretence of assisting at the baptism; this in effect he did, and was later sent back to France without disguisement, to present the excuses drawn up for Mary for her disastrous marriage with Bothwell.

period was not directly composed by him. Still, if Father Edmund had been openly in Scotland, some mention of the fact could hardly fail to have found a place. Knox returned in June 1567 in time to take part in the demand for Mary's life. How far he and Cecil were in agreement in this, one can only guess from similar previous conjunctions.

[1] Pollen, p. 369.

[2] The late Father Pollen, some years ago, kindly lent me his notes from an unfinished Memoir by Father Hay, written between 1589–91, from which it appears that Hay spent three years in Scotland from August 1585. "His business," says Father Pollen, "was evidently religio-political, and he had much communication with his brother Peter Hay, then at the Court of James...he was banned and searched for, and passed under various disguises....The English Court had a special 'down' on him...." Spottiswood, *Hist. Ch. Scot.* II, p. 392, indicates that Hay had been imprisoned at one time in the Tower; this is probably an error, as, though a certain Father Edmondes, a Jesuit, was imprisoned in the Clink in 1587, it is not certain that this meant Edmund Hay.

What, then, was the part taken by this most zealous priest Edmund Hay? Recently admitted as "professed of the four vows," which included submission to the will of the Sovereign Pontiff, "dead to the world, he sees naught but our Lord who takes the place of parents, brothers, and of all things[1]." Doubts have been cast on the constancy of the Bishop of Dunblane, but on that of his companion Edmund the idea of doubt is impossible; to him no danger, no sacrifice would weigh against obedience in the Holy Cause. The question above cannot be answered other than by induction from indirect evidence.

The evidence is abundant that both Chisholm and Hay were sent over to bring to effect the "useful and prudent counsel that I (Mondovi), in the name of our Lord the Pope, offered to give some necessary aids (towards)[2]." Ostensibly, this was to be done by persuading the Queen to act; actually, as has already been said, such an attempt was known to be hopeless before the envoys started. Not only had she refused, but, if Buchanan is to be trusted, she had shown the letters on the subject to the principal victims[3]. To a man of Father Edmund's intensity of spiritual exaltation this was a minor hindrance, for he had already a low opinion of the Queen's orthodoxy, "May God grant that she may lay to her heart this fatherly correction, and that it may lead her to carry out with greater diligence the work which hitherto she had only begun...[4]," and this was probably less than he felt of a lady who had declared for liberty of conscience[5]. He may have been a loyal and affectionate subject, but such feelings

[1] Fouqueray, I, p. 106.

[2] Pollen, p. 323. See also the same purpose in many of the letters collected in the same volume, relating to Laureo's nunciature.

[3] I do not think that Buchanan is to be trusted, this part of his history is nearly everywhere at variance with truth. I doubt if there were any letters to show, more probably a "credit" or verbal communication brought by the younger du Croc. What is more likely is that Darnley's letter received at the same time was shown to Moray. Possibly it came to much the same thing in putting the Protestant nobles on their guard.

[4] November 1566, shortly before starting for Scotland.

[5] The view taken by Hay of such a transgression is exemplified in a later letter after the marriage with Bothwell: "I hear," he says, "that both religions (God have mercy on us!) are approved...."

would not weigh one grain when confronted by want of firmness in the cause to which he was dedicated. In such circumstances Father Hay would be unlikely to waste time in useless addresses to Mary; even if she had been disposed to listen, which it is clear she was not, he would have proceeded at once to act independently. He had once before had a similar task and failed; this time there should be no failure.

Before the course followed by Father Hay is considered, it is convenient to draw attention to some features of his mission, and the curious reticence in reporting the result. Following Laureo's letters, we are to believe that Hay had orders to return to Paris after a few days' sojourn in Scotland[1], to report on the state of affairs. Weeks passed and the Nuncio continued to express hope of early news. From the 4th to 24th January, 1566/67, he apparently did not write at all to Rome; on the latter date he mentioned having had a letter from Hay dated 23rd December, but he tells us nothing of what it contained other than that the writer promised an early return. There was another long interval on Laureo's part, and his next letter to Rome was dated 13th February. He is still expecting Hay "at any hour," but has not heard from him.

During all this time, Rome repeats orders for the Nuncio to return to his Diocese, yet he remains in Paris, reiterating his intention to go to Scotland when, on Hay's return, he shall hear that the way is clear. The suspicion grows that Laureo was less expectant of Hay's return than of hearing of an event in Scotland that would enable him to make an entry with all the pomp due to a Papal Nuncio. That event could only materialize through the fulfilment of Hay's mission.

A week later (19th February) news came, but certainly not what was expected; Darnley and his father were dead, the Protestant lords were safe[2]. A letter had also been received from the Bishop of Dunblane[3]. Unfortunately, the letter is not forthcoming; but, as it was written before the death of Darnley, it may

---

[1] Pollen, p. 333.   [2] The part as to Lennox being of course an error.
[3] The date of receipt is not mentioned, but I think we may assume that it was carried by du Croc, who left Edinburgh on the 22nd January.

be surmised that it contained an account of his audience with Mary, which must have taken place between her arrival in Edinburgh on the 14th January and her departure for Glasgow on 21st January. For reasons of his own the Bishop gave a rosy view of this conversation[1] which does not accord with the more serious account of it already quoted on p. 261 above. Father Edmund Hay wrote also, but he addressed his letter to his Superior in the Society, Father Manare, and its contents were evidently pessimistic; apparently no progress had been possible in the great matter. At the time of writing these letters, Darnley was sick at Glasgow, the Queen was at one with her nobles, and Moretta had not yet arrived at Edinburgh. "All the harm," exclaims Laureo, apparently still harping on Hay's letter, "comes from her Majesty having shown herself opposed to doing what was proposed to her...."

On 23rd February letters arrived by the hand of Clerneau[2], who left Edinburgh on the 10th or 11th February, the first official messenger from the scene; Hay wrote by this messenger and his letter must have been dated the day of the murder, 10th February; again he neglected the Nuncio and addressed himself to his Superior, Father Manare. Complete secrecy was maintained as to what was said, and if the Nuncio knew he said nothing, except that Hay would return with Moretta. It must be supposed that Hay gave opinions or statements which would be of the utmost importance, but the silence regarding his letter indicates contents which Manare thought better suppressed; at the least it can be said that the favour shown to Hay on his return indicates that he was held to have faithfully played the part assigned to him to his utmost power.

On 15th March, 1567, Hay and Moretta arrived in Paris in company, and Laureo reports their news in his letter of 16th. They could hardly have Scottish news later than of 28th February, and what they told the Nuncio seems rather designed to conceal than to impart truth; one can understand de Silva's re-

---

[1] Pollen, p. 351.
[2] Pollen suggests that Clerneau sent a courier forward and came himself a day or two later.

mark, "he (Moretta) gives signs that he knows more than he likes to say[1]." In London Moretta had taken the line of hinting at the Queen's complicity, but the Nuncio does not suggest that he gave similar colour to his conversation with him; he seems content to reiterate that Mary's danger was due to her refusal to do what "was recommended and proposed to her from our side, with promise of all the aids necessary.... But she would never hear of it...."

On 8th April, 1567, we come to the Nuncio's last letter from Paris. He still harps on the want of "sincerity" on the part of the Cardinal of Lorraine, in failing to urge the destruction of the Protestants; it seems evident that his whole plan of operations depended on this, and on Mary as the instrument to carry out the advice tendered. Father Edmund had evidently imparted no more to him (*i.e.* the Nuncio) than bare facts known to all the world; he had promised to leave an account in writing of what he did, but it appears fairly certain that he never did so, for, so late as 9th June, the Secretary-General of the Society writes to Manare to the effect that the fuller relation promised had not been received. What reply Manare made to this is not recorded, but he appears to have been alone the recipient of Father Edmund's confidence. As Father Pollen in his prefatory remarks says: "Considering all these envoys (he includes the Bishop of Dunblane) saw, heard and *presumably reported upon* ...we cannot but feel that there is no other lacuna in the correspondence which we should be better satisfied to see filled up."

It would be too much to say that Father Pollen believed that the silence of Hay covered knowledge regarding the explosion at Kirk o' Field which would put the same complexion on the affair that has been suggested in this work; but it is clear that his deep study of the question, and his knowledge of many papers other than those which he printed in his *Papal Negotiations*, led him to believe, it might even be said to know, that something was concealed. In the eyes of Edmund Hay, Mary was a sinner, a recusant, and, if he had known that she had taken part in a step, the murder of Darnley, which in effect was playing

---

[1] *Simancas*, date 1st March, 1567.

into the hands of Cecil and the English Protestant party, it is impossible to believe his opinions and his knowledge, which he surely must have expressed, would have been kept secret.

The evidence of his rôle is admittedly negative, but this much is patent; at or about the time when Moretta appeared on the scene, first in Paris and then in Scotland, Hay seems to have found him a more competent leader, and to have ceased to regard the Papal Nuncio with confidence. The attitude of the latter lacked that adaptability to change which, to a man of Hay's temperament, left no choice but independent action in conjunction with Moretta the "Spaniard," as he was in effect.

THE SHADOW OF SPAIN

When Moretta and Hay met in consultation on or about 25th January, 1567, with perhaps the Bishop of Dunblane as third party—though nobody seems to have trusted the last—what were the materials at hand? The Queen was pursuing a course opposed to Religion; Darnley was exerting himself in Spanish interests, and posing as the champion of the Catholic Church, with the Earl of Lennox behind him; Sir James Balfour, long a secret agent of the Catholics, was ready on payment for any desperate deed; the Protestant lords were primed for the murder of Darnley. Hay himself was commissioned for the murder, or "justification," of the Protestant lords; Philip was "coming" to the Netherlands; the Pope was ready to find money for something "signal"; the whole devilish stew was on the boil.

Darnley's intimacy with Philip's Ambassador in Paris and his obvious intercourse with the Duchess of Parma have already been referred to; it cannot be doubted that Moretta came with instructions in which the name of Darnley or his father figured. Whether the reader accepts my reason suggested above for Philip's attitude of indifference towards Mary[1] or not, it is certainly the case that he was indifferent[2].

[1] That he suspected her of intrigue against his sovereignty in the Provinces, as well as of leanings to a composition in religion.
[2] Some of the evidence which justifies this statement has been cited; another instance may be added, which occurs in the examination of one

On a previous page[1] the terms have been mentioned in which the Bishop of Dunblane alleged that he put the case to Mary, "How easy it would be to purge the kingdom of heretics, foreign troops ready, money available, no such opportunity likely to recur." Even if it be accepted that this was put to and refused by Mary, is it not probable that it was also put to Darnley? It was hardly necessary to do so, for this was already his line, and quite unnecessary to talk him over to consent to action against the Protestant lords, which evidence of a trustworthy kind shows was his nearest wish, a wish accentuated by the knowledge that these same lords were banded to destroy him. We know that he had this knowledge, from the Lennox manuscript[2]. Certainly Darnley had every reason to hasten his *coup* and to fall in with whatever scheme was now in hand. At any time, Moretta, Hay, Balfour, Dunblane, would have found him ready to listen, but now more so than ever.

It may well be asked if these offers of men and money were in fact substantial. As to money, they probably were so, for, with Mary out of the way, and Darnley with his father heading a Catholic revival, both Spain and Rome would contribute generously. The 20,000 crowns already at Antwerp were, as Pius

James Young, alias Dingley, a Jesuit, in the year 1591 : "After the death of the Queen of Scotland, both Allen and Parsons sought to stir up the Spanish King, who never could be persuaded to attempt anything against England in her (Mary's) lifetime, objecting that he should travail for others." Which means that he would do nothing for Mary, who was not likely to be less "English" than Elizabeth. Father Pollen also notices Philip's many refusals to help Mary; see *The Month*, January–June 1911, p. 22.

[1] p. 261.

[2] "In this meantime his father being advertised that at Craigmillar, the Queen and *certain* of her Council had concluded an enterprise... that he should be apprehended and put in ward...did give him warning thereof..." (see Mahon, *Mary Queen of Scots*, p. 124). The insertion of the Queen as an assenting party is of course merely an addition of Lennox; we have the other side of the story, that the Laird of Minto told him of the Craigmillar talk, and Mary had refused the proposal (Camb. MS. Dd. 3. 64, No. 36). It is beyond doubt that Darnley knew himself safe so long as the Queen was with him.

himself had said, only a part of what he would do for something really "signal." As to men, the prospect was less certain. Margaret of Parma was herself hard pushed by the ever-growing rebellion. She could have sent a stiffening of Spanish troops, and money would attract others; but, for real business, that overwhelming force that rumour reported to be on the move from Spain was essential. But no one but Philip himself knew whether, or when, this force might start. It was collecting in December, very secretly. Fourquevaux had reported it, and Charles IX in reply had expressed his anxiety at the preparations, "for they are so concealed and difficult to discover, yet the preparations are so great, that it is impossible to proceed so secretly that one does not see and hear of it[1];" and in another letter he says, referring to the alleged intention of Philip to make a descent on Algiers: "It may well be some conquest more near or else an intention to proceed direct to Flanders. Employ your five senses to find out the truth." Real or not, these preparations were believed in at the time, and neither Darnley nor Lennox would regard the talk as chimerical. From England they counted on support on a greater scale than they would probably have received, but one is justified in saying that at the close of the year 1566 Darnley recognized that his last opportunity had come, and believed that Philip's power was not far off.

On 21st January, 1566/7, Mary left Edinburgh for Glasgow to bring back her now ostensibly contrite husband; enough has already been said as to why it was that she should go in person. She was due to start back on the 27th, and to arrive at Craigmillar at the end of the month. The French Ambassador du Croc left Edinburgh on the 22nd, and on the 24th, when some twelve miles from Berwick, he met Moretta posting to Edinburgh, a month late to fulfil his mission as sponsor for the Duke of Savoy; and, so much had these two to say to each other, that "the aged and discreet" du Croc turned back and accompanied Moretta to Dunbar, after which he resumed his journey to London and France. They were old acquaintances; "The one (Moretta,

---

[1] Letters of Chas. IX dated 7th December, 1566.

probably) seemeth very desirous of the other's company homewards.... I think he will overtake the other (du Croc)[1]."

Why did this "aged" Ambassador of France undertake an
extra thirty-mile ride for the express purpose of having conversation with the Envoy of Savoy, which is much the same as
saying, of Spain? Their national policies were poles apart, but
they were friends and had a common ground in religion; the
Savoyard was, it appears, somewhat extreme; in Mary's early
days in Scotland he had been sent to her "to confirm her what
he could in her opinion touching religion[2]," and then he had
left her that legacy of Riccio, productive of much evil. Du Croc
is variously described as a "creature" of the Queen-Mother and
as a client of the house of Guise. De Silva says of him[3]: "They
tell me he is a good catholic, and he professes to be one, but he
is considered—*algo inquieto*," *i.e.* rather restless or unreliable,
something not quite what was desirable. He passed as a Queen's
man, but his interference in Mary's affairs wrought more harm
than good. Moretta, on the other hand, was indifferent to King
or Queen, so long as he furthered religion and his master's orders.

It is probable that du Croc had more to tell Moretta than the
latter was likely to tell him. The knowledge that Mary had
refused "the test" was common to both, for Moretta would have
heard that before leaving Paris; he had reached that place about
1st Janauary and spent several days there, before coming to
London about the 18th. He had been in the Nuncio's company
and in that of de Alava, and from the latter would have heard
much, but would pass on very little of it to his companion.
Du Croc could tell how troublesome Darnley had been, about
his wanting to leave Scotland, his doings at Stirling, something
about the Cecil-Moray-Morton bond; but this cannot all have
been new to Moretta. The main item would be that Mary was
at the moment in Glasgow, and that Darnley was coming back
to Edinburgh with her in a week's time, news he may have heard
the day before in Berwick, but not earlier.

[1] *Border State Papers*, XII, under date 26th January, 1567.
[2] December 1561, in Keith, II, pp. 125–6.
[3] *Doc. Ined.* LXXXIX, p. 462.

On 25th January the companions separated, Moretta towards Edinburgh, du Croc to resume his interrupted journey towards London, but with the expressed intention of travelling "at much ease"; he dropped hints in Berwick and London, that he was not without expectation of the tragedy that followed. But the question to which one would like a certain answer is whether the catastrophe anticipated by du Croc was the same as that in the mind of Moretta. It may very well be that the latter left du Croc in possession of his own view, based on the knowledge of the intention of the lords towards Darnley, and it may be, too, that the leisurely journey of the Frenchman, and the arrangement of the flying courier to catch him up, was due to Moretta. It would be immensely useful to him to get *his* news to Paris by the convenience of an Ambassador travelling with full facilities.

It is not unlikely that Moretta did know something about the plot against the Queen which Archbishop Beton's belated warning specified. Beton's letter to Mary was dated 27th January, and was sent by one Robert Dury, who arrived in Edinburgh on the morning of the 10th February; the gunpowder tragedy had taken place only a few hours previously. It contained this:

For none of the heads precedent thought I to have despatched expressly towards your Majesty, if by the ambassador of Spain (de Alava) I had not been required thereto; and specially to advertise you to take heed to yourself. I have heard some murmuring in like wise by others, that there be some surprise to be trafficked in your contrary, but he (de Alava) would never let me know of no particular, only assured me he had written to his master to know if by that way he can try (learn?) any further, and that he was advertised and counselled to cause me haste towards you herewith. Further in this instance, and at his desire partly, I spake earnestly at the Queen Mother, if she had heard any discourse or advertisement lately, tending to your hurt or disadvantage, but I came no speed, nor would she confess that she had gotten nor heard any such appearance[1].

Out of this extract arise several questions. It would be quite in accordance with Philip's methods to send a warning timed to

---

[1] Keith, I, p. ciii.

be too late. De Alava had his information on a certain date which enabled him to write to his master and to receive his answer; this correspondence would probably have required not less than twenty-two days in transit. He then apprised Beton of the matter in such a way that a hint is conveyed of the Queen-Mother's complicity, or knowledge, coupled with a suggestion that she should be sounded; and that would carry the matter back another day or two, say to the beginning of January, at which time Moretta was in Paris and in touch with de Alava, and very probably the sharer of his secrets; and it must not be forgotten that de Alava was intimate, at least by correspondence, with Darnley.

De Alava tried to imbue the Archbishop with the notion that Catherine knew a good deal about the plot against the Queen of Scots, and a sidelight throws an interesting and useful solution of this piece of by-play. On 26th January, 1566/7, Catherine, writing to Fourquevaux, tells him that de Alava has fallen into "great choler," she thinks he cannot be well, and when he is better he will be more polite[1]. The fact is she has had his postbag rifled, the necessity for ascertaining Philip's intentions being no doubt the moving cause; on at least two other occasions, once before and once later, she did the same thing[2]. This occurred at precisely the time that de Alava was imparting to Beton his warning about Mary's danger, so that it may reasonably be concluded that, in pushing the innocent Archbishop into cross-questioning the Queen-Mother, de Alava hoped, if she fell into the snare, to have a proof that she had possessed herself of his papers. Catherine was, however, far too wily, and the Archbishop "came no speed," and she, who loved a ruse, no doubt fully

[1] *Lettres, C. de M.*, of dates 26th and 30th January, 1566/7.

[2] The first occasion was in August 1564, at a time when Philip had apparently become aware that the marriage negotiations carried on by Mary with Don Carlos were not without ulterior motives. Cardinal Granvelle had recently been dismissed from the Netherlands. The second time was in September 1568 when the mysterious death of Don Carlos was on the *tapis*. When Catherine enquired about the prince, de Alava replied that she knew as well as he, for she had seen his letters (*Lettres, C. de M.*, 8th September, 1568).

enjoyed his attempt. But the importance of the affair is the conclusive proof it affords that Alava's budget from Spain did in fact contain reference to the question, couched in terms that the Ambassador would have preferred to keep to himself. It is also a justifiable inference that Alava might have apprised Mary much earlier than he did of the threatening danger; and, if Moretta, too, was in possession of the secret, he also might easily have communicated it to Mary at Glasgow after his arrival in Edinburgh.

When Moretta came to Edinburgh on 25th January he found the town comparatively empty; the Queen and her train were in Glasgow; Moray, if one can trust the 'Detection,' was away; Bothwell on the frontier; Morton, newly pardoned, was still forbidden to come within seven miles of the Court; others were probably taking advantage of the Queen's absence. His arrival seems to have been unaccompanied by any of the marks of honour usually accorded to an Ambassador; it suggests that the Queen was by no means inclined to overlook what seemed intentional discourtesy in his belated arrival long after the baptismal ceremony, and from other things[1] she seemed suspicious as to what he was now come about. He had at least ample leisure and opportunity to consult with those of the extremist Council in Scotland who were pledged to carry out the programme of the Nuncio, such as the Bishop of Dunblane, Father Edmund Hay, Sir James Balfour, possibly also the Bishop of Ross.

It is remarkable, if it is merely a coincidence, that it was after Moretta's arrival that Balfour tendered that advice to Darnley, which, as already stated, led to the substitution of Kirk o' Field for Craigmillar as the place of residence during his convalescence. The precise date on which the change was made is not known; when dealing above with the question of the "Choice of Kirk o'

---

[1] According to de Silva (*Simancas*, 1st March, 1567) Darnley had expressed a wish to see Moretta during the time he was at Kirk o' Field, but Mary by various shifts had prevented a meeting. No other reason for this action on her part can be suggested than that, with a general knowledge of Darnley's plotting in England and on the Continent, she thought it better to keep him from contact with a man of whom she was not very sure.

Field" the evidence of Nelson has been quoted, to the effect that it was "devisit" in Glasgow; but there is another evidence, that of Thomas Crawford, which shows that the question of the actual date was undecided. Among the Cambridge MSS.[1] there appears to be the original draft drawn up for Crawford's evidence; it has many corrections, and his reference to the matter in question ran as follows, showing the dubious mind of the authors: "The Kinge asked me at that present time what I thought of his voyage. I answered y^t I liked it not because she tooke him to Craigmillar...."

It does look as if Crawford, left to his own devices, would have said that the Royal party left Glasgow with the intention of going to Craigmillar, and, combined with the hasty preparation of Kirk o' Field, it appears likely that the change of programme took place on the journey and probably during the halt at Linlithgow, that is, on the 30th or 31st of January[2]. If this hypothesis is correct, Moretta and his friends Hay and Balfour had had four or five days in which to perfect their plans, and to communicate with Darnley.

The plot of nine months ago was to be repeated, with the actors, or some of them, interchanged as regards their parts; *then* the Protestant lords employed Darnley as figure-head to triumph over the Catholic cause; *now*, with the same figure-head, the sentence of the Church was to be executed against the same lords.

It was an ingenious plan, nothing in it unlikely to succeed; with Moray recalled to meet the Ambassador, all those on the black list except Morton would be present in Edinburgh; if steps were taken to bring him in, they are not recorded. If all these persons could be assembled in a convenient place offering facilities

[1] Press mark Dd. 3. 64, No. 36.

[2] The "enemy press," of course, has a different story, viz. that the halt at Linlithgow was to await arrival of news from Bothwell, and we are told that Hob Ormistoun did in fact bring that news. Still, there seems no good reason why Bothwell's presence or absence should affect the "settling in" at Kirk o' Field; there would be time enough for his rôle later on. Ormistoun's coming to report the evil success of the expedition on the frontier, and the capture by the rebels of his brother, was natural enough.

for general destruction the great desideratum would be attained. Innocents might suffer with non-innocents, but that was a consideration which affected the zealots but little. There were many gunpowder plots, and, except in some isolated cases of individuals, no attempt was ever made to confine the victims to one or the other Religion; all of them relied on the confusion resulting from a wholesale massacre, thus enabling some political *coup* to be brought about[1]. Certainly Kirk o' Field, with its assembly of Protestant nobles for the festive Sunday, offered peculiar opportunities.

To suppose that either Mary or Bothwell or the Protestant lords would choose so public an occasion for action of this sort, without any special reason for profiting by the ensuing confusion, would be to write them down as fools. To Darnley, on the other hand, the confusion meant everything to his success.

Had secrecy been maintained it seems probable that the plan would have succeeded. As was expected, *mutatis mutandis*, in the English plot of 1605, in the confusion consequent on the anticipated death of the Sovereign and the leading nobility and councillors, the triumphant ringleaders, masters of the heir-apparent (whose capture from Holyrood would not be difficult), could hold their own in the west until the first Spanish troops arrived, the signal for the uprising of all the latent Catholicism in the country. It must be clear that all the clues were carefully laid to prove this to be a Protestant plot, from which Darnley escaped by a miracle, while the Queen lost her life; one can imagine the skill with which this story would have been developed. If something could be added of Elizabeth's assent to the Cecil-Moray bond, which might very likely have been the case, the proof would be complete; and all Europe, hardened as it was, would cry out.

It is easy to understand that both Catholics and Protestants

---

[1] At or about this period there were plots to blow up the Prince of Parma and the nobility in the streets of Antwerp; an alleged plot to blow up Elizabeth in Parliament (Abbot's *Antilogia*, p. 137); to blow up the Duke of Florence in church; and the English Gunpowder Plot of 1605.

desired to cover up any trace of their connection with the affair[1]. The Nuncio and his agents wished nothing less than publication of their intention to destroy the lords on the black list; Cecil must cover Elizabeth from all stain of an attempt against Darnley; as regards Philip—those who know of his extraordinary ingenuity in concealing his tracks in other cases will not be surprised at how little is heard of his interference now. General accusations of one party by the other were not convincing, but to choose a scapegoat and "prove" a case would set curious tongues wagging on a wrong quest. It suited Philip to condemn the Queen of Scots through the innuendoes of Moretta, and it suited Cecil to get together an elaborate process for the same purpose. Helpless Mary, escaped from Kirk o' Field, must be destroyed still more cruelly.

The silence of Philip is more expressive than abundance of smooth words. He must have had the news from de Silva, who wrote on 17th February, yet, though we have letters of Fourquevaux from Spain of 3rd and 15th March, he makes no mention of the reception of the news; nor is there any letter extant from Catherine to her Ambassador making the announcement. It

---

[1] Frequently quoted against Mary by her enemies, and glossed over by her friends, is the letter of the Archbishop of Glasgow, dated 9th March, 1567 (in Keith, 1, p. civ). He tells her that she is greatly and wrongly calumniated as "motif principal of the whole, and all done by your command." But the rest of the letter shows clearly enough what is in his mind. He adjures her to do "such justice as the whole world may declare your innocence, and give testimony for ever of their treason that has committed, without fear of God or man, so cruel and ungodly a murder...." Beton was, it must be remembered, a party to the action against the Protestant lords, he knew of Mary's refusal to participate, he knew but too well the reasons for supposing Mary to favour these same lords, he had heard on all sides the rumours put about that this was a Protestant plot, and he had probably heard from de Alava that she had a hand in it. He urges her now, late though it be, to execute the "justice" long since pressed on her, and so prove that she is no heretic. He never thought Mary was guilty, see several of his letters in Stevenson's *Selections* (Maitland Club). Curiously enough, the idea that Mary would now execute the purpose urged on her is mentioned in a letter by Laureo of 8th March, practically the same date as that on which Beton wrote. (Pollen, p. 361.)

cannot be believed that the Catherine who was so anxious to hear how Philip received the news of the death of Riccio was indifferent on this much greater occasion. Secret communications must have passed, and the secrecy is significant. Writing to de Silva on 8th March, when he had certainly had the news from Paris, Philip makes no comment at all, his principal theme on that occasion was, "To note what you say with regard to the Queen's pleasure when you informed her of my decision to go to the States." In fact he makes no real comment until 2nd June, and then in the baldest language: "It has given me much sorrow, on account of my friendship with the Queen."

CONCLUSION

An attempt has been made in this concluding chapter to show, as briefly as possible, the accumulating pressure which led the Catholic Church to make a great effort to regain Scotland, and the means taken to achieve success. Of the facts there is no doubt whatever; as regards the interpretation of the method followed there may be dispute. At least it may be hoped that future investigators will not neglect the evidence of external Cause, as has been the case in the past.

An attempt has also been made to show, that, during her residence in France, Mary was not in contact with influences of the kind that the narrow outlook of some historians would have us believe; that her attitude in Scotland was the outcome of her innate moderation, and not a pose; that the incident of Kirk o' Field, with its accompaniment of studied publicity, requires an explanation widely removed from that accepted hitherto by friend or foe; that the religious strife of the age with its complement of violence, working through the disordered intellect of a youth, requires a place in the foreground of any true picture of the event.

Darnley was capable of the part which has here been given him; of that there can be no doubt. On him had been heaped the goodwill and forbearance of a woman anxious to give him a leading part and to display a happy union; but in him there was no response, nor any compunction. It would be charitable to suppose him "frantic," that is, mad, as Camden declares the Earl of Moray stated him to be, but the modern term "degenerate" would describe him more aptly.

An endeavour has been made to penetrate the veil which shrouds the Cause of Kirk o' Field—that term has been deliberately chosen, because, whether Cecil is regarded as guilty only of intention, Darnley of action, and Lennox of abetting, there was behind each an impelling power.

The disruption in the outward forms of the faith of Christians controlled or affected every political act of the period.

The notion that the death of Darnley was the direct result of a carnal lust between Mary and Bothwell is a grotesque fiction, a reflection of sixteenth-century animalism. Nor can it be admitted that any scheme of Bothwell to attain power through the Queen was the cause of the tragedy; at that time, his power was insignificant and his personal following and influence too small for such an idea.

The Counter-Reformation movement, aimed against the Protestant lords and the Queen, was the basis of the intended tragedy of Kirk o' Field; and Darnley, Lennox, and Balfour were the moving spirits, encouraged by the foreign envoys who came over to represent Philip of Spain and the Nuncio. In this connection the words of the English Ambassador in Paris, Sir Henry Norris, already quoted, may here be repeated: "As at first I thought, therein I remain not to be removed, that the original of that fact came from hence [Paris]."

Unfortunately for Darnley the plans failed, and he himself was the totally unexpected victim of those nobles whom he had insulted, and who were determined to prevent his attaining the Crown of Scotland.

The two plots coincided in time and place, and the result was the mystery of Kirk o' Field.

INDEX

Abbey of Holyrood, 3, 6
Adam, Robert, 18
Adamson, Principal John, 14
Ainslie Bond, the, 133, 173
Ainslie's map of Edinburgh (*c.* 1780), 15
Alesius, Alexander, *Collegium Sacerdotum* mentioned by, 6, 21
Anglo-Scottish Commission, 228
Arschott, Duchess of, 206, 207
Argyll, Duke of, 38, 142; pardoned by Mary, 222
Arran, Earl of, 134
Austin Friars of Holyrood, 3, 6

Bacon, Sir Nicholas, 164
Balfour, Gilbert, 74
Balfour, Sir James, 38, 49, 64, 68, 73, 81, 126, 139, 226, 243, 267, 273; and Esme Stewart, 162; exercise of his secret power, 160–4; given Priory of Pittenweem, 160; his connection with Bothwell, 151–5; his connection with the gunpowder plot, 148–50; his intrigues with the Catholic party, 135–40; letter to Killigrew, 163; receives the King's pardon, 161; responsibility for plot, 119; source of his power in Scotland, 141–7; takes command of Edinburgh Castle, 152
Balfour, Robert, 83, 118
Barrel, the tale of a, 60–66
Bastian, messenger, 181
Beanston and Brunstane, Lairds of, 155–7
Bedford, Earl of, 144, 175, 185, 188, 190
"Beith, Raid of", 210
Bellenden, Sir John, 68, 80
Beton, Archbishop, letter to Mary, 182, 183; warns Mary, 271
Beton, John, 73, 211, 237, 251
Beton, Lady Janet, 130
Beton family, 131
Bewick, John, 22 *n.*
Beynstoun, the Laird of, 176

Binning, John, 65, 66
Biographia, 71–78
"Black list" of Catholic party, six persons on, 252
Blackfriars Wynd, Cowgate at, 7
Blackwood, Adam, 54 *n.*
Bond, Cecil-Moray-Morton, for the "removal" of Darnley, 250
Bond, the Ainslie, 133, 173
Bonkil, the cook, 53, 70, 117
Borromeo, Cardinal, 218
Borthwick Castle, attack on, 158–60; flight of Bothwell to, 155
Bothwell, Adam, Bishop of Orkney, 74
Bothwell, Earl of, 38, 41, 64, 68, 97, 142, 225; carries the Queen to Dunbar, 134; flight of, to Borthwick Castle, 155; his attitude in the crisis, 131–4; his connection with Sir James Balfour, 151–5; his movements on the 9th Feb. 1567, 121–4; marriage suggested with Mary, 133; marriage with Mary, 188; the ubiquity of, 66–68
Bothwell, Margaret, 74
Bothwell's Narrative, extract from, 63
Brand, John, minister, 76
Brief addressed to Mary by Pius V, 234
Briefs for the King and the Queen-Mother of France, 236
"Bristo, Lands of", 34
Brunstane and Beanston, Lairds of, 155–7
Bryce, W. Moir, 33
Buchanan, George, 78, 101; account of what the women saw and heard, 107; condemns the Catholics, 89; evidence of, 35
Burns, Mrs George, 52

Carberry Hill, 73, 159, 186
Carnival Sunday, Feb. 9, 1567, 38
Casket Letters, 77, 79, 97, 127
Cassillis, 38
Castelnau, 225, 226

Catholic and Protestant elements combine for Mary's downfall, 167, 168

Catholic Church, Darnley champions, 267

Catholic party, "black list", 252

Catholicism, some envoys of (1564–5), 204–9

Cause of Kirk o' Field, 201 *sqq.*

Cecil, 51, 129, 146, 164, 174; condemns Mary, 276; document of 24 Oct. 1566, 223, 224; letter from Cockburn to, 96; letter from Drury to, 108; letter from the Earl of Sussex to, 1

Ceneda, Bishop of, 236

Cessford, Walter of, 112, 113

Charles, Archduke, as suitor for Mary, 200

Charles IX, 269

Chatelherault, Duke of, 42; "Great Lodging" of the, 17

Chisholm, William, Bishop of Dunblane, 207, 208, 221, 227, 259, 263, 267, 273; granted audience with Mary, 261

Cholmeley, Sir Richard, 250

Clarke, Captain, 77

Clerneau, M., 90, 91, 165, 265; report on the explosion at Kirk o' Field, 46

Close Head, Sandy Bruce's, 61

Cockburn, Sir James, of Skirling, 172; given command of Edinburgh Castle, 152; letter to Cecil, 96

College of St Leonard, 9; St Salvator, 9

Collegium Sacerdotum, 21; mentioned by Alesius, 6

Commission, Anglo-Scottish, 228

Commissioners, Elizabeth's, 51, 79

Condé, Servais de, 23, 37, 40, 82

Conspirators, the, and handling of the gunpowder, 52, 53

Correr, Giovanni, Venetian Ambassador, 47, 91

Council at Edinburgh, 253

Council, Lords of, 251, 252; letter after explosion at Kirk o' Field, 45

Council of Trent, 201, 202

Counter-Reformation in Scotland, 201–4; persons engaged in, 216

Cowgate at Blackfriars Wynd, 7

Craig, John, minister, 134

Craigmillar, 79, 80, 83, 124, 179, 269, 273, 274; Council at (1566), 141

Crawford, Thomas, 20, 79, 274; his *History of Edinburgh University*, 13

Crichton, Alexander, 147

Crichton, Father William, 205, 261

Crichton, John, 157

Crichtons, the, of Brunstane, 156, 157

Crisis, the, 199, 200

"Crown Matrimonial", 189, 191, 227

Cullen, James, 157, 176; biography of, 72; captured by Morton and hanged, 75

Curia, the, 233

Custody of the heir to the throne, 171, 172

Dalgleish, George, 61, 121; biography of, 71

Dalzel, Andrew, 15; and ghost of Darnley, 43

Dançay, M. de, French Ambassador in Denmark, 77

Dare, Martin, 249

Darnley, 227, 237; and Spain, 243, 252; and the Pope, 252; and Riccio plot, 138; arrives at Kirk o' Field, 37; arrival in Edinburgh, 82; as a plotter against his Queen, 188–199; Cecil - Moray - Morton Bond for "removal" of, 250; champions the Catholic Church, 267; Earl of Morton executed for murder of, 47; escape from Kirk o' Field, 90; ghost of, 42; letter to Lennox, 115; letter to Mary, 256; news of death conveyed to Paris, 100; official story of murder of, 48; plotting in England, 258; reconstruction of the murder of, 104; servants of, 115–18; stories of murder of, 92, 93, 94; unofficial story of murder of, 45 *sqq.*; where murdered, 70

David I, King of Scotland, and Abbey of Holyrood, 3, 6

de Alava, Francis, 258, 259, 272; Spanish Ambassador in Paris, 238
de Brienne, Comte, 188, 255
de Foix, Paul, letter to Catherine de Médici, 212
de Gouda, Father Nicholas, mission of, 203, 204
de Médici, Catherine, 192, 272; letter from Paul de Foix to, 212
de Pimodan, M., 188 n.
de Silva, Guzman, Spanish Ambassador in London, 80, 215, 258
de Toweris, Nicholas, 22 n.
de Villemont, Clerneau, 226, 227
Defamatory placards, the, 173–8
Depositions of Hepburn, 61, 62; Paris, 54; Powrie, 50, 51, 52
Dickson, Thomas, 22 n.
Dolu, M., Mary's treasurer, 181, 182
Douglas, Archibald, 64, 65, 101, 144, 145, 147, 258; letter to Mary, 143
Douglas, Gavin, Bishop of Dunkeld, 22, 24
Douglas, George, 140, 150
Drever, Dr James, 187 n.
Drury, Sir William, 49, 51, 60, 133; and the placard makers, 177; letters of, 80, 81, 102; letter to Cecil, 108
du Croc, M., 90, 251, 255; accompanies Moretta to Dunbar, 269, 270
"Duke's House" or great lodging, 7, 8, 12, 42, 43
Dunbar, du Croc and Moretta at, 269, 270
Dunblane, Bishop of. See Chisholm, William
Dunkeld, Bishops of, dwelling-house of the, in Edinburgh, 22
Durham, Alexander, 86 n., 117, 149 n.
Durham, Sandy, 38
Dury, Robert, 271

Edgar's maps of Edinburgh (1742 and 1765), 15
Edinburgh, Council at, 253; dwelling-house of the Bishops of Dunkeld in, 22; early maps of, 15; Treaty of, 164, 223; University of, 3; University, houses occupied by Principals of, 13
Edinburgh Castle, Balfour in command of, 152; Mary at, 249
Edmonstoun, James, 176
Egmont, doom of, decreed, 258
Elizabeth, 165, 181; letter from Mary to, 146; reconciliation with Mary, 222, 223
Elizabeth's Commissioners, 79
Embassy of William Chisholm, Bishop of Dunblane, to Pius V, 228–31
England, Darnley and his father plotting in, 258; West of, 248, 249
Envoys of Catholicism (1564–5), 204–9
Erskines, the, and custody of heir to the throne, 171, 172
Evidence of Buchanan, 35; Thomas Nelson, 34, 36

Fata texunt, 258–67
Fawdonside, Andrew Ker of, 111, 112
Fawkes, Guy, 58, 59
February 9, 1567, 66; night of, the story and the reality, 69, 70
Flodden, disaster of (1513), 9
Flodden Wall, 33 sqq.
Foreign negotiations of Scotland (1565), 209–16; (1566), 221–8
Forfeiture, Summons of, 73 n.
Forster, Sir John, 149, 188; letter of June 1581, 64
Fourquevaux, 193, 222, 272
France, King and Queen-Mother of, Briefs for, 236
Friday, 7th Feb. 1567, day of exceptional happenings, 125–31
"Friday letter", the, 127, 128
Furniture of Kirk o' Field, 37, 38

Galloway, John, 121, 123, 124
Gardens east and south of Kirk o' Field, conspirators in, 41, 42
Geddes, William, 75
Glasgow, Archbishop of, letter from Mary to, 148
Glasgow, Mary's visit to, 80, 198; Provand's Lordship in, 12, 26
Gordon, Lady Jean, 130

Grant, James, 33; *Old and New Edinburgh*, 6

Granvelle, Cardinal, 206, 207

Gray, Master of, letter to Walsingham, 65 *n*.

"Great House", 25

"Great Lodging" of the Duke of Chatelherault, 17

Grey de Wilton, Lord, 134

Guests at supper party, Feb. 9, 1567, 38

Gunpowder, the, conveyance by the conspirators, 52, 53; effect of, 58, 59; quality of, 57; quantity of, 56; source and conveyance, 49–51

Gunpowder plot, Sir James Balfour's connection with, 148–50

Gwynn, Henry, 117, 138, 215, 243, 249, 250

Hamilton House, 83

Hatfield papers, letter found among, 129

Hay, Father Edmund, 46, 94, 95, 122, 136, 231, 259, 260, 261, 263, 264, 267, 273; companion of de Gouda, 204

Hay, John, 30; biography of, 75; his "evidence", 28; his story, 66

Hay, John, of Tallo, the younger, 176

Hay family, 204

Henderson, Thomas, 121 *n*.

Henry VIII, 229; and the Scottish traitors, 147

Hepburn, John, 30, 122, 176; biography of, 75; depositions of, 61, 62, 80, 142 *n*., 177, 178; his story, 67

Hepburn, Patrick, 157

Hepburns, the, of Beanston, 156, 157

Herrera, Anthony, 54 *n*.

Herries, Lord, 172 *n*.

Hertford, Earl of, 147

Hog, Christina, Mary's faithful waiting-woman, 181

Holy League, 162

Holyrood Abbey, 3; founded by David I, 6; residence for Royalty, 8

Holyrood, and Kirk o' Field, "secret" way between, 43, 44; King James' Tower, 17

Home, Lord, attacks Borthwick Castle, 158

Hubert, Nicholas (called "Paris"), biography of, 76–78. *See also under* Paris

Huntly, Earl of, 38, 133, 142

Inchkeith, the Captain of, 159

Inchtok (Blakstok), Francis, 22 *n*.

James IV, 9

James, King of Scotland, accepts bribe, 65 *n*.

Jedburgh, 254, 255; Mary's illness at, 179; "Queen Mary's house" at, 12

Kelso, Abbot of, 113

Ker, Andrew, of Fawdonside, 111–14, 120

Ker, Matthew, 8

Keys, false, 178

Killigrew, Sir Henry, letter from Balfour to, 163; the mission of, 164–73

Kincaid, Archibald, 22 *n*.

King James' Tower at Holyrood, 17

Kirk o' Field, Cause of, 278; choice of, 79–84; Darnley arrives at, 37; Darnley escapes from, 90; east and south gardens of, 40, 41, 42; furniture of, 37, 38; last hours at, 84–95; physical features of the ground at, 17, 18, 19; plan of, and other contemporary buildings, 16; plotting at, 274, 275; precincts of, 10 *sqq*.; Provost of, 12; quadrangle, ruined or south side of, 19 *sqq*.; Queen's intention to remain all night at, vouched for, 95; reproduction of part of original sketch, 11; "secret" way between Holyrood and, 43, 44; substituted for Craigmillar, 273–4; tapestries at, 39

Kirkaldy, William, of Grange, 174

Knox, John, 135

Lainez, James, Father-General of the Society of Jesus, 202

Laing, Malcolm, 48, 51, 59, 67

Lairds of Beanston and Brunstane, 155–7
"Lands of Bristo", 34
"Lane of St Mary in the Fields", 7
Lang, Andrew, 12, 44, 78
Laureo, Vincenzo, Bishop of Mondovi, Nunciature of, 231–42
League, Holy, 162
Lennox, Earl of, 47, 114, 116, 125, 161, 238, 243, 267; concurrence in Riccio plot, 138, 139; letter from Darnley to, 115; his MSS, 44; on the night of the murder, 105–6
Lennox, Lady Margaret, 220, 238, 247, 249
Lennox Narrative, 86, 90
Leslie, John, Bishop of Ross, 164; condemns the Protestants, 89
Letter, "Short" Glasgow, 79
"Letter, the Friday", 127, 128
Letters, Casket, 77, 79, 97, 127
Lindsay, Lord, 143
Linlithgow, 106, 274
Lochleven, Mary Stuart at, 83, 185
Lords of Council, the, 251, 252
Lorraine, Cardinal of, 229, 234, 236; wooing of, by the Bishop of Mondovi, 239–42
Low Countries, 248
Lumley, Lord, 223

Maitland, Secretary, 133, 142, 167, 185
Manare, Father, 265, 266
Maps of Edinburgh, 15
Mar, Earl of, 171
Mary Stuart, and baptism of her son, 243, 244; Archduke Charles as suitor for, 200; at Edinburgh Castle, 249; at Glasgow, 80; at Lochleven, 185; at Seton, 183; between the hammer and the anvil, 217–20; carried to Dunbar by Bothwell, 134; Catholic and Protestant elements combine for downfall of, 167, 168; condemned by Cecil and Philip of Spain, 276; gives audience to the Bishop of Dunblane, 261; grants pardons for the Riccio murder, 112; health of, 178–88; inclined towards Rome, 243; in man's apparel, 99; letter

after explosion at Kirk o' Field, 45; letter from Archbishop Beton to, 182, 183; letter from Archibald Douglas to, 143; letter from Darnley to, 256; letter from Pius V to, 230; letter to Archbishop of Glasgow, 19, 148; letter to Elizabeth, 146; marriage with Bothwell, 188; offers of reconciliation to Elizabeth, 222, 223; opposed to Religion, 267; pardons Argyll and Moray, 222; plotted against by Darnley, 188–199; reconstruction of the scene of the tragedy of, 1 sqq.; suggested marriage with Bothwell, 133; taken by Bothwell to Borthwick Castle, 155; visits Glasgow, 198; warned by Archbishop Beton, 271
"Matrimonial Crown", 227
McEwan Hall, 17
Megginch, 205
Meggotland, hunting in, 250
Melville, Sir James, 90, 134; conveys news of the birth of a son to Mary to London, 100; Memoir, 153
Melville, Sir Robert, 80, 105, 170, 180, 198, 251
Mertin, Mistress Barbara, 107
Mildmay, Sir Walter, 223
Minto, Laird of, 268 n.
Mondovi, Bishop of, 91, 103; arrives in Paris and makes his first report, 233–39; his character, 231–3; wooing of the Cardinal of Lorraine by, 239–42. See also under Laureo, Vincenzo
Moray, Earl of, 47, 101, 116, 142, 161, 190; letter of, 74; pardoned by Mary, 222
Moretta, Signor di, 90, 91, 109, 235, 259, 262, 267, 273; and du Croc at Dunbar, 269, 270
Morton, Earl of, 31, 64, 65, 101, 126, 190; attacks Borthwick Castle, 158; confession by, 146; executed for murder of Darnley, 47; proclaimed Regent, 160
Murray, James, of Tullibardine, 172, 174
Murray, William, 77

Narrative, Lennox, 86, 90
Narratives, physical impossibilities of the accepted, 45 *sqq.*
Nau, Claude, 112; *Memoirs*, 80, 90, 126, 134
Nelson, Thomas, servant of Darnley, 26, 30, 79, 87, 274; evidence of, 35, 37
Norris, Sir Henry, 103, 174, 217, 278
Northumberland, Earl of, 76
Nunciature of Vincenzo Laureo, Bishop of Mondovi, 231–42

Ochiltree, Margaret Stewart of, 113
"Old Provost's House", plan and section of, 28
Ormistoun, James, 113, 121, 176; biography of, 76
Ormistoun, Robert, biography of, 76
Oxe, Peter, 77

Pachecho, Cardinal, 209
Paris, French page, 30, 53, 54, 69, 85; deposition of, 151 *n.*
Parma, Duchess of, 267, 269
Pearson, Professor Karl, 129
Philip, King of Spain, 192, 228, 234, 258, 267; and Darnley, 252; and the Netherlands, 246, 247; condemns Mary, 276; projected journey to the Netherlands, 222
"Picture", the 1567, 4, 109–14
Pittenweem, Priory of, given to Balfour, 160
Pius IV, 9, 202; Scotland in the Pontificate of, 204–16
Pius V, 203, 259; and Darnley, 252; Brief addressed to Mary, 234; embassy of the Bishop of Dunblane to, 228–31; letter to Mary, 230; Scotland in the Pontificate of, 217–31
Placards, the defamatory, 173–8
Plan and section of "Old Provost's House" and the "Salle", 28
Plan of Kirk o' Field, and other contemporary buildings, 16
Playfair, W. H., 43
Plot, the rationale of the, 79 *sqq.*
Polanco, Father, 232
Pole, Arthur, 249

Pole, Edward, 249
Pollen, Father Joseph, 217
Potterrow, 7
Powrie, William, 52, 60, 61, 68, 121; biography of, 72; depositions of, 50, 51
Protestant and Catholic, combine for Mary's downfall, 167, 168
Protestant party, 64
Provand's Lordship, 26; house in Glasgow, 12
Provost of Kirk o' Field, 12
Public Record Office, London, "picture" of 1567 preserved in Museum of, 4

"Queen Mary's house" at Jedburgh, 12

"Raid of Beith", 210
Randolph, Thomas, 136, 137, 179, 190, 212, 224
Rapperlaw, William, 22 *n.*
Rebel leaders against Mary, 237
Religion, Mary opposed to, 267
Reres, Lady, 38
Riccio murder, 229; initiated, 225; pardons granted by Mary, 112
Riccio plot, Darnley and the, 138; Lennox concurs in, 138, 139
Robertson, Dr, 188
Robertson, Joseph, 27, 37, 39
Rogers, William, spy, 249
Rokesby, 173
Rome, Mary inclined towards, 243
Ross, Bishop of, 273
Russale, Thomas, 8
Russell, Dr J. S. Risien, 178 *n.*
Ruthven Narrative, 191 *n.*

St Andrews, 9
St Leonard, college of, 9
St Mary, Church of, 3 *sqq.*; drawing or "picture" of (1567), 4, 5. *See also* Kirk o' Field
"St Mary in the Fields, Lane of", 7
St Salvator, college of, 9
"Salle", plan and section of, 28
Savoy, Duke of, 235
Scarborough Castle, 248, 250
Scilly Isles, 248

Scotland, Counter-Reformation in, persons engaged in, 216; foreign negotiations of (1565), 209–16; foreign negotiations of (1566), 221–28; in the Pontificate of Pius IV, 204–16; in the Pontificate of Pius V, 217–31; the situation in, July to November 1566, 242–57

Scottish traitors and Henry VIII, 147

Scrope, Lord, letter of, 73

"Secret" way between Holyrood and Kirk o' Field, 43, 44

Seely, Sir John, 201

Sempill, Lord, 105

Servants of Darnley, 115–18

Seton, Mary at, 183

Shaw, John, 112

Solaro, Bertino (Moretta), 235

Somerset, Protector, 42

Spain, and Darnley, 243; the shadow of, 267–77

Standen, Anthony, 214, 243, 253

Standen, Anthony, Junior, 117, 243

Stanley, Sir William, 214 n.

Stevenson, Father, 229

Stevenson, John, 117

Stewart, Esme, and Balfour, 162

Stewart, John, of Traquair, captain of the Queen's guard, 69, 97, 120 n.

Stewart, Lord Robert, 85; discloses plot to Darnley, 116

Stewart, Margaret, of Ochiltree, 113

Stirling Castle, 171, 251; the "quarrel" at, 195

Stirling, Mistress May, 107

Summons of Forfeiture, 73 n.

Supper party, Feb. 9, 1567, guests at, 38

Sussex, Earl of, letter to Cecil, 1

Tapestries at Kirk o' Field, 39, 40

Taylor, William, 120

"Test", reception of the, November 1566, 254–7

Texunt, fata, 258–67

Thornton, James, 226, 227

Throckmorton, 185, 225, 226

Throplow (Thraples), 66

Time, consideration of, 52 sqq.

Tragedy, reconstruction of scene of the, 1 sqq.

Treaty of Edinburgh, 164, 223

Trent, Council of, 201, 202

Tournon, Cardinal, 232, 234

Town Wall, 33 sqq.

Turpin, Dick, 100

Vocat, David, 8

Walker, William, 195

Walklot, George, 22 n.

Wall, Flodden, 33 sqq.

Wall, Town, 33 sqq.

Wallace, Edgar, article "The New Crime", 187

Walsingham, letter from the Master of Gray to, 65 n.

Warbeck, Perkin, 25

Welch, John, 22 n.

Westminster, judicial enquiry at, 108

Whittinghame, meeting at, 146

Wilson, Dr, translates "Friday" letter into Latin, 128

Wilson, Dr Thomas, 107

Wilson, Stephen, 205, 206, 215, 221, 228, 230, 251, 253, 256, 260

Yaxley, Francis, 213–15, 243; missions to Spain and Rome, 137, 138

Young, James (alias Dingley), 268 n.

www.ingramcontent.com/pod-product-compliance
Ingram Content Group UK Ltd.
Pitfield, Milton Keynes, MK11 3LW, UK
UKHW010348140625
459647UK00010B/924